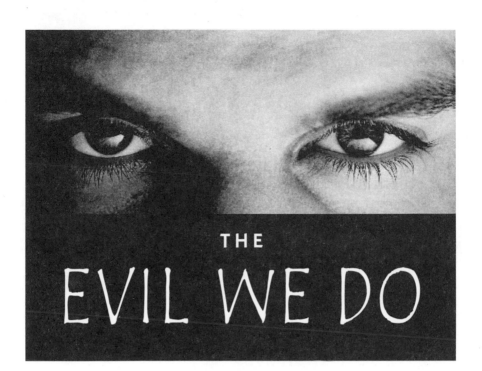

THE
EVIL WE DO

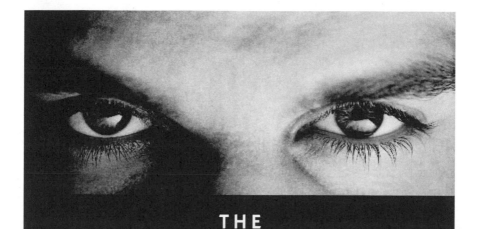

THE
EVIL WE DO

the psychoanalysis of
destructive people

CARL
GOLDBERG, Ph.D.

 **Prometheus Books**

59 John Glenn Drive
Amherst, New York 14228-2197

Published 2000 by Prometheus Books

The Evil We Do: The Psychoanalysis of Destructive People. Copyright © 2000 by Carl Goldberg. All rights reserved. No part of this publication may be reproduced, stored in a retrieval system, or transmitted in any form or by any means, digital, electronic, mechanical, photocopying, recording, or otherwise or conveyed via the Internet or a website without prior written permission of the publisher, except in the case of brief quotations embodied in critical articles and reviews.

Inquiries should be addressed to
Prometheus Books
59 John Glenn Drive
Amherst, New York 14228–2197
VOICE: 716–691–0133, ext. 207
FAX: 716–564–2711
WWW.PROMETHEUSBOOKS.COM

04 03 02 01 00   5 4 3 2 1

Library of Congress Cataloging-in-Publication Data

Goldberg, Carl.
The evil we do : the psychoanalysis of destructive people / Carl Goldberg.
p. cm.
Includes bibliographical references and index.
ISBN 1–57392–839–9 (cloth : alk. paper)
1. Psychoanalysis—Case studies 2. Good and evil. 3. Social sciences and psychoanalysis. 4. Philosophical anthropology. I. Title.

RC509.8 .G65 2000
616.89'17—dc21   00–042166
                                                                           CIP

Printed in the United States of America on acid-free paper

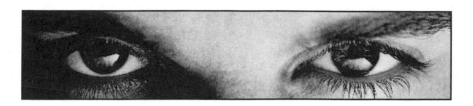

CONTENTS

THEORY AND METHOD

The evil men do lives after them.
The good oft interred with their bones.
                              —William Shakespeare,
                                        Julius Caesar

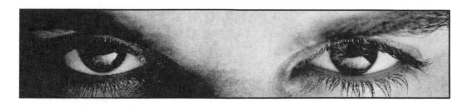

ACKNOWLEDGMENTS

THE AUTHOR WISHES TO EXPRESS HIS APPRECIATION TO THE FOL-
lowing colleagues who were generous with their time and thoughtful-
ness in reviewing the manuscript: Virginia Crespo, M.S.W., Royal
Huber, Peter Olsson, M.D., Myron Weiner, M.D., and Heward
Wilkinson, M.Sc. I am also grateful for the research support of the
librarians at Albert Einstein College of Medicine and Stern College,
both affiliated with Yeshiva University.

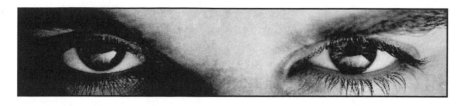

AUTHOR'S NOTE

IN ACCORD WITH MY PROFESSIONAL ETHICAL MANDATE AND MY OWN scruples, I have disguised the identities of the people I have treated in psychoanalysis or psychotherapy who I present in this book by making changes in their descriptions and case histories. In addition, I have altered the exact circumstances of some of the vignettes in order to accentuate the critical issues under discussion. Finally, some of the dialogue has been condensed from what actually was said by my clients and myself.

I need also to mention that I have always found difficult the choice of the proper term for the people I treat. During my clinical training and through most of my professional career I worked in hospitals and medical schools. The only allowable term for the people treated there is "patient." As a humanistic and existentially oriented psychologist, I found the label too suggestive of the authoritarian relationship of doctor and patient to be appropriate for the type of relationship I seek to establish in my clinical practice. In private practice as a psychoanalyst, I initially used the terms "analysand" and "client" for those I treated in psychotherapy. The former I now regard as too clinical and the latter suggests a formal business arrangement—that eschews the complex and often difficult personal relationships that evolve between myself and the people I treat. In my previous books, I have used the term "the people I work with" to designate those I treat. But this term can be confusing— understood to refer to my professional colleagues as well as those I treat. In this book I use the term "client" as the best of problematic choices for those I have treated in psychoanalysis and psychotherapy.

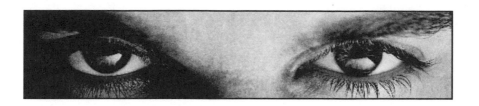

FOREWORD

D R. CARL GOLDBERG'S *THE EVIL WE DO* IS A WAKE-UP CALL TO ALL PSY-choanalysts as well as to psychotherapists who are influenced by psychoanalysis. Speaking from a social and moral perspective, this analyst urgently appeals to the profession to reexamine its dispirited, moribund, and negativistic status as an amoral, individualistic psychology. He awakens us to its responsibility as a cultural institution that inescapably generates values to others for which it must own its responsibility. Too often, these values have been negative, largely, according to Goldberg, because of the idiosyncratic nature of its founder, Sigmund Freud, against whom the author marshals considerable evidence as to his autocratic indifference to human beings and to human values. Freud only valued the "truth of the drives," according to Goldberg. Moreover, as we have reason to believe, Freud was probably a hysteric, who polarized, who was subject to hyperbole, who was charismatic, who was vulnerable to slights, and who was irritable, self-conscious, and subject to introspection (in the sense of being preoccupied with oneself) rather than truly gregarious, considerate, or loving.

THE EVIL WE DO

Not unlike Martin Luther and his posting of his ninety-three theses on the gates of the Cathedral at Wittenberg, Goldberg posts his own theses, really antitheses, to some of the traditional canons of current psychoanalytic practice to enjoin psychoanalysts to adopt what *I* would call a valorization of such concepts as innocence, goodness, virtue, altruism, truth, caring, moral responsibility—and a demand to free these qualities from their hitherto ignoble connotation in psycho-analysis as *defenses* against the "real" truth of the drives, which Freud considered to be primary and defining.

If I read Goldberg correctly, "The Evil We Do" classical psychoan-alysts may be in danger of enfranchising the primacy of evil within us at the expense of dismissing our inherent potential goodness, as well as our desire to love and protect.

Perhaps a credible reconciliation between Goldberg's views and those he attributes to Freud would be as follows: What Freud stated may be essentially correct when confined strictly to the domain of his own explorations. What Goldberg and the sources he depends on for his thesis state is also correct. What psychoanalysis needs is a larger, more expansive, and more embracing vision for the innumerable per-spectives of truth, i.e., emotional truth, objective truth, human truth, unconscious truth, Absolute Truth, and so on and on, each existing on different planes and yet holographically united.

What I believe that Goldberg utmostly recommends is that psy-choanalysis take more seriously than ever its social and moral dimen-sions. The profoundest message I get from his evocative work is that psychoanalysis and its practitioners must explicitly and continuously renew their dedication to their implicit higher purpose.

Goldberg writes with a messianic zeal tempered with unusual clarity and objectivity about these lost souls who have been condemned both by society and by psychoanalysis as morally bad and untreatable, respectively. His utmost theme is a resounding one; psychoanalysis should extend hope and compassion to these patients and not shrink from its responsibility to understand them. Goldberg's concept of virtue and the moral imperative establishes bridges between psychoanalysis and philosophy and ethics. A single statement he makes is emblematic: "Orthodox psychoanalysis focuses almost exclusively on the develop-ment of skills in recouping what one has failed to gain earlier in life (the *patient* role); it totally eschews the role of *helper*. The psychoanalytic neglect of the helper role in healing is bonded to its lack of concern for the client's social and moral responsibility" (p. 42). These are philosophical, psychological, ethical, and even spiritual issues which psychoanalysis has steadfastly skirted. The title of Goldberg's book, *The Evil We Do*, paradoxically tells a double story: not only is it our responsibility to do our utmost to understand the origins of evil; it is almost as evil for us not to try to do so.

This is a wonderful, inspired, and inspiring book for professionals and laymen alike. I shall recommend it highly wherever I go.

James S. Grotstein, M.D.
Clinical Professor of Psychiatry, UCLA

INTRODUCTION

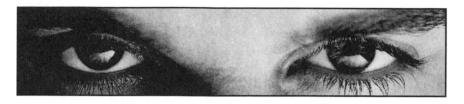

SOCIAL AND
PSYCHOLOGICAL
CHALLENGES TO
PSYCHOANALYSIS
IN THE
NEW MILLENNIUM

*For this is the journey that men make: to find themselves. If they fail in
this it doesn't much matter what else they find.*
—James Michener, *The Fires of Spring.*

IAM COMMITTED TO THE SOCRATIC DOCTRINE THAT ONLY THE EXAMINED
life is worth living. For the past thirty-five years I have identified with
psychoanalysis as a social revolution imbued with important ideas about
the role of self-examination in a life lived fully and well. Psychoanalysis's
mission a century ago was to transform society from a hostile, fearful place
to a world in which goodwill and reason prevail (Freud 1914, 1927, 1930,
1933).[1] But psychoanalysis has come upon hard times. Caught in the
snare of political, bureaucratic, and economic issues on the one side,
accused of clinical inefficacy, social irrelevancy, and a lack of moral
responsibility, on the other, psychoanalysis has lost the sweep and pro-
fundity of Freud's vision (Goldberg 1996). The general public no longer
regards psychoanalysis as the panacea it was touted as for decades. Today
psychoanalysis stands behind short-term therapy and psychopharma-
cology as the treatment of choice for psychological problems.

THE EVIL WE DO

Psychoanalysis's tarnished reputation is unfortunate in light of our contemporary societal issues. Psychoanalytic theory has the capacity to provide profound insights to enable us to understand and competently deal with these difficult social problems. For example, as potentially the most knowledgeable discipline for seeking out the motivations that encourage us to cooperate with and rejoice in others' well-being, analysts are well-appointed as trusted advisors in the establishment of a well-functioning society. It is in regard to the capacity of psychoanalysts to recognize the underlying factors that foster societal salubrity that I speak out about the role psychoanalysts can and must assume to address the social and psychological challenges of the new millennium. I don't want the "light to fail": I wish to see realized the vital ideas and intentions that psychoanalysis early in its history held up as a guide to a more constructive society.

But there are built-in barriers that analytic theory and practice have imposed on itself that currently stand in the way. In short, a number of serious dilemmas in how analysts view human existence cast an oscillating shadow on the significance of psychoanalysis's impact on contemporary society. I am referring to a set of important metapsychological and philosophical issues that psychoanalysts and psychologists have not dealt with successfully. It is precisely a deficiency of knowledge in regard to these issues, as I show in the chapters to follow, that is at heart of the limitations in current psychoanalytic practice.

These limitations are no less problematic to others who practice psychotherapy, regardless of their theoretical persuasion. Consequently, the issues I address in this book are of importance to all who practice psychotherapy, as well as to every person concerned with the role psychology will take in the new millennium. I am referring to such questions as:

- How much free will does each of us have? And its attendant concern: how responsible are we for our behavior?

- Why are the psychodynamics of self-deception (the behavior that seems to be central to most psychological and interpersonal conflicts) so difficult to describe and understand in noncontradictory terms?

- Will a better understanding of self-deception enable us to formulate a useful and coherent theory of memory and of consciousness?

- To what extent are psychological defenses conscious strategies and to what degree are they automatic (unconscious) processes?
- Is it possible to provide a valid explanation for love and intimacy that does not attribute its development to unresolved infantile patterns?
- Similarly, is there evidence that virtuous behavior has its own development and isn't simply a derivative of partially successful endeavors of the person to defend against his forbidden urges?
- And, do we have a reasonable basis for determining what are the crucial tasks of living a virtuous and responsible life? If so, do we have the wherewithal to use this knowledge to help enable destructive people to overthrow their malevolent lifestyles?

In the chapters to follow, these and other important psychological issues are explored by tracing their involvement in the lives of the clients whose case studies I present. Whereas Freud sought to show the validity of orthodox psychoanalysis through his presentation of largely unsuccessful cases, I provide successful cases to demonstrate the utility of a more humanistic psychoanalysis than most contemporary analysts ascribe to in their clinical practices. Based on my clinical experience, I explore what clinical practitioners must specifically do to rekindle the torch of hope, compassion, and responsibility in the contemporary theory and practice of psychoanalysis.

Admittedly, meaningful revision of psychoanalysis and social theory is not a modest endeavor. I assume the commission of revisionist with the recognition that no single publication will fully accomplish the task. As a social theorist, as well as an analytic practitioner, I am primarily concerned with what each of us as a member of a troubled society[2] can gain from a thorough study of very seriously destructive people about the underlying causes of our complex social problems, and the practical and tangible ways enlightened analytic thought will enable us to successfully address these issues.

The theme of this book is the struggle between good and evil in all of us. I provide case studies of men and women from all walks of life, who I, as a psychoanalyst and social theorist, have enabled to escape from evil. I do not mean evil in a trivial or even metaphorical sense. Some of the fascinating—yet highly dangerous—clients I have treated over the past four decades have committed horrible crimes: murder, rape, mayhem in heinous ways—even involvement in atrocities.

Not many other analysts share my interest in working with this population. At first glance this attitude is understandable. Forensic psychologists/psychiatrists and criminologists recognize that the likelihood that a seriously destructive person will reverse his or her adverse behavior is poor. Neither conventional psychoanalysis nor any other form of psychotherapy or rehabilitative program has been consistently effective with these clients and inmates.

On the other hand, we have a deeply ingrained tradition in our society of trying to salvage lives no matter how deplorable they have been. Since childhood, as a result of personal experiences (discussed in chapter 2), I have been mindful of the havoc malefactors wreak on society. As an analyst I have found that my extensive clinical work with destructive clients has provided me with insights into the important metapsychological and philosophical problems that I have raised above. My primary intent in this book is to use the case studies of people I treated to show that even those who have lived destructive lives can be restored to a virtuous existence by a probing psychological examination of these metapsychological and philosophical issues. My second aim here is to show how a better understanding of these issues can lead to a psychology Freud promised a century ago that can transform society from a hostile, fearful place to a world in which hope, compassion, and responsibility prevail.

There are, of course, significant differences among analytic theorists and practitioners in regard to how they go about trying to understand human behavior. It is necessary, therefore, for me to define specifically the analytic position I take in the clinical cases I explore in this book. Of foremost concern, in this regard, is the analyst's ontological assumptions.

PSYCHOANALYTIC ONTOLOGICAL CONCERNS

Ontological concerns refer to a priori notions about the essential nature of existence. That is to say, these assumptions appear to defy verification, and are therefore based upon belief rather than empirical evidence.

Psychoanalytic theory consists of two interlocking dimensions. At its core there are ontological notions of human nature describing the presumed social and psychological principles that govern the vicissitudes of human existence. Second, based on these core notions, analytic clinical theory consists of methodology and techniques to liberate the client from dysfunctional emotional, cognitive, and behavioral patterns, by a delineation of what the person must do to influence his or her behavior constructively and that of others. Obviously, efficacious analytic treatment requires ontological notions of human behavior crucial to enlightened functioning.

Throughout their history, psychoanalysts have debated what should be the ontological basis for an analytic inquiry of mental life. Following Freud, most have opted for a depth psychology based on the scientific methodology of the natural sciences.[3] This psychology is normative and reductionistic—in that it seeks to discover the crucial variables that *determine* behavioral events, discarding all the rest as irrelevant. The key psychological variables of this position are those factors that interfere with an individual's correct *perception* and *knowledge* of his own motivation. I refer to those who hold this position as *orthodox analysts*.

In contrast, there have always been analytic theorists and practitioners who have claimed that the deterministic position is inappropriate because it regards the individual as having less free will and choice of behavior than he is actually capable of exercising. Their perspective is idiographic, based on the premise from romantic and existential philosophy which holds that people are best understood holistically and in-depth rather than by those attributes they superficially share with others. The key psychological variables of this position are those of *volition* and *purposefulness*. I refer to practitioners with this approach as *humanistic analysts*.

For the most part, this position includes analysts whose orientation is interpersonal, existential, and humanistic. These analysts are crucially influenced by the writing and teaching of psychoanalysts Carl Jung, Harry Stack Sullivan, Karen Horney, Erich Fromm, Alfred Adler, Sandor Ferenczi, Otto Rank, Erik Erikson, D. W. Winnicott, W. R. Fairbairn, and John Bowlby.

Most readers may accept my statement that there are two rival psychoanalytic positions as historically accurate; but some may question its validity for contemporary psychoanalytic theory and practice. There is merit in questioning my contention. Clearly, the schools of psychoanalysis are more diversified than they were thirty years ago. In fact, the perspectives of most analysts on the principles governing human existence probably fall somewhere between the two viewpoints I outlined above. Arguably, the position most practitioners take is inconsistent—dependent upon the particular clinical or theoretical problem with which they may be wrestling, or to some event existent in their personal life which has a particularly painful impact. Nevertheless, I believe that there still exist crucial ontological differences among analysts. To explore the contrasting utility of these two existential perspectives on human behavior, I discuss them in their extreme forms.

FREUD'S ORTHODOX POSITION

The importance of mutuality and intimacy is central to all psychological systems. But, according to Freud (1905), there are deterministic limits to mature intimacy cast by the phylogenetic nature of human nurturance. In other words, in Freud's view (1905), mature attempts at intimate relations fail because they are driven by *inherent* infantile patterns to secure satisfactions native to the infant-mother bonding; as such they result in *inevitable* narcissistic hurt and depression.[4] In essence, Freud (1921) dismisses mature love as a desperate pretense at affection because men cannot experience genuine affection for those women toward whom society legitimizes sexual relations; insofar as men desire intimate connections not with strangers, but with women who have been tenderly loved since childhood.

Women, according to Freud (1918), are no more fortunate than men in this regard: "A husband is, so to speak, never anything but a proxy, never the right man; the first claim upon the feelings of love in a woman belongs to someone else, in typical cases to be the father; the husband is at best a second."

A number of other factors influenced Freud's choice of a deterministic explanation in regard to the principles governing human existence. I confine my discussion here to five factors:

1. Freud hoped to establish a social movement for the ethical liberation of society's superior people. It was to be based on unalterable principles of human behavior, which would guide these people away from the irrationality and ignorance of existing institutions (Fromm 1959). Although religion in modernity had a lesser hold on the populace than in the past, it was still potent enough in his day that Freud regarded it as his archrival (Rieff 1966). The view that an individual has free will and is therefore responsible for his actions is central to each of the major world religions. Freud took a position in opposition to free will.

2. Freud needed the mantle of science to gain respectability for his ideas (Roazen 1968). The numerous accounts of Freud's background describe significant influences on his ideas from romantic and intuitive philosophy (for example, Wain 1998). And his early work is written in German in the poetic and romantic language of his Victorian age (Bettelheim 1983). But Freud had a wily political mind (Roazen 1968). He was acutely aware that if he were to continue to express his ideas in romantic terms the intellectually elite for whom he primarily wrote would not take his ideas seriously (Wain 1998). He needed, he believed, to demonstrate that the basis for his ideas was scientific.

3. Freud was forever fighting contradictory tendencies in himself (Jones 1953). Early in his career, he claimed that he had no interest in philosophy (Robinson 1969). Later when he expounded most of his work on culture and society, he admitted that at heart he was always a philosopher and explorer, not a physician, or even an able scientist (Roazen 1968). His deception may have been as much inner negation as denial. According to Jones (1953), Freud went to considerable effort to counter in himself what he regarded as his excessive interest in philosophy. Attempting to erect psychoanalysis as a science was an effort of inner negation.

4. Freud was often discouraged in the early years of his work. Despite what he regarded as correct interpretations, patients' symptoms remained, or were replaced by still other symptoms. Especially puzzling to Freud was that the interpretations offered to patients he regarded as cooperative did not always have the desired therapeutic effect: they didn't help the client get better. Freud sought a way to indicate that his psychological theories were valid despite mixed clinical results (Hale 1995). By showing that an analyst's correct interpretations were insufficient for personality change because of the tenacity of the patient's unconscious resistances, Freud could logically contend that his theories were valid despite limited treatment success.

5. Freud's primary mission was a social agenda, not a therapeutic one (Bettleheim 1983). He believed that society could change for the better only through the mass instillation of psychological knowledge about raising and educating children, and by means of a deep understanding of social and psychological issues derived from the individual's self-analysis (Roazen 1968). But psychoanalytic education did not seem to make any decisive societal changes. Freud's pessimism grew as he became increasingly reconciled to the idea that human nature was largely intractable—regardless of whether the influence attempts addressed society or the individual (Rieff 1966).

PREMISES HUMANISTIC PRACTITIONERS SHARE WITH ORTHODOX ANALYSTS

Since humanistic analysts have different ontological notions about human nature than do orthodox analysts, the question of relevance must be addressed; that is to say, do humanistic practitioners *share* common psychological assumptions with orthodox analysts about the conceptual tools analysts have available to them to fulfill Freud's therapeutic mission: to remove the blinders the individual has imposed on his conscious awareness in order to hide painful truths about his desires? I believe that they do, although the importance given these tools varies in accordance with the differing ontological notions of each of the two analytic positions. The important conceptual equipment that differentiates both humanistic and orthodox analysts from other schools of psychotherapy includes such beliefs as:

1. Freud's revolutionary idea that there is no qualitative difference between normal and abnormal minds: every mind is aberrant in certain ways and like every other mind in still other ways. This notion has important redemptive implications: no malfunctioning mind theoretically is beyond repair.

2. Psychoanalysts are unique among psychotherapists as their central concern is the revelation of the individual as a meaning-seeking being. It is the conscious recognition of one's uniqueness as a person rather than the removal of dysfunctional behavioral symptoms that is primary to all psychoanalytic inquiry.

3. There is rationality in archaic and irrational mental processes. Since analysts of both positions see psychopathology as an attempt at a coherent orientation toward the world, all behavior is regarded as purposive and meaningful. Even seemingly irrational behavior has a supposed logic in regard to how the individual views herself.

4. Because our most disturbing experiences are those that threaten our relation to time, the patient's anxieties are venues of access to the patient's mental life. In this regard, there are three temporalities of ontological anxiety: guilt (past); shame (present); anticipatory anxiety (future). Guilt is experienced as behavior already chosen and committed; what is unclear is when the person will deal with the guilt. Shame is felt as a loss of the safe and familiar; time seems frozen, endless: with no place to hide. Anticipatory anxiety is teleological—the sufferer's sense of purpose is obsessed with what he or she regards as decisive-to-be moments in the future. Orthodox analysts, for the most part, seek to enable the patient to experience fully the present by probing the guilts of the past. Humanistic analysts, in contrast, focus on anticipatory anxiety. ·

5. Important clues to our suppressed fears and desires are symbolically encoded in such psychological productions as our mannerisms, posture, speech, dreams, fantasies, and so forth. Humanists, however, believe that this symbolic material is more accessible to conscious effort than do orthodox analysts, who because of their ontological belief

in repression hold that the meaning of human behaviors is largely inaccessible to untrained conscious scrutiny.

6. The symptomatic act—such as any sort of failure in life—is an attempt to ward off fearful, forbidden urges. They are indicative of the individual's ambivalent (opposing) motivational forces. Humanists hold that these motivational factors are accessible to consciousness. Orthodox analysts don't.

7. Both analytic orientations adhere to what I call the "Hamlet principle": the relativity of psychological experience. "There is nothing good or bad," Shakespeare's *Hamlet* tells us, "but thinking makes it so." Consequently, our fantasized fears and desires often shape our behavior more impactfully than do actual experience. Humanists contend that these fears are not necessarily repressed; more often they simply lack an expressive language in order to be recognized and understood. Emotionally articulate language, they claim, promotes personal freedom and responsibility by means of a widened reflection, diminished need for self-idealization and resistance to irrational authority. In contrast, orthodox analysts firmly hold to the belief that human intentionality is unavailable to conscious reflection without trained analytic probing.

8. All analysts believe that far more than any other influence— genetic or environmental—relationships with significant others decisively shape our personalities. However, the experiences of the pre-oedipal and oedipal years are regarded as less crucial to humanists than to orthodox analysts, in that the former hold that psychological growth is continuous throughout the lifespan, whereas orthodox analysts believe that personality is decisively set in the first few years of life.

9. All analysts hold to what I call the "mirror of the psyche" principle: we get to know ourselves best through a dialogue with others. For orthodox analysts, however, there is generally a greater concern than for humanists that relationships outside of analysis can contaminate ongoing analytic work.

10. Transference plays a role in all interpersonal encounters—brief or enduring. Humanists put less emphasis than do orthodox analysts on the role of transference in analysis, because humanistic analysts contend that the actual attributes and behavior of the analyst are usually more influential in how the client perceives the analyst than is transference distortion.

11. Psychological defenses in the form of resistances in treatment must be resolved before progress can be made toward the treatment goals. Humanistic practitioners contend that positive/proactive strategies can be employed through the resistances to reach the core existential concerns of the analysand. For example, according to the humanistic analytic position, despair is representative of the individual's teleological anxieties rather than his guilt feeling about the past. Consequently, the humanistic practitioner contends that by probing the patient's future concerns the analyst is given a more authentic view of the patient's choices in his being-in-the-world than by seeking repressed memories of the patient's past—the bailiwick of orthodox analysts.

12. Insight alone is not sufficient for psychological change: working through is required. In humanistic analysis there is a belief that working through must include attention to the patient's social and moral responsibilities. The orthodox analyst, in contrast, takes a neutral position in regard to values, contending that the only legitimate ethic in psychoanalysis is the pursuit of intrapsychic truth.

The position I take is that of a humanistic analyst. As humanistic analysts hold that the person of the analyst is as important as his theoretical assumptions, the reasons I became an analyst are discussed in chapter 2.

The Evil We Do is organized in the following way: in chapter 1 I take a critical look at why and how psychoanalysts have failed their social and moral obligations, not only to their clients, but to society-at-large as well. I make a number of suggestions for addressing the psychoanalytic profession's indifference to social and moral responsibility, which are discussed more specifically in subsequent chapters. In chapter 2 I explore why I became a psychoanalyst who treated very destructive people throughout my career. In all of the chapters except 7 and 10, I explore the case studies of my clients whose treatments raised important philosophical and metapsychological issues. Chapter 7 is a personal vignette of my encounter with an unfortunate child in a foreign country. I examine the effect the experience had on my subsequent clinical work with malevolent and destructive people. Chapter 10 is a discussion of the specific ways analysts can improve their theory and practice so that psychoanalysis can fulfill its promise of hope, compassion, and responsibility.

So not to bog down the clinical vignettes with excess theoretical discussion, I have placed these discussions in a "Theory and Method" section. Moreover, insofar as some of the terms and concepts I mention may not be familiar to the reader, I have included a glossary at the end of the book.

NOTES

1. A controversy has persisted from early in the history of psychoanalysis as to whether Freud had a societal mission, or was primarily concerned with the individual's mental life. This controversy is due to a certain dualism in Freud's writings: while the overall aim of his account of human behavior is explicated on the activities of innate biological drives, his description of mental processes and their functions is explained as activities developed in response to the problems and challenges which society imposes on the individual (Aronoff 1962). My position is that Freud had a societal mission.

2. Princeton University public policy professor John J. DiIulio reports in an article in the *New York Times* March 12, 1999, that currently there are about two million inmates in U.S. prisons.

3. This is not the place to fully evaluate psychoanalysis as a science. Harvard Medical School psychologist Drew Western (1998) has provided an extensive review of the status of psychoanalysis as a psychological science. He concludes that attacks on psychoanalysis are misconceived because they focus on "an archaic version of psychodynamic theory that most clinicians (today) similarly consider obsolete . . . (in contrast) an enormous body of research in cognitive, social, developmental, and personality psychology now supports many of (Freud's) propositions." University of California at Berkeley psychologist John Kihlstrom (1999) contests Western's evaluation of these empirical studies, arguing that "Freud's legacy is not to be assessed in terms of ideas which emerged since Freud died, but rather in terms of the ideas propounded by Freud himself through the twenty-four volumes of his collected works. Chief among these is a particular view of unconscious mental life—a view which, to date, has found little or no support in empirical science." Psychologists Seymour Fisher and Roger Greenberg (1985, 1996) and Yale University professor of philosophy Barbara Von Eckardt (1982) also have provided

extensive reviews of the empirical studies that have attempted to test specific hypotheses derived from Freud's theories. This data is mixed in regard to a support of Freud's suppositions. Overall, far more writers castigate psychoanalysis as a scientific endeavor than defend its empirical validity. No less an orthodox British analyst than Edward Glover (1952) admits: "It cannot be denied that there is an increasing tendency *not* to apply to the data of (psychoanalytic) observation or to the methods of interpretation such scientific controls as *are* available."

Glover's statement is hardly surprising when we realize that Freud was ambivalent about science (Bettleheim 1983). According to Holton (1988), Freud claimed that one must not be misled by clinical data. But Freud was far too well-trained in the philosophy of science not to recognize that his use of a single case to test his theories meant that psychoanalysis was not an empirical science competently modeled after the natural sciences. It is a *semantic* (logical) discipline, and as such requires its explanations—whether offered in clinical interpretations or in theoretical assumptions—to be stated in such a way that its premises are subject to refutability by logical deduction (Edelstein 1984). Yet, analytic theorists and practitioners have rarely concerned themselves with this methodological requirement. Instead, they use analytic clinical methodology to "prove" that analytic doctrine is valid: a practice that raises a host of ethical and moral problems in addition to the methodological ones. For example, it has become a well-known occurrence that the disillusioned analyst, who regards her theory and practice as limited, is told by her supervisor or colleagues that her disillusionment is not a legitimate challenge to analytic theory and practice but a product of her repetitive infantile conflicts (Goldberg 1990). She is urged to "return to the couch" to deal with her professional concerns. There is a thorny problem here: can a practitioner meaningfully find answers to questions about the limitations of that practice by using that practice to evaluate her dissatisfactions? For in doing so, is the analyst not tacitly confirming that all questions and doubts are not real but simply a product of psychopathology? Psychoanalyst Allen Wheelis (1962) cautions us about the folly of assuming that despair is synonymous with psychopathology, for if this was true then all moral questions are dismissed and relegated to intrapsychic conflict. Unethical behavior by analysts is usually handled in a similar way. The practitioner accused of unprofessional conduct is sent back for more analysis.

4. Humanistic analysts contend that Freud's invective against mature love is misconceived. They indicate that failures in mature intimacy are *not* necessarily due to inherent infantile patterns; more likely they are a result of the lack of knowledge and skill the subject has in negotiating equitable and balanced

adult relationships. The humanistic analytic position in regard to love and intimacy is explored in chapter 9 and section C.

REFERENCES

Aronoff, J. 1962. Freud's conception of the origin of curiosity. *Journal of Psychology* 54: 39–45.

Bettleheim, B. 1983. *Freud and man's soul*. New York: Knopf.

Edelstein, M. 1984. *Hypothesis and evidence in psychoanalysis*. Chicago: University of Chicago.

Fisher, S., and R. Greenberg. 1985. *The scientific credibility of Freud's theories and therapy*. New York: Columbia University Press.

— — —. 1996. *Freud scientifically reappraised*. New York: Wiley.

Freud, S. [1900] 1965. *The interpretation of dreams*. Reprint, New York: Avon.

— — —. 1905. My views on the part played by sexuality in the aetiology of the neurosis. In *Sigmund Freud: Sexuality and the psychology of love*, edited by R. Rieff, 1–9. New York: Simon & Schuster.

— — —. [1914] 1990. The history of the psychoanalytic movement. In *The standard edition of the complete psychological works of Sigmund Freud*, edited by James Strachey, 14: 3–44. Reprint, New York: W. W. Norton. Hereafter referred to as the *Standard edition*.

— — —. [1918] 1990. The taboo of virginity. In *Sigmund Freud: Sexuality and the psychology of love*, edited by P. Rieff, 60–76. New York: Simon & Schuster.

— — —. [1921] 1990. Group psychology and the analysis of the ego. *Standard edition*. 18: 67–134.

— — —. [1927] 1990. The future of an illusion. *Standard edition*. 21: 3–34.

— — —. [1930] 1990. Civilization and its discontents. *Standard edition*. 21: 59–134.

— — —. [1933] 1990. New introductory lectures on psychoanalysis. *Standard edition*. 22: 3–158.

Fromm, E. 1959. *Sigmund Freud's mission*. New York: Grove Press.

— — —. 1964. *The heart of man*. New York: Harper & Row.

Glover, E. 1952. Research methods in psycho-analysis. *International Journal of Psychoanalysis* 33: 403–409.

Goldberg, C. 1990. The role of existential shame in the healing endeavor. *Psychotherapy* 27: 591–99.

— — —. 1996. Critical issues confronting the profession of psychotherapy:

now and into the new millennium. *International Journal of Psychotherapy* 1: 23–33.

— — —. 1997. *Speaking with the devil: Exploring senseless acts of evil*. New York: Penguin.

— — —. 1998. The indifference of psychoanalytic practice to social and moral responsibility. *International Journal of Psychotherapy* 3: 221–30.

— — —. 1999. A Psychoanalysis of love: The patient with deadly longing. *American Journal of Psychotherapy* 53: 437–51.

Hale, N. G. 1995. *The rise and crisis of psychoanalysis in the United States: Freud and the Americans 1917–1985*. New York: Oxford University Press.

Holton, G. 1988. *Thematic origins of scientific thought*. Cambridge, Mass.: Harvard University Press.

Jones, E. 1953. *The life and work of Sigmund Freud*. New York: Basic Books.

Kihlstrom, J. F. 1999. Empirical perspectives on the psychoanalytic unconscious. *Contemporary Psychology* 44: 376–78.

Rieff, P. 1966. *The triumph of the therapeutic*. New York: Harper & Row.

Roazen, P. 1968. *Freud: Political and social thought*. New York: Knopf.

Robinson, P. A. 1969. *The Freudian left*. New York: Harper & Row.

Von Eckardt, B. 1982. Why Freud's research methodology was unscientific. *Psychoanalysis and Contemporary Thought* 5: 549–74.

Wain, M. 1998. *Freud's answer: The social origins of our psychoanalytic century*. Chicago: Ivan R. Dees.

Western, D. 1998. The scientific legacy of Sigmund Freud: Towards a psychodynamically informed psychological science. *Psychological Bulletin* 124: 333–71.

Wheelis, A. 1962. *The seeker*. New York: New American Library.

1

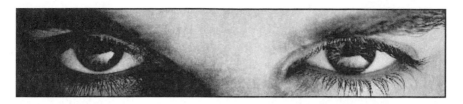

THE CASE OF THE
UNPATRIOTIC
PROSTITUTE

Psychoanalysis and Moral Responsibility

"Responsibility educates."
—Wendell Phillips, "The Press"

SALLY JAMES WAS REFERRED TO ME THIRTY YEARS AGO DURING MY apprenticeship as an analyst. A beautiful black woman in her early fifties, always artfully dressed, usually with pastel scarfs, turn-of-the-century blouses, and slit skirts, Sally was the illegitimate daughter of a white judge and his black mistress in the deep South. She knew her father only from afar. Her mother had little interest in mothering, leaving Sally as a five-year-old child to be raised by her sharecropper grandparents. As a naive and alluring teenager, Sally was continuously pursued by men—black and white alike. Rather than "giving it away," her mother encouraged her to charge for her favors. When Sally was seventeen, her father, perhaps concerned that he might be identified as the sire of a black prostitute, had the town sheriff hand her an envelope with five hundred dollars and put her on a bus for Los Angeles.

Despite only a few years of sporadic attendance at a rural, all-black school, Sally matured quickly in the big city. She was highly intelligent;

her keen observational skills enabled her to recognize that in her circumstances—without family, friends, formal education, or financial support—she needed to build a life in Los Angeles that was well-rounded; that is to say, to be "street smart" was necessary for her to stay alive, but insufficient for "a bountiful existence" (an expression she brought with her from the black South)—it would restrict her to the underlife of the city. To become sophisticated about style, culture, and the arts also was limited, since she had no means of supporting herself. But practical intelligence and culture combined would enable her to live well.

Her growing sophistication as a young woman served to refine her natural beauty. She became a highly paid call girl, who after a few years ran her own escort service. Several of her clients were in federal government service. On a number of occasions she and her girls were asked by these men to entertain foreign businessmen and dignitaries visiting California.

The turning point of her life occurred the day she was asked to meet a 10 A.M. client. She was greeted at the door of the hotel suite by a distinguished-looking, middle-aged man in a black pinstripe suit. Highly unusual clothes and time of day for sex in Los Angeles! she thought. But he wasn't interested in sex for himself. He introduced himself as a U.S. State Department official who was acquainted with several of her clients. He was there, he told her, to offer her unofficial employment as a hostess for his foreign dignitary guests. He wanted her to relocate to Northern Virginia and to hire a dozen or so beautiful, intelligent, and sophisticated young women. All would require high-security clearances, of course. But he promised to pay her a monthly retainer that exceeded her earnings on the West Coast. The arrangement held for three decades.

I asked Sally what she believed was the State Department's intention for the men she and her girls entertained. "It varied, of course. I know in many cases, they simply wanted these foreign diplomats and businessmen amused and favorably inclined toward our policies. In a few instances, I suspect that my employers were part of the Central Intelligence Agency."

"What did the CIA want with your clients?"

"I guess to compromise them and render them more vulnerable to their policy objectives."

"Were any of your clients ever seriously harmed during the time of your assignments with them?" I asked, aware that if Sally was as astute as she appeared, she had a reasonably accurate idea of what happened to her clients.

"At least one client, I'm sure, was assassinated or whatever is the proper term for murdering one's country's enemies."

"How did you feel about your participation in a murder?"

"What should I feel? I did not participate or even know ahead of time about the plans for any murders. In fact, some people would say that I was a patriot; I helped my country. But none of this is any concern of mine. What's in it for me to be a patriot? To tell you the truth, I have been as violent as I needed to be to survive."

"Meaning what?"

"Early during my life in Los Angeles I and the woman who ran the escort service I worked for became involved in an angry argument about the amount of time I was spending with my boyfriend. I thought to myself, Why not "bag two badgers with one stone?" I had my boyfriend take her for a ride, beat her up plenty, and put her on a bus for the South—the reversal of my trip, eh! And then I took over her business."

"Sally, I'm still not clear why you have phoned me for a consultation."

"Just to set the record straight, I have no problems with guilt. I am here because I am concerned with my daughter, Betty. Alex, your patient who works in the State Department [Alex's case is presented in chapter 9] is a friend of mine; he knows my background and believes that I have lingering resentments because of how I was treated as a child. I don't feel this is true. But I trust Alex, and I told him I would see you and find out."

Betty, her adolescent daughter in boarding school in Rhode Island, had no idea about the actual source of her mother's affluent lifestyle. She was led to believe that her mother was a highly paid interior decorator, who grew up in California and had been an aspiring but unsuccessful young actress. Her father, she was informed, had been a fellow actor. The parents' marriage, Sally added to the story she told her daughter, survived only slightly beyond Betty's birth. In fact, Betty, even more light-skinned than Sally, was the offsring of Sally's long relationship with a married State Department official.

Sally told me that she felt no regret in how she lived her life: she learned quickly that she was on her own; she could not afford to feel sorry for herself because there was no one who cared about her and would protect her. She claimed that she had done reasonably well under these circumstances. But her daughter had a clear slate; there was no good reason that she had to know about Sally's past and bear a stigma. She told me that if there was a specific reason for consulting with me it was to get some idea about how to keep her daughter from finding out about Sally's past.

Although Sally had no previous psychoanalysis or any other psychotherapy experiences, I assumed—given her intelligence—that she was aware that consulting with me would no better enable her to hide her past than she herself had done on her own. So for what psychological reason was Sally here?

In discussing Sally's case with my analytic supervisor, who I will call Drew Avery, I conveyed my belief that Betty represented for Sally her second self—an innocent self that she was trying—without awareness—to remake. What concerned me most was my anticipation that she sought to reconstruct her personal identity with the same social and moral apathy with which she had subsisted in her present identity. I didn't mean in terms of her choice of profession, but that she had lived her whole life, as best I could ascertain, only for herself. I felt that Sally's analytic treatment would be incomplete without examining the source of her moral indifference and helping her gain a social and moral perspective: not only in regard to herself, but for her daughter as well. In short, I was concerned that Sally's moral apathy would adversely shape Betty's social and moral development.

Drew Avery vehemently disagreed with me. With considerable indignation, he told me that my first concern—actually, my only analytic responsibility—was to enable Sally to recognize her unconscious motivation: to realize that she was using her daughter to undo her guilty image of herself as a fallen woman, and then to trace the etiology of her neurotic guilt to her childhood conflicts. With a disdaining flip of his wrist, he added that whether or not Sally lacked a sense of social and moral responsibility was not my proper concern as an analyst. Analytically, I was suppose to be a scientist, not a moral philosopher. He told me that Freud's metaphor of the detached, impenetrable surgeon "like a mirror reflecting nothing but what was shown to him" (Freud 1912) was the only appropriate model for a competent analyst. "Save your concerns about social values," Avery cautioned, "to political rallies in your private life and discussions about philosophy with your friends." (Washington, D.C.—where this conversation between my analytic supervisor and me took place—was at the time in the midst of the political rallies and turmoil of the Vietnam War.)

"But what about Sally's possible deleterious effect on her daughter?" I asked.

"Sally is your analysand, not Betty. Let Betty's analyst, if she ever enters analysis, concern himself with her!"

A review of the literature on the role of the analyst readily evinces that my supervisor's statements are consistent with psychoanalytic doctrine: the analysand has experienced moral doctrine all of her life; if moralizing was useful, it would have been so earlier. She needs to form her own conscience. Moral probing may hinder the analysand from a free inquiry of her mental life. Consequently, the psychoanalyst must extricate himself from all moral demands except the recognition that an examination of the unconscious motivation for one's behavior is the highest aim of human conduct.

Adherence to moral neutrality is still central to psychoanalytic doctrine. Consequently, whether or not my supervisor's statements were an exaggeration of conventional analytic doctrine is less important here than their implications for the question: Who, as analysts, are we actually responsible to in our clinical endeavor—the ostensible requests of the client at the inception of analysis or to the "better nature" (her submerged or undeveloped sense of conscience, compassion, and responsibility)?

I believed then and still do today that the analyst's responsibility is to his client's "better nature," no less than to the needs she articulates at the onset of analysis. Consequently, to continue to treat Sally under the conservative aegis of my analytic supervisor was a serious compromise of what I regarded as my clinical responsibility to my client. Therefore, with the reproach of my supervisor, I referred Sally to another analyst.

With the publication of his monumental work *The Interpretation of Dreams* in 1900, Sigmund Freud began the psychoanalytic revolution. **37**

He sought to demonstrate that the most authentic method for discovering how to live fully and well is to decipher the symbolic meanings in one's thoughts and feelings. This interpretive endeavor, he believed—if done competently by enough people—would transform society from a realm in which instinctual drives dominate to a place in which modulated reason can successfully compete with these powerful instincts.

We have now experienced a century of psychoanalysis. Our culture is saturated with its theories. Vast numbers of people have been recipients of its treatment services. And yet, in the postmodern world—the period that has followed the Second World War—we are less optimistic about our future than were people prior to the psychoanalytic era (Hillman and Ventura 1993).

I will cite three important sources of evidence of our contemporary societal malaise. A century ago Americans still took pride in their achievements and those of their community. For the most part, they felt a moral obligation to assist neighbors and strangers alike: indeed, anyone less fortunate than themselves. Most importantly, they believed that the capacity to be of help to others was the essence of a life lived well. Gradually, we have become an affluent society in which capital and material possessions rather than our labor and generosity are regarded as reflections of the fulfilled life. For too many Americans, concern with the problems of those less fortunate is no longer seen as necessary to a well-developed life, but a time-consuming activity that interferes with enjoying the benefits of affluence. According to the new American ethos, the reward of successful living is to be indulged by others; the less one is involved in the life of another, the more one is seen as an achiever rather than a person of servitude (Goldberg 1997b).

The second indication is the problem of evil. The most important problem humankind has ever faced is vicious destructiveness. Each of us as private citizens can attest to the calamitous presence of malevolence in our society—the "senseless" acts of cruelty and destructiveness that have become a ubiquitous component of daily life. Yet psychoanalysts along with other behavioral scientists have acted for the most part as if the problem of evil could be safely ignored by regarding it as a moral issue best handled by theologians and philosophers, or that the character structure of perpetrators could be reduced to known and well-understood psychological concepts and psychiatric diagnoses. It cannot! Psychological denial and reductionism have not served well the psychoanalyst's mandate to provide meaningful explanations and effective psychological intervention of social problems for the public. We still are not clear why people do appalling things to each other and to themselves. Because psychoanalysts and other clinicians have only treated the symptoms of malevolence, ignorant of its causes, evil remains elusive, able to exert virtually the same awesome and perplexing power as it has always done. Even today, perpetrators of atrocity vanish into history with their dreadful secrets still undisclosed (Goldberg 1997b). Not surprisingly, our age has been called "One of the most frightening in the history of the world" by the eminent theologian and social activist Cornel West.[1]

Third, reflective of our societal malaise, the first international study of major depressive illness reported in 1992 in the *Journal of the American Medical Association* that there has been a steady increase in clinical depression throughout the world in the present century. For example, people born between 1945 and 1955 were more than twice as likely to incur serious depression in the course of their lifetimes than people born between 1905 and 1915 (The Cross-National Collaborative Group 1992).

The increasing occurrence of serious emotional problems during the age of our greatest psychological sophistication causes one to wonder if our sophistication is more apparent than real: a cover-up for the reality that psychoanalytic public education sheds weak light and provides insubstantial help with society's serious problems. Obviously, all of our societal ills cannot be put at the doorstep of the psychoanalyst. These problems are overdetermined by a complex of social and cultural forces.[2] Nevertheless, as the most influential contemporary theory of American society,[3] psychoanalysis must be held accountable for its substantial impact on society's malaise. I seek to show that psychoanalysis —both as education and as treatment—has had little beneficial effect on society's serious social problems. My thesis is that Freud's lack of responsiveness to the importance of social and community responsibilities of analytic patients has prevented psychoanalysis from developing a theory of moral imperatives for human behavior. Moreover, this insufficiency has not only hindered analysands from their social and moral obligations to others, it also has had a subversive impact on American society. Contemporary social theory is more influenced by psychoanalytic thinking than by any other authority. For the last several decades, psychology and psychoanalysis have replaced the former pillars of society—religion, science, and education—as the sine qua non application in all matters in which human endeavor is involved. One need only glance at current periodicals, view cinema or television, or take a purview of the vast number of shelves in bookstores to readily appreciate that in postmodernity most complex human problems and concerns have been reduced to the level of psychological and psychoanalytic explanation. Indeed, the ideas of Sigmund Freud and his followers have been more influential than any other persons who have lived in the current century. In short, we have looked to psychology and psychoanalysis to provide us with a viable perspective on how to live the good life in an age of cynicism (Goldberg 1997a). Clearly, psychoanalysis has not yet provided a sound social theory.

My criticism of psychoanalysis is not intended to diminish its role in society, but rather to extend its vision by showing its blindness to the position of the psyche in the outer world. I argue here that psychoanalysis's most serious error is the notion that the psyche is located within the encapsulated self, removed from a deteriorating social world. The controversial Sanskrit scholar and onetime psychoanalyst, Jeffrey Masson in his *Assault on Truth* (1984), states: "... by shifting the emphasis from an actual world of sadness and cruelty to an internal stage on which actors performed invented dramas for an invisible audience, Freud began a trend away from the real world. . . . [It is this that] is at the root of the present-day sterility of psychoanalysis and psychiatry throughout the world" (114).

THE ROLE OF EQUITY AND BALANCE IN HUMAN EXISTENCE

To enable psychoanalysis to broaden its vision it must first redefine its premises. Essential to this endeavor is the psychoanalyst's understanding of the crucial role of equity and balance in human existence.

Social, psychological, and literary evidence (Goldberg 1977) reveals that the concept of *fairness* (equity) is a basic issue that runs through the course of human history in all cultures. Indeed, it is rather difficult to conceive of any notion that is more fundamental to the transactions of people involved with one another than the concern that they be treated in a just, right, and honest way—be these exchanges brief encounters with strangers, or durable, lasting relationships with significant others.

Consequently, both aberrant and emotionally disordered behavior are generated by disturbances of regulated and common systems of expected and proper (equitable) behavior. If an individual cannot derive desired material and emotional exchanges in accordance with what he has come to expect and feel entitled to by the system of equity from which he operates, aberrant and/or emotionally disordered behavior results. In contrast, living fully and well comes from a composite of balanced relationships: this is to say, an overall sense that one has given sufficiently of himself to balance the care and goodwill one has received from others (Goldberg and Kane 1974).

Accordingly, it is my observation that people who seek mental-health services are essentially concerned with establishing equitable and balanced relations with others. My clinical experience has shown that for this to happen three crucial roles must be competently assumed by the client. These roles are of patient, student, and helper. The *patient* role is based on the clinical awareness that without the emotional recognition of dysfunctional aspects of our behavior we cannot ameliorate problem areas in our lives. Equity theory asserts that those who are deficient in some important area of their functioning deserve to be given to by those abundant in these areas. The *student* role is based on the understanding that without utilizing the cognitive skills of the learner we could not generalize from one life experience to another or gain from other peoples' experiences. Equity theory assumes that the student is pursuing normal psychosocial development: as a learner he acquires knowledge, later he will teach others what he has learned. Finally, the *helper* role indicates that without the experience of being of assistance to others and recognized and appreciated for these efforts, our lives would remain sterile and unsatisfying. Equity theory claims that the helper should give because he himself has been accorded, and now is overabundant in some important area of function in which others are in need of his help.

All three roles are essential to healthy psychological and social functioning at appropriate times. People who incur difficulties in life are those who have rigidly maintained one role to the exclusion of others. The implications of the principles of equity and balance for constructive interpersonal relationships are presented in chapter 9 and in section C of the Theory and Method Appendix. The role of equity theory in humanistic analytic treatment in illustrated in Vincent's case in chapter 8 and section C.

Orthodox psychoanalysis[4] focuses almost exclusively on the development of skills in recouping what one has failed to gain earlier in life (the *patient* role); it totally eschews the role of *helper*. The psychoanalytic neglect of the helper role in healing is bonded to its lack of concern for the client's social and moral responsibility.

THE IMPORTANCE OF A THEORY OF MORAL IMPERATIVE

A system of morality is a statement of how a person ought to behave. As such, morality is derived from a conception of the necessary responsibilities members of an ideal society must establish and maintain in concert with one another.[5]

Encouraging moral responsibility rests upon a knowledge of virtue. Consequently, to perform a constructive role for the society it serves, a theory of human behavior needs to competently explain how virtuous behaviors develop.

Unfortunately, psychoanalysts have turned their attention more inclusively than seems warranted to examining human ills, as if we could understand virtue by studying misfortune alone. In short, current analytic theories emphasize loss and psychopathology in how people live their lives. They pay relatively little attention to the admirable and constructive mainstream of human development—the capacity for empathy, identification with others, affection, caring, compassion, and altruism—that foster moral responsibility.

The lack of a psychoanalytic theory to explain the development of human virtue is closely related to Freud's puzzlement about his own morality. In a letter July 8, 1915, to J. J. Putnam, a Boston physician, Freud wrote: "When I ask myself why I have always aspired to behave honorably, to spare others and to be kind whenever possible, and why I don't cease doing so when I realized that in this way one comes to harm and becomes an anvil because other people are brutal and unreliable, then indeed I have no answer. . . . Why I—and incidentally my six adult children as well—have to be thoroughly decent human beings is quite incomprehensible to me" (E. L. Freud 1960, 308–309).

Could Freud's own moral questioning have so profoundly straitjacketed psychoanalysis for the past century so that it could not develop a moral theory? Viewing Freud as a powerful paradigmatic leader suggests it could and has done so.

THE PARADIGMATIC LEADER

It can be argued that psychoanalysis is not the exclusive intellectual property of Freud alone. And as such he should not be held accountable for the deficiencies of his followers. Such a thesis has merit. Clearly Freud was a highly complex and enigmatic figure. Writers for the past century have interpreted him in a variety of ways. Nevertheless, as a powerful leader (no one has questioned the potency of Freud's charisma), Freud influentially shaped his followers' behavior. Freud needs to be compared here with the world's foremost religious prophets, since no other important social or psychological movement has been so narrowly defined on the basis of the founder's sacrosanct statements as a justification for the conduct of its members as has psychoanalysis. One must go to religious movements to find a comparable practice.

Karl Jaspers (1962), the German psychiatrist and philosopher, and a contemporary of Freud, in his renowned study of the personalities of those he regarded as true prophets—Jesus, Socrates, Buddha, and Confucius—indicates that for each, human love was unlimited and universal. Thus, although the prophet may feel fear and doubt (as Jesus apparently did on the cross) or resolute enlightenment (as Socrates did

43

on choosing his existential death), he never pushes his followers to validate his beliefs. Instead, each patiently creates by personal example a psychological sanctuary in which his disciples can choose for themselves what to believe. This was hardly true of Freud!

Freud's personality seems to be responsible for a lack of interest in affirmative behavior among psychoanalysts. Stefan Zweig, the poet—who knew Freud when Zweig was a young man and kept in close contact with him for the rest of Freud's life—describes Freud as "unfailingly autocratic and intransigent [94]. . . . Courteousness, sympathy, and considerateness would have been incompatible with the revolutionary thought-trend of Freud's creative temperament, his essential mission being to make extremes manifest, not to reconcile them" (93). Moreover, according to Erich Fromm (1959), the humanistic psychoanalyst, Freud was a person who exhibited a "lack of emotional warmth, closeness, love, and beyond that, of enjoyment of life" (11). For example, according to his nephew Harry, Freud was toward his own children "always a bit *formal* and *reserved*. Indeed, it rarely happened that he kissed any of them; I might almost say, really never" (Gay 1988, 162).

FREUD'S PERSONALITY PREDILECTIONS

Freud's puzzlement about moral conduct is related to his personality attributes in at least the following five ways:

1. *Freud did not trust love*. Viewing moral conduct as an autonomous act of healthy striving comes from the belief that its expression is a manifestation of affection for others rather than compelled from the fear of punishment for wrongful behavior.

According to the psychoanalytically trained historian Peter Gay (1988), Freud believed that "virtually all sentiments of love are ambivalent, virtually all contain elements of rage and hostility" (372). Freud frequently made statements about human nature that probably were more accurate judgments of his own personality than of universal applicability. His view of love appears to be an example of this tendency.

Freud, Fromm (1959) tells us, "was a very insecure person, easily feeling threatened, persecuted, betrayed, and hence, as one would expect, a great desire for certainty. To him, considering his whole personality, there was no certainty in love—there was certainty only in knowledge . . ." (11).

Mistrusting love as a binding force in mature relationships, Freud (1905) rejected affection as a healthy mainspring of human behavior. He viewed it as a seductive, repressive, magical wish inflicting everyone. He believed that intimate attachments were the rediscovery of the lost object—behaving as if lovers possess the same personal characteristics as the oedipal parent—so that the experience of love repeats infantile patterns. Predicated upon the mother-child bonding, disappointments in adult attempts at love result in inevitable narcissistic hurt and depression. As such, love sentiments were for Freud an unreliable guide for moral conduct (Goldberg 1989a).

2. *Freud did not trust altruistic behavior.* Two of Freud's strongest statements of the supremacy of destructive human instincts are found in his *Civilization and Its Discontents* (1930) and in his reply letter to Albert Einstein in the late 1930s. Einstein had written Freud, asking whether the massive human destructiveness of war could somehow be averted. Freud replied in the negative.

In his response to Einstein, as well, as in his other writings, Freud reduces all human strivings to conflicting drives; and by doing so he eschews altruism and other virtuous behaviors as fundamental human attributes. He claims instead that these apparent virtues are actually psychological defenses compelled by feelings of guilt and/or grandiose fantasies of heroism to mask feelings of emotional impotence.

Freud's basis for denying the benevolent character of apparent virtue is a powerful paradoxical explanation in which he reverses the conventional views about *thought* and *deed*. In other words, Freud contends that psychical reality, not material reality, is the basis for psychological life. Consequently, dreams and "forbidden" fantasies can be of such illicit tenor that they can even exceed the import of actual villainous deeds. This is exemplified in Freud's (1900) explanation for the anguish of Shakespeare's noble character Hamlet. Freud tells us that Hamlet suffers from a guilty conscience of oedipal origins. Hamlet unconsciously senses that he desires to do precisely what his uncle, Claudius, the King, has consummated—doing away with Hamlet's **45** father and seducing Hamlet's mother. Consequently, were Hamlet to carry out his revenge against Claudius, the man who fulfilled the repressed wishes of Hamlet's own childhood, then Hamlet, according to Freud's interpretation of the oedipal metaphor, would have also to castigate himself (as did Oedipus). Hamlet's self-abnegation egresses from his unconscious realization that he is no better in his heart than Claudius was in his deeds.

The interpretive problem here is that Freud often disregards the manifest text and interprets "below" the surface in what he regards as the "true meaning" of the text. He does this in his explanation of Hamlet's enigmatic behavior. In other words, Freud finds evidence of Hamlet's oedipal complex by disregarding several important contraindications.

First, it is highly questionable that Hamlet's attachment to his mother was either prolonged or unusually strong. Evidence of enmeshed bonding is a primary necessity for verification of an oedipal conflict. The Shakespeare scholar Henry Goddard (1960), among others, indicates that Hamlet's vibrant male friendships, especially with Horatio, and his falling in love with Ophelia, a woman rather different in temperament and personality from his mother, seem to have occurred at what psychologists would regard as appropriate times in Hamlet's development. This information serves as negative evidence that Hamlet was suffering from an intense pathological oedipal conflict.

Second, another primary consideration in validating an oedipal conflict is the presence of destructive impulses toward the father. Nowhere in the play is there any evidence that Hamlet desires his father's death. Actually, there is more evidence to share psychoanalyst Frederic Wertheim's (1941) contention that Hamlet's considerable rage and resentment is evoked by his mother.

Third, the most important circumstance in the Oedipus story indicates that the myth has little relevance to Hamlet's situation. We need to return to the original Oedipus myth to help us see how little attention Freud generally gives to the whole fabric of a literary work in appropriating the material in support of his theories. We find that Freud does only a perfunctory job of examining the Oedipus story. His interpretation totally disregards the first half of the myth in which Oedipus's parents express extreme fear and hatred of their child (Bloch 1966). Nor does he mention that they actually attempt to murder their helpless child. These sentiments and behavior are contradictory to that of Hamlet's familial relationship (Goldberg 1989).

Four decades of clinical experience have impressed upon me the realization that a patient's overriding need in treatment is to find positive qualities about himself and his life, and to use this information to establish his personal identity in a self-enhancing way. In short, the most difficult task, indeed, the turning point in a patient's road to psychological healing, is to gain a *trust in his own goodness*.

Unfortunately, Freud's reversal of the importance of thought and deed encourages clients to turn away from examining their personal morality. In other words, psychological systems that reduce affirmative behavior to defensive behavior subvert human virtue. They contribute to a selfish focus rather than to one's responsibilities to others. By telling us that by nature we are a seething cauldron of lust, conflict, and hatred, psychoanalytic theory gives all of us "permission" to express ourselves in egocentric and mean-spirited ways. This trend in psychoanalysis Peter Marin (1975) calls "a deification of the self . . . in which selfishness and moral blindness now assert themselves in the larger culture as enlightenment and psychic health."

3. *Freud devalued friendship.* Freud, psychoanalyst Michael Eigen (1993) tells us, felt that his creative work was the only pursuit that made his life worthwhile. By creative work, Freud was referring to the solitary journey in search for inner truth. If Eigen is right, then what was Freud saying about the value for him of his patients, his close friendships (especially with his intimate friends, the physician Wilhelm Fliess and the psychoanalyst Sandor Ferenczi), and his family?

Freud, it appears, viewed relationships as adaptive—making life manageable—but if held too highly they may diminish one's chances for profound psychic transformation (Eigen 1993).

In contrast, it can be argued that both friendship and the pursuit of inner truth are of comparable value. The philosopher Fredrich Nietzsche certainly bonded the two together on the grounds that only the truthful are capable of deep friendship. Personal integrity was of paramount importance to Nietzsche's view of truth; in friendship, he believed, integrity or its lack is best revealed. But for Freud his obsession with inner truth was all-consuming. Consequently, I believe that it is a solipsistic foreclosure of human potential to adopt what I regard as

Freud's seriously myopic vision: the belief that the intrapsychic world holds more wisdom and truth than the world of other people. Whereas it is mandatory that we search our inner depths in seeking our identity, nevertheless it is in the world we share with others that our identity is of significance.

A serious scrutiny of a client's lack of a social and moral sense is unlikely to take place with a therapist who believes that the realm of the mind is far more significant than the world of others. This is exemplified in the instances of generosity Freud extended to his patients. For example, not only did he not charge a fee to the Wolf Man, his impoverished Russian patient (Freud 1918), he collected funds from his friends and colleagues to help the Wolf Man meet basic needs. But on the other hand, I have not heard of a single instance in which Freud said to a patient who he had previously shown generosity, something to the effect: "Once you were in need and you were showed kindness. Now you are no longer in dire plight. I believe you *should* give to others who could use your help."

Generosity that is one-sided is patronizing: in no way does it contribute to the patient's sense of social and moral responsibility. Being of help to others is not only a social and moral responsibility of enlightened citizenship, it is therapeutic, as well, for those whom we call emotionally disturbed, but who are actually emotionally impoverished. The so-called emotionally disturbed person has been deprived of equitable and balanced relationships with others. These relationships serve as a *lifeline* that sustains and maintains the individual, keeping him alive and well. When a person performs needed social and emotional services for others and is recognized for his help, he is valued both by others and himself. Concomitantly, he experiences legitimate entitlement to ask for needed or desired responsiveness from others.

4. *Freud confused conscience and superego.* One who believes that neither affection nor altruism is genuine is left with only fear and threat as moral guardians. Freud (1923) held that the superego—predicated on fear and threat—is the agent of morality. Psychoanalytically trained sociologist Eli Sagan (1988), in contrast, persuasively argues that for the superego to be moral it needs the services of the conscience: because the *superego always collaborates with its own corruption*.

Freud's conjoining of superego and conscience has made it difficult to make psychological sense of heinous acts by individuals with strong superegos. As Sagan (1988) points out, "The mechanisms of the superego make it possible to use almost any virtue in the most horrible of human projects. . . . The Nazis used all the trappings of the superego to promote genocide" (13). The "good" Nazi was loyal, obedient, even willing to sacrifice his life to carry out the prescriptive norms of his society.

"The relative health or pathology of the superego is (actually) dependent on how much or how little of conscience is operative in its functioning" (Sagan 1988, 14). Conscience is fostered in love, derived from the child's early compassionate nurturing—including the child's relationship with the father. In his writings, Freud ignores the importance of the preoedipal father-son relationship (Goldberg 1991). His notion of oedipal rivalry between the father and son regards the child's experience of the father as inordinately negative, namely, a powerful barrier in the way of the child's libidinous reunion with the mother. But surely the child's growing identification with his father is much more than a defense against paternal punishment that stems from the oedipal situation.

Child analyst Peter Blos (1985) indicates that Freud's interpretation of the oedipal situation inaccurately overemphasizes the son's wish to replace the father. Freud's oedipal thesis is opposed to the realization that the father establishes a sense of trust and safety in the preoedipal child. This early bond of love between father and son, Blos points out, frequently continues despite the conflicts of the oedipal period.

5. *Freud used the wrong model for the competent analyst.* Those who believe that human motives are essentially mean-spirited are more apt to trust peoples' minds rather than their hearts. Freud's inability to recognize that warmth, compassion, and genuineness rather than intellectual grasp of some profound psychological truths about the patient were the essential ingredients in psychological healing required him to find a therapeutic model that would neutralize the untoward critical proclivities of the analyst from harming the patient. He chose the metaphor of the detached, impenetrable surgeon that my supervisor Drew Avery insisted is the only proper analytic position. Here Freud has presented as his ideal type an analyst model who would be reluctant to reveal his own values and consequently would take no stance in regard to the client's social and moral responsibility.

THE IMPLICATIONS OF FREUD'S SOCIAL ATTITUDES FOR PSYCHOANALYSIS

Does it really matter what are a person's "actual" motives—deep in his unconscious—for his caring and altruistic behavior? What is more important is that the expression of these affirmative behaviors makes the world a better place to live for all of us. Since we cannot properly promote moral responsibility if we reduce virtue to a defense against our inherent destructive nature, I submit that psychoanalysis—by rendering virtuous behavior suspect and base—serves as a subversive force in society.

Lacking interest in the complex social problems of the external world, analysts unwittingly have become conservative agents of the societal status quo. From this perspective, the psychological problems of their clients are regarded as failures in successful social adaptation due to intrapsychic conflict, rather than, or as well as, symptoms of an unjust, oppressive societal power structure.

A preponderance of our societal problems are moral, economical, and political. They are due to societal philosophies that justify maximizing profit at the expense of the safety, health, and happiness of those who lack social, political, and economic power. We are a nation in which the gap between the rich and the poor is rapidly expanding. These issues are ignored by a psychoanalytic practice that focuses inordinately on dreams and other intrapsychic preoccupations. Today there is less concern by analysts about the needy and the deprived than ever before (Jacoby 1983).

Troublesome societal issues are ignored in large part because psychoanalysis is *elitist*—rendering most of its service to those who pay the most and need it the least. "Those persons who pay the highest fees for psychotherapy (and psychoanalysis) will tend to have the mildest degrees of maladjustment" (Schofield 1964, 19).

Although many analysts in my acquaintance are among the most socially concerned and compassionate people I know, as a profession, analysts leave unexplored the legitimacy of the social and political power of their affluent and influential clients. They help them, complains Peter Marin (1975), "avoid the demands of the world, to smother the tug of conscience. They allow them to remain who and what they are, to accept the structured world as it is—but with a new sense of justice and justification, with the assurance that it all accords with cosmic law. . . . [Yet try] as as we do, we cannot ignore the routine inequalities of consumption and distribution which benefit us and condemn others to misery. Each of us must feel a kind of generalized shame, an unanswered sense of guilt. So we struggle mightily to convince ourselves that our privilege is earned or deserved, rather than (as we must often feel unconsciously) a form of murder or theft. Our therapies become a way of hiding from the world, a way of easing our troubled conscience." In short, currently the psychoanalytic enterprise helps very few—mostly those who need help the least. And the help that those advantaged few receive is not what they need the most: a tug at their social conscience.

Freud in his mistrust of affection and relationships has guided psychoanalysis away from addressing the fundamental paradox in human development. The paradox is this: healthy human development requires that we take responsibility for ourselves and not remain overly dependent upon others; at the same time, we are keepers of our brothers and sisters and they of us. The poet John Donne warned: No one of us is an island onto himself. We all belong to one solidarity. An act that involves one person inevitably has moral impact upon us all (Goldberg 1997b).

For psychoanalytic practice to become a viable agent for social and moral responsibility, analysts must relinquish their claim that the cause of human unhappiness is solely a matter of intrapsychic issues. Analysts must help their clients recognize a simple fact of human nature: none of us can live satisfying and meaningful lives in the midst of others' suffering. All who have tried have failed. Since none of us exists alone, a life lived well is concerned with helping foster the conditions that extend justice and concern to every member of society. Only when each of us feels that his or her personal worth as a person is based on our compassion and responsibility to others, rather than on affluence and influence, will we have a just and harmonious society. This was eloquently stated in a rare statement by a psychoanalyst. As a Dutch citizen, J. A. Meerloo had been a prisoner in a Nazi concentration camp during World War II. On the basis of this experience he points out: "Justice can be looked on as a guiding moral value only if it can be severed from man's private interests. If man is motivated not merely by his own suffering, not merely by his own self-pity, not merely by the wrong inflicted upon himself, but more by the suffering and pains of others— weaker ones and minorities, etc.—then indeed we could speak of justice as a guiding principle" (Meerloo 1959).

In the next chapter I present a vignette of my formative years to account for why my childhood best friend became a convicted killer, and I, from a similar background, a psychologist and psychoanalyst, who for much of my career studied and treated those who subsisted as highly destructive people.

NOTES

1. In a lecture in 1995 at the Church of Saint John the Divine in New York City.

2. Many of these factors I discuss elsewhere (Goldberg 1997a).

3. In this chapter I discuss the impact of psychoanalysis on American culture, the society I know best. This perspective may be less accurate for other postmodern societies.

4. Other psychotherapies, such as behavior therapy, group therapy, and family therapy, sometimes address the helper role—in order to develop the patient's competence in getting what he seeks from others—but not because of a social and moral responsibility to be of help to others.

5. More Americans regard the major source of society's serious problems as moral (45 percent) than political (28 percent) or economic (17 percent) (Horowitz 1997).

REFERENCES

Block, D. 1966. Some dynamics of suffering. *Psychoanalytic Review* 53: 31–54.

Blos, P. 1985. *Son and father: Before and beyond the oedipal complex.* New York: Free Press.

Cross-National Collaborative Group. 1992. The changing role of major depression: Cross-national comparisons. *Journal of the American Medical Association* 268: 3098–3105.

Eigen, M. 1993. *The electrified tightrope*. Northvale, N.J.: Jason Aronson.

Freud, E. L., ed. 1960. *Letters of Sigmund Freud*. New York: Basic Books.

Freud, S. 1900. 1965. *Interpretation of dreams*. New York: Avon.

———. [1905] 1990. *Three essays on the theory of sexuality*. In the *standard edition of the complete psychological works of Sigmund Freud*, edited by James Strachey, 7:231–43. Reprint, New York: W. W. Norton.

———. [1912] 1990. Recommendations to physicians practising psychoanalysis. *Standard edition*. 12: 109–20.

———. [1918] 1990. From the history of an infantile neurosis. *Standard edition*. 7: 1–104.

———. 1927. *The future of an illusion*. New York: Norton.

———. 1930. *Civilization and its discontents*. New York: Norton.

Fromm, E. 1959. *Sigmund Freud's mission*. New York: Grove.

Gay, P. 1988. *Freud, a life for our times*. New York: Norton.

Goldberg, C. 1977. *Therapeutic partnership: Ethical concerns in psychotherapy*. New York: Springer.

———. 1989a. The role of passion in the transformation of anti-heroes. *Journal of Evolutionary Psychology* 9: 216.

———. 1989b. The shame of Hamlet and Oedipus. *Psychoanalytic Review* 76: 581–603.

———. 1991. Why Hamlet could not love. *Psychoanalysis and Psychotherapy* 9: 19–32.

———. 1996. Critical issues confronting the profession of psychotherapy: Now and into the new millennium. *International Journal of Psychotherapy* 1: 23–33.

———. 1997a. Chautauqua Institution lecture: The responsibilities of virtue. *International Journal of Psychotherapy* 2: 179–91.

——— 1997b. *Speaking with the devil: Exploring senseless acts of evil*. New York: Penguin.

Goldberg, C., and J. D. Kane. 1974. Toward an equitable therapy for the poor. In *Mental health issues and the urban poor*, edited by D. A. Evans and W. L. Claiborn. New York: Pergamon.

Goddard, H. C. 1960. *The meaning of Shakespeare*, vol. 1. Chicago: University of Chicago Press.

Hillman, J., and M. Ventura. 1993. *We've had a hundred years of psychotherapy and the world's getting worse*. San Francisco: HarperCollins.

Horowitz, I. L. 1997. Social science and the citizen. *Society* 35: 2.

Jacoby, R. 1983. *The repression of psychoanalysis*. Chicago: University of Chicago.

Jaspers, K. 1962. *Socrates, Buddha, Confucius and Jesus: The paradigmatic leaders*. New York: Harcourt, Brace & World.

Marin, P. 1975. The new narcissism. *Harper's Magazine* (October): 45–70.

Masson, J. 1984. *Assault against truth*. New York: Farrar, Straus & Giroux.

Meerloo, J. A. 1959. Justice as a psychological problem. *Archives of Criminal Psychodynamics* 3: 7–51.

Sagan, E. 1988. *Freud, women, and morality*. Englewood, N.J.: Fish Drum Press.

Schofield, W. 1964. *Psychotherapy: The purchase of friendship*. Englewood Cliffs, N.J.: Prentice-Hall.

Wertheim, F. 1941. The matricide impulse: Critique of Freud's interpretation of *Hamlet*. *Journal of Criminal Psychopathology* 2: 455–64.

Zweig, S. 1973. Portrait of Freud. In *Freud as we knew him*, edited by H. M. Ruitenbeek, 90–97. Detroit: Wayne State University Press.

2

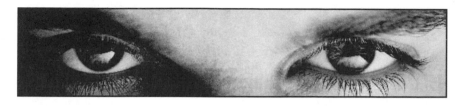

THE CASE OF THE
ADOLESCENT MURDERER

The Refusal to Self-examine

*Of all exercises there are none of so much importance, or so immediately
our concern, as those which let us into the knowledge of our own nature.*
—Bishop William Warburton,
Church sermon, eighteenth-century England

IT WAS NOT BY CHANCE THAT I BECAME A PSYCHOANALYST WHO
during my career was engaged in an arduous psychological struggle with
seriously destructive patients. My work was impelled to a considerable
degree from my efforts to understand why Nicky, my closest friend in
childhood, became a convicted murderer in his late adolescence.

At the age of seven I was a student in a boarding school set in a
dense forest in Westchester County, just north of New York City. At
the school, with its German accent and the love of books, Mozart,
and the outdoors, I first heard the word "psychology." My teachers,
who had recently fled to the United States from the Nazi Holocaust,
were well educated and trained in psychoanalytic ideas. They conveyed an understanding of human behavior that was for me mysteri-
ously powerful: the capacity to articulate the shadowy fears that sus-

tained periods of silence for my classmates and me. Indeed, they seemed able to read our minds.

Each of us was assigned to a teacher with whom we met weekly in a private counseling session. Asked about my thoughts and dreams during the week, I was often reluctant to reveal my private world. When I did describe my dreams, more than once I was told that they indicated that I had a special interest in one or another of the girls at school, or that I harbored competitive feelings toward male classmates. Uncannily, I found these assertions to be accurate.

My experiences with these European teachers stimulated my interest in psychology. The house in which my counseling sessions were held was tucked snugly in a grove of graceful weeping willow trees on the edge of the school grounds. On my casual walks back to my class-room, pausing for a few moments at the school's small languid pond, adorned with water lily rush, I reviewed what had occurred in my ses-sion. I said to myself many a time: Wow, this psychology thing is pow-erful stuff! Maybe I can use it to try to figure out why my parents always seem so angry at each other.

I began attending the school toward the end of the Second World War. My father never made enough money at jobs at different times on the railroad, as longshoreman or taxi driver to support himself, my mother, and me. In an era in which most mothers stayed home to take care of the household, mine worked as a secretary in a young adult education pro-gram. My parents had serious marital problems. Their personalities and interests were at odds. My mother was far more ambitious; she wanted to rise from a working-class style of living to a more middle-class exis-tence. My father's limited education frustrated her ambitions. He spent his few free hours at Broadway shows, films, and sports events.

My mother sought to "better" herself by taking continuing education classes. Wanting to be helpful and needed by people besides her family, she did volunteer work for civic and political organizations. At one of these meetings she met a woman better educated than she. They became friends. My mother told her about the problems at home. Her friend knew the director of a progressive education boarding school. Before she introduced them, she told my mother: "Send your son to boarding school. He will learn more from the European teachers there than from the public school he is now attending. Besides, he won't be exposed every day to arguments in your house between you and your husband."

In my fourth year at the boarding school I was assigned a new roommate. Nicky was also eleven. We had much in common. Unlike most of our classmates, we were from working-class families: mine a Jewish family living in South Brooklyn; his, a black family residing in Newark. The school was as liberal in its financial policies as it was educationally progressive. Nicky and I were on scholarship: our families paid less tuition than our classmates' parents. We also were the best athletes at school.

What we didn't share was an attitude about the weekly psychological sessions. Nicky was one of the few youngsters in school who resisted his sessions. He often didn't show up.

"I don't need anybody to tell me what they think I'm thinking. If I have something to say, I know how to say it," he told me after he skipped a session.

"But what are you thinking about that you don't want anyone to know?" I asked.

"Hey, if you're really my buddy, don't bug me with that psychology crap!" he shot back. I was taken aback—and felt hurt—that Nicky did not trust me enough to recognize that I was his ally, not his enemy. I would learn later that one of the most significant human characteristics is that we are more decisively shaped by what we do not know about ourselves than by what we recognize and understand. It is costly for a person to be unwilling to explain himself to those who care about him. A trusted relationship serves as a reliable mirror. Those who are unable to see themselves accurately are as much strangers to themselves as they are to others.

The ethos of progressive education held that students were not compelled do anything they didn't want to do. Our teachers, whatever they might have believed were the motives for Nicky's behavior, accepted his right to attend sessions only when he wanted to be there. I, in contrast, was intrigued by exploring my mind. Of all the gifts my mother gave me, the most valuable of all, I believe, was the encouragement to know myself. "It's a good thing to learn about yourself," she would say. "You'll be a better person for the time you spend getting to know who you are." **57**

THE EVIL WE DO

A few nights a week, Nicky and I lowered ourselves down from our second-floor dormitory window to the grassy turf below. We trotted down the dark, winding road from the high hill on which the school sat to Main Street in town. There we hung out in the general store, reading comics and sports magazines, and drinking sodas.

I can still see Nicky's amused face, illuminated by the porch lights of the homes along the way, as we jogged back to school and conspired about ways to beat the rich boys at school in games like marbles, and in informational quizzes in class at which prizes were given. Beating my classmates with my personal resources indicated to me that I could do as well or better than those from more privileged families. Because we lacked the nice clothes and material possessions of our classmates, Nicky and I were determined to use our personalities, good looks, and intelligence to do better than our classmates at all forms of competition.

At sports we never had to conspire; as long as we were on the same team we were unbeatable. At other types of games we developed a secret code: a sign language that enabled us to give each other information and instructions about the right moves or the correct answers. The code was a modification of the signals we used on the baseball field. We also made up rules that gave us an advantage. If the others complained that they had never heard of these rules, we shrugged our shoulders and told them that they didn't know the game as well as we did. They usually accepted our rules.

It wasn't because they were unaware. They recognized that we had made up a new rule. I suppose we were able to get away with so much because they were intimidated by our daring. None of them took the risks we did. We smoked cigarettes. I stopped when my parents found out. Nicky continued. On occasion, Nicky and I would "borrow" a car of some neighbor of the school. We would go on night-time "joyrides" lasting about an hour. Nicky was a competent driver. The other boys at school were afraid to drive. Sometimes Nicky let me take the wheel. Our classmates knew about our drives, but none ever told. I guess they were concerned that if they "ratted" on us, we would no longer have anything to do with them. Frankly, they were a rather boring group of kids. They sat around a great deal after school, until Nicky or I took charge and organized an activity.

I left out another consideration. No doubt Nicky's ability to act differently from the others stemmed from his striking good looks: Nicky was a tall, graceful youngster, with a quick, charming smile. In fact, my mother often remarked after he visited my home in Brooklyn, having ridden his bicycle over two major bridges and miles of city streets: "Nicky looks like Harry Belafonte, only better looking." It has been my experience that very attractive people, with the charm that seemed so facile for Nicky, can get away with selfish behavior that more ordinary-looking people cannot.

Despite the admiration he received, Nicky seemed to have an unrelenting need to tell boastful and contradictory stories about himself and his family. There was a mysterious shroud that cloaked his father's identity and whereabouts. According to one story, he was the then popular white bandleader Spike Jones. And, in another account, he was a black war-decorated army master sergeant, whom Nicky had not seen in a long while. In the eight years I knew Nicky, I never met his father or heard that he was home visiting.

The two relatives of his who I did meet were oddly complementary: his mother, a short, stout, talkative woman, who always seemed caught up in giggles; and his schoolteacher, maiden, maternal aunt, a tall, slim woman with a stern face. She rarely spoke.

I found it strange that they seemed unaware that Nicky was an active and independent child. They behaved as if he had only a past. His mother would gush breathlessly, statements to the effect, "Oh, that Nicky! You should have seen him as an infant: he was so cuddly and beautiful!" On one occasion I heard her speak to her son in baby talk. Nicky's cheeks flushed, but he did not voice to her the indignation he was quick to express to others.

The majority of Nicky's stories involved married women who wanted to leave their husbands for him. Once when I asked him why a grown woman would prefer a boy of twelve, he quickly turned away to conceal a menacing sneer. But an instant later he recovered, drew his face back to me, leaned forward, and said in his soft amicable baritone, "I'm as good with a woman as I am with a car."

I listened politely, keeping to myself my amusement about the lack of credibility of his yarns. But what did trouble me was that I, along with Nicky, took advantage of our classmates. I recognized that **59** although my other classmates were not as close to me as Nicky, never-theless, they were also my friends.

About once a month I spent a weekend at one or another of their affluent homes in Westchester. Nicky, as the most popular boy at school, also frequently stayed at their homes. He was a spellbinding charmer; his easy comradery and amusing stories of his forays into the adult world disguised his lack of respect for his classmates and their parents. There was hardly a parent, I'm sure, who didn't regard Nicky as a delightful and intelligent child.

Yet in looking back, I suspect, as important as expressing kind-ness and decency to any child, these politically liberal parents also wanted to be seen as people who were as kind to a disadvantaged Negro child (as African Americans were referred to then) as to a Jewish child from Brooklyn.

"I'm not faked out by their niceness to me," Nicky told me one Sunday evening as we listened to a professional basketball game on his battered radio and compared notes about our weekend visits. "Andy's father [a reknowned corporate attorney] can't wait to shock the stuffed shirts with whom he works. When he tells them that a colored friend of Andy's slept in his house, they'll piss in their pants," he expressed with a deadpan look.

I am sure most of my classmates turned out to be good, decent people, but as children, they tended to be very opinionated spectators rather than doers. That is why my resolve to be fair to them evaporated quickly. Ashamedly, I admit that Nicky's friendship was far more important to me than my sense of fairness. He was my very best friend. With him I didn't have to concern myself with acting properly as I did with the others. I still remember my feelings of irritation when I was around many of my classmates. They continually evaluated each other's behavior by absolute standards of mental health they must have acquired in their counseling sessions. For instance, if I wanted to listen to a ball game after class alone in my room, it was unacceptable to them. "It's not healthy to spend your time alone when you could be with the group," Ellen, a precocious ten-year-old with large horn-rimmed glasses and an authoritative manner, would say.

The importance of the most opinionated group members' notion of healthy behavior over my deciding what was right for me was a negative

consequence of the psychological mind-set at school. I didn't have to justify my behavior with Nicky. He accepted me as I was. This was a tolerance he didn't seem to extend to anyone else, except maybe his mother.

A strong curiosity also interlaced my bonding with Nicky. What I
mean is that he showed me a dark side of himself that I believe few
others saw. Perhaps, prior to meeting Nicky I lived in a protective
cocoon. Besides, my parents' periodic outbursts, I had rarely seen the
resentful side of the human psyche before I met Nicky. I had grown up
with cousins and the children of my parents' friends who came from
more affluent families than mine. In their homes I was treated warmly
and caringly. As for my parents, they struggled to meet their obligations, but I knew they were giving me the best they could. I had little
sense of early deprivation in my life.

Nicky's sense of the world was quite different from mine. At
unguarded moments, his mellow voice, facile smile, easy and smooth
movements were gone. In their place I heard an indignant tone and saw
the staccato gestures of resentment. Nicky made it clear to me that he
felt entitled to whatever he could get.

"Who has the right," he virtually hissed, "even if they were physically capable of stopping me, to keep me from getting what those soft,
lazy classmates of ours get for just being born to rich, fat parents?"

Was Nicky's resentment simply the result of being born into less
affluent circumstances than his classmates? Nicky's answer was: "Those
kids are just ordinary nobodies. None of them is ever going to go any-
where. Me? I'm going to be a *Somebody* some day. Just watch me!" I shud-
dered when he told me that. I realized that Nicky was capable of just about
anything to be recognized as a superior person. At those moments I sensed
that his resentment would some day cause him a great deal of trouble.

To my knowledge, Nicky never stole money or possessions. His
modus operandi was to manipulate others with his charm and cleverness: telling people what they liked to hear about themselves, e.g., that
he regarded them as a confidant, a best buddy, or (when he was with a
girl) someone he admired and would like to marry. He rarely meant his
compliments. As an analyst, I now recognize Nicky's deceit as a derivative of extreme contempt for other people. As I show in the case
studies to follow, one's virulent contempt of others is always an expression of one's unexamined self-hatred.

THE EVIL WE DO

People who are too fearful to examine unknown aspects of themselves frequently resort to *magical thinking*. This dangerous mind-set involves a suspension of one's critical reasoning faculties, enabling them to behave *as if* the world is the way they want it to be rather than as how others experience it. When a child is unable to consciously acknowledge and find words to express his feelings of helplessness in achieving or maintaining a close and loving relationship with parents (Nicky's absent father, his emotionally unavailable mother) and other significant others (Nicky's aunt), he feels condemned to a world of pretense (Nicky's strange stories). In other words, children who cannot express their upset over their lack of control over their lives are compelled to find ways of pretending that they are not as helpless as they feel. This explains Nicky's claim that: "I don't need anybody to tell me what they think I'm thinking."

In other words, when warm, caring, and trusting relationships with early caretakers are lacking, children use magical thinking to compensate for their feelings of vulnerability and lack of self-worth. As adults they transform their emotional frailty into a position of invincibility. Thus, Nicky's "Me. I'm going to be a *Somebody* some day. Just watch me!" Rather than making an effort to improve their character—e.g., Nicky's disdain for counseling—those who magically change themselves from vulnerable people to superior people by magical thinking do so by convincing themselves that they are already perfect. One who is complete requires no self-improvement. From their narcissistic point of view, it is only other peoples' flawed perceptions that prevent their superiority from its rightful recognition.

In the throes of magical thinking, people impressed with their own superiority will use any means available to their imaginations to convince others of their inferred special status. As we will see, Nicky's destructive behavior as an adult was an attempt to show that he could do whatever he pleased.

The next to last time I saw Nicky was when I was a junior in college. He was then six-foot-three in height and dressed impeccably in the latest European-style clothes. He lived on the Upper East Side of Manhattan, in a low-rent building the owner hadn't found time to renovate in order to raise the rent. He worked part-time for an escort service. I assume either the service or his women clients bought most of what he wore. He never seemed to have any money of his own.

I had gone to his apartment to go out to dinner with him, talk about our friends from school, and to lend him a few dollars. It was still early in the evening when we returned to Nicky's apartment. The wintry streets were dark and bleak. But when he opened the door of his apartment it was more dim inside than in the street below.

"Nicky, why don't you turn some lights on? Didn't you pay the electric bill?" I kidded. Nicky was always out of money and rarely paid his bills until he was compelled. He ignored my question. He searched the outside hallway furtively. Then he quickly pulled me inside the apartment.

"This guy is gunning for me. He has a 32-caliber pistol. I laid his old lady. What a 'knockout' she is! But she 'came on' to me. . . . Believe it or not, the guy once thought," Nicky snickered, "that he was my best buddy!" Nicky seemed to have no fear. Indeed, he seemed to be enjoying the whole scenario.

The amusing situation turned deadly. But I did not learn about this for some time. A couple of months later I tried to reach Nicky at his apartment. His phone was disconnected. I called a mutual friend from boarding school who was more in regular contact with Nicky than I was at the time, since I attended an out-of-state college. I was told that the cuckolded husband had come after Nicky. In self-defense, Nicky had knifed him in the liver. He bled to death. At Nicky's trial the court apparently had serious doubts about Nicky's emotional stability. He was only nineteen and had already been involved in several acts of serious violence. Nicky was sent to a hospital for the criminally insane.

I have often wondered why Nicky and I, who had much in common, went such separate ways: he became a killer, and I a psychologist who has spent many hours in an effort to understand and help people like Nicky. The root of my answer lies in Nicky's mistrust of psychology. I recognize now that he feared encountering parts of himself that he had suppressed: his hurt, his vulnerability, his rage. Without this awareness he could not deal reasonably with his acute sense of contempt for ordinary people. The only legitimate role for ordinary people, according to the Nickys of this world, is to admire the self-acclaimed superior and give them what they demand. And if people resist, the Nickys make them pay dearly. My severe condemnation of Nicky is a product of the sadness and disappointment I felt in realizing the last time I saw him that he wasn't the special person I once believed him to be. But, then, I, too, had difficulty being around people I regarded as ordinary. From continual self-examination I had to admit ashamedly that, like Nicky, I wasn't entirely comfortable with my parents' identity, especially on visiting day at school. My parents weren't well educated or articulate, nor did they have the respected professional positions my classmates' parents held: professions such as psychiatrist, physician, attorney, stage and screen actor and actress. Further probing brought me to a frightening realization: the chagrin I experienced with my parents came from a feeling that as their child, I, too, would turn out to be an ordinary person.

But are people who lack wealth and celebrity necessarily unimportant? I began to ask myself after the initial shock subsided from uncovering the source of my discomfort with my parents. Evaluating my parents' lives during this troubling period of my life, I realized that they had not only given me far more education than their own immigrant families had given them, but also something at least as important: the opportunity to observe their generosity of spirit. Although each had a quite different personality from the other, that which they shared was their compassion and concern for others. In my presence I never saw either turn away from someone in need.

I am not certain whether my father never spoke of his generous deeds because he was inarticulate in expressing his feelings or because he was a modest man. I heard about them from my mother. One report I remember best told of his experiences as a taxicab driver in New York City. According to my mother, he quickly knew that the frightened young man or woman in the backseat had run away from home and was uncertain what to do or where to go. Inevitably, he would buy a bus ticket and put these passengers on a bus to their hometown, urging them to work out their problem with their family.

One of the most memorable incidents that showed my mother's compassion and concern occurred the evening she and I, as a child, visited my maternal grandmother in a city-operated hospital. All of the patients on her ward had visitors but one, a frightened, blind old woman. The nurses' aide had simply put out her food on a tray and left her to her own resources. The old woman fumbled with the food, spilling it all over herself and on the bedcovers. My mother said in Yiddish that it was a pity to be treated like an old rag. She went over to the woman, fed her, and spoke comfortingly to her as she did so.

The value my parents placed on the lives of people who suffered was shown in their generosity and compassion; it was their most important legacy to me. It has attuned me to search for the implicit good in others, no matter how wretched their lives. I am in agreement with Shakespeare's words, "The evil men do lives after them, the good oft interred with their bones." Throughout my career as a psychologist and psychoanalyst, I have sought to find the wellspring of virtue in my patients, even those who have committed the most egregious of crimes.

In the next chapter I tell of my clinical treatment of Mike, a powerful and vicious inmate I met in my capacity as a consulting psychologist to a forensic facility for dangerous criminals. His face scarred from brutal assaults and abuse from foster parents and correctional school guards, Mike had been incarcerated many times for severely beating up those who insulted him. My clinical work with Mike raises the crucial question of how free any of us are to exercise our will.

3

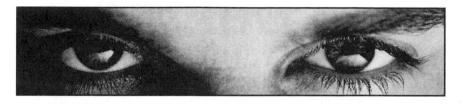

THE CLIENT WHOSE
RAGE LACKED A VOICE

Sin or Sickness?

If I could have used my tongue, I would not have struck him.
—Herman Melville, *Billy Budd*

EVERY DAY SCORES OF MEN AND WOMEN, BY MEANS OF PHYSICAL FORCE or persuasive behavior, cause others the outrage of undeserved suffering. Many of these acts are violations of criminal statutes, still others are more appropriately defined as immoral. Nevertheless, all are malevolent in that they have in common treating other people with a lack of respect and consideration for the victim's humanity (Goldberg 1999).

I first met Mike in my capacity as a consulting psychologist to a psychiatric facility for vicious criminals. He was thirty years of age; nearly half of his life had been spent in correctional institutions. Physically imposing, he had multiple facial scars from cigarette burns and brutal beatings inflicted by sadistic foster parents and correctional facility personnel. Deeply embarrassed about his appearance, Mike had been incarcerated numerous times for severely beating those who insulted him. With so many losses in his life, he found it easier to express rage at his deprivations than regret and bereavement. Nevertheless, Mike was intelligent; psychological tests administered in prison placed him in the superior range of intellectual functioning: clever at understanding human behavior—except in regard to his own motives. His lack of self-insight was compounded by a considerable difficulty putting his feelings into words. He explained his actions by reference to external circumstances. For example, rather than identifying his feeling state at the time of his violent behavior, he pointed only to the victim's provocative behavior— as if his own actions were justifiable automatic responses.

Many of the violent incidents in his life followed his substantial intake of alcohol. For example, the event that brought him back to prison was his violent attack on a bouncer in a supper club. As Mike was leaving the club, the bouncer had insinuated that Mike's very attractive companion could do better than Mike. Without a moment's hesitation, Mike lifted up the man and hurled him through a glass door. The man nearly bled to death from his injuries.

OUR LACK OF KNOWLEDGE ABOUT THE REDEMPTION PROCESS IN ADULTHOOD

Mike, after each incident in which his violent rage caused him to hurt another person, returned to therapy with me and continued to plead his case. He was a victim of his upbringing; he was only doing what he had been painfully taught—to protect himself from a potentially lethal attack from others; indeed, not to defend his honor would serve to maximize that threat. Nonetheless, he stated that he wished he could live his life in a less violent way.

For the past thirty years I have treated a number of patients who have committed murder, rape, and mayhem in heinous ways, and like Mike, claimed they wished to transcend the indifference, viciousness, and cruelty that informed their daily existence. In short, they expressed the desire for a psychological and spiritual transformation. But none had any idea where to begin.

We have a tradition in our society of trying to salvage peoples' lives no matter how egregious their existence has been. As a psychoanalyst concerned with moral issues, I wondered what psychological assistance I could provide Mike.

At first glance the prognosis for people like Mike is poor. Most criminologists and forensic psychologists, as I indicated already, are dubious about a person's capacity to reverse the conditions that promote destructive behavior. They point out that there is no empirical evidence to support the efficacy of psychoanalysis for turning criminals away from crime, nor, for that matter, any other rehabilitation approach, such as psychotherapy, group therapy, social-work counseling, educational classes, or vocational training (Silberman 1978). This view is confirmed by Jack Abbott (1991), a violent convict who wrote of the years he spent with legions of embittered men who left prison more hardened and criminally proficient than when they first entered.

Pessimism about rescuing destructive lives is due to the inchoate state of our knowledge about adult moral development; we know far more about children. For example, there is a considerable literature on the early backgrounds of exemplary people, including studies by psychologists David Levy (1946), Nancy McWilliams (1984), Elizabeth Midlarsky (1968), and Kristin Monroe (1991). In contrast, there are no normative data about how adult lives are transformed.

Psychoanalysis is held largely responsible for our lack of understanding of adult moral development. The theory of personality development that evolved from classical analytic notions discourages developmental exploration of adulthood. It employs clinical evidence to contend that all important aspects of personal character are inexorably set within the early years of life. This psychoanalytic bias has plagued all of the behavioral sciences (Goldberg 1996).

The psychoanalyst concerned with recovery ethics[1] can respond to this charge with the observation that the skillful, well-trained analyst is in the fortunate position to understand the individual best—for no other profession possesses the exquisite skills to listen and comprehend, and no other has the time to probe in such depth. Psychoanalysts, by means of their clinical skills, have the opportunity to describe the motivations and psychodynamics of destructive people about whom they have indepth, firsthand knowledge. As a psychologist and psychoanalyst who has spent many hours (indeed, many years!) with people who have committed crime and mayhem, my psychoanalytic practice has provided me with a perspicacious view of the conditions in the lives of people from all walks of life that interfered with their capacity to behave in cooperative and caring ways toward others. It is this bald view of the struggle between good and evil that has enabled me to recognize that a destructive client's overriding need in treatment is to find positive qualities about himself and his life and to use this information to establish his personal identity in a self-enhancing way. The most difficult task, indeed the turning point in Mike's road to psychological healing, was to gain a *trust in his own goodness* (Goldberg 1992).

In this chapter I am concerned with two basic questions: first, to what extent people have choice and are responsible for the acts they commit or influence; and second, what are the factors that if recognized and competently acted upon can change destructive lifestyles. Because we lack empirical data about changing destructive lives, I will use clinical and anecdotal evidence to examine these questions.

THE CAPACITY FOR CHOICE AND RESPONSIBILITY

To change one's destructive behavior one first must be convinced that one's way of life is dysfunctional, and, second, be able and willing to pursue constructive behavior: this is to say, capable and desirous of acting in ways in which one's own and others' best interests are respected and protected.

The crucial question of how free we are to exercise our will is a very old and controversial concern. Most theorists contend that the issue of human will is inaccessible to empirical investigation and therefore is not a proper study for psychological investigation (for example, Lapsley 1967). I take issue with this thesis, agreeing with Heinz Kohut (1959) that the psychoanalyst has phenomenological evidence for the freedom of will. Consider the following:

70   We can observe in ourselves the ability to choose and to decide.

The question, then, is: can further introspection reduce this sense into more fundamental components? In other words, can we by introspection separate the experience of making a choice into the experience of compulsion, indecision, and doubt? My personal introspection suggests it cannot. For example, an exploration of the motivational basis for my own experience of being able to choose leads me to a wider and more vivid sense of freedom. On the other hand, the converse psychological configuration, namely, my sense of being compelled and feeling indecision and doubt, can usually be broken down by means of introspection. As I proceed to examine these phenomena in myself by means of resistance analysis[2] of my underlying motives, I simultaneously experience an increasing capacity to choose and decide.

When I examine the psychological processes that follow my increased sense of my ability to choose I find that the freedom I experience is made possible by the fact that exercising my belief in psychological freedom enables me to act rather than remain passive. In short, if an individual believes that he has some freedom over his behavior, he generally acts in ways to maximize his capacity to choose. If, in contrast, he believes that he has little or no choice, then he generally behaves in ways to minimize his decisional activity. "To act," says University of Glasglow philosopher John Macmurray (1957, 134), "is to determine; and the Agent is the determiner." To act upon a belief in free will, I contend, provides a person with *agency*—the existential sense that he is capable of becoming the person he seeks to be (Goldberg 1977).

A belief in freedom of will, then, is a *functional* position; it serves to maximize the extent of our ability to choose. But in no way does it detract from determinism as a principle governing human behavior: this belief itself is induced by the recognition that one seems to be able in some aspects of life to have some control over one's behavior; and these actions could not take place in an indeterminate universe.

Nevertheless, it is highly unlikely that we will ever produce definitive evidence to discount free will as an *epiphenomenon*—the notion that we have considerable influence on what happens to us when in fact we don't. The position I take is that if indeed none of us has any freedom of choice, then it is pointless to continue to explore the capacity to overthrow a destructive life. Therefore, for purposes of our exploration, we must grant two assumptions: few or none of us have no choice, **71** although some of us may be more able than others to freely choose how we behave; and, the capacity for free will is not an innate attribute. Consequently, we would do well to learn why some people appear to have more free will than others.

FACTORS THAT IMPEDE THE ABILITY AND DESIRE TO LIVE A DECENT LIFE

My clinical work with children suggests that there are a small number of specific factors in raising children, when found together, that adequately explain why as adults they fail to develop a capacity for emotional connectedness and mutuality with others. Their interpersonal incapacity is related to destructive tendencies. Of course, the more prominent the presence of all these factors, the greater is their impact on the child, and the more likely that the individual as a child and/or an adult will be inclined toward destructive behavior. The five factors I found most important (all readily present in Mike's background) are: shame vulnerability, benign neglect,[3] an inability to mourn, linguistic difficulty in expressing feelings, and witnessing significant people who behave as if rageful anger is a legitimate means for dealing with frustration and conflict. I refer to these as *the primary factors of destructiveness* (Goldberg 1997b). I discuss each briefly here and more extensively in Section B of the Theory and Methodology Appendix.

Shame Vulnerability

Pride and shame are the monitors of our personal identity. When a child can feel pride in his competence and knows he has won the esteem of others, he forms a positive personal identity. But if instead he is disregarded and mistreated, and indeed subjected to a pattern of humiliation and shame, he will acquire a negative personal identity (Goldberg 1991b). Each shaming experience, especially those that involve disregard and mistreatment, as Mike's story shows, depletes the child's sense of personal worth, painfully informing him that he is inadequate. As such, these experiences undermine the child's interpersonal relation-ships and his feelings of well-being and security.

Benign Neglect

Deprivation of parental attention, guidance, and compassionate concern can be as devastating to a child as physical abuse, as shown in Vincent's case in chapter 8. The extensive empirical research inspired by Attach-ment Theory indicates that not having caretakers emotionally available impedes the security and well-being necessary for a child's constructive sense of personal identity (Ainsworth 1962; Bowlby 1953).

Inability to Mourn

This concept refers to the child's reactions to parents who discourage him from grieving disappointments. As shown in Nora's story in chapter 5, to the extent that a child is unable to consciously acknowledge and give words to his inability to achieve or maintain a desired relationship with significant others, he may feel the need to create a fictional world in which he feels safe. In other words, children who cannot express their upset over their lack of control over their lives are compelled to find ways of pretending that they are not as helpless as they feel. Destructive behavior, in an important sense, is an attempt to show that the perpe-trator can run his own life—he can do whatever he pleases.

Linguistic Difficulties in Expressing Feelings

Our most important drive is the striving to find *personal meaning* in our lives. Meaning is a common dimension of people: one that sum-marizes the way in which we relate to our personal world and to the world of others.

It is from our ability to use language intelligently that we acquire a facility in obtaining personal meaning for ourselves in relationships with others. In other words, it is meaningful language that enables us to become human rather than brute and solitary beasts. Language dis-

73

orders are frequently found in people who commit violent crimes, as exemplified in Mike's case.

Witnessing Significant People Who Behave as if Rageful Anger Is a Legitimate Means for Dealing with Frustration and Conflict

Parents, of course, model behavior for their children: their actions are more powerful guides than their words. A parent might tell her child that being angry is wrong, while at the same time reacting to frustration and conflict with rage.

My clinical experience (Goldberg 1997a) has shown that the primary factors taken together influence an individual toward destructive behavior in the following development: the destructive personality begins in childhood as a state of extreme vulnerability to mistreatment by early caretakers, proceeds to feelings of impacted self-hatred and then to self-protection by an indifference to other people, followed by attempts to feel better about one's self by acting as if one is a superior person, and finally to a transformation of the shamed person's self-contemptuous personality to that of perpetrator of outrage against others in order to demonstrate one's superiority. This profile may suggest an inevitable progression in becoming and remaining destructive. In fact, those patients with whom I worked, who to some significant extent were able to change their destructive behavioral patterns, did so by their persistent willingness and courage in struggling to recognize the adverse impact of some or all of the above destructive factors. In contrast, most behavioral scientists hold that early traumatic experiences prevent an individual from constructively modifying destructive behavior (for example, Menninger 1968). What is the basis of their claim?

COMMONSENSE NOTIONS
ABOUT HUMAN BEHAVIOR

Most behavioral scientists seem to believe the psychological fiction that people who commit heinous behaviors suffer from a mental disorder, and this illness causes them to have less free will available to them than do "normal" people. As psychologist Maurice Temerlin (1963) indicates: "Since both neurotic and psychotic persons tend to experience determinism rather than choice, their perception of the conditions under which choice may be experienced becomes distorted" (42).

We can best understand this statement by examining commonsense assumptions about the human mind. First, common sense tells us that human beings possess a faculty of "self-control" (which we call "free will"). Second, people assume that free will, present in all psychologically normal people, is impaired to a greater or lesser degree in psychologically abnormal people. This is because we believe that abnormal behavior—due to early trauma—has its origins in the deeper and unaware parts of the psyche, whereas more conscious and controllable factors are involved in normal behavior. Third, people believe that psychological conflicts—the presence of traumatic childhood experience—cause the person to suffer *irresistible urges* that cannot at the moment the offender is acting wrongfully be set aside and overridden by free will. Fourth, insofar as an offender is unable to control his impulses, he should not be held responsible for his psychological helplessness.

I show in the remainder of this chapter why these commonsense notions are fallacious, and how by changing them we provide the destructive person with access to constructive behavior.

THE REASONS FOR MIKE'S
DESTRUCTIVE BEHAVIOR

Mike tried to impress upon me from the start of our clinical work together that the numerous violent altercations he had been involved in—before and during the time I was treating him—were typical of **75** prison life, or, for that matter, of any protracted period in a confined space. They occur as an automatic response to the reality of confinement: a person threatened by another cannot walk away. The prisoner has to face another inmate with whom he is in conflict every day, perhaps for many years. At that moment when one is most vulnerable and unprepared, the dangerous other may attack with deadly force. It is far better, Mike indicated, to be the first to strike and to do it forcefully: that is, intimidate and reduce the enemy to cowering timidity. In short, Mike's viciousness was based on the pernicious belief that the victim is so threatening to his well-being that any proactive destructive action he takes is justified.

Of course, Mike could have walked away from the nightclub incident that brought him back to prison. Moreover, whatever insult he perceived from the bouncer surely didn't carry a death threat. Rather, it called attention to some aspect of his demeanor that a socially assured person would have likely ignored or dealt with in a more benign way.

Mike was unsocialized as a result of his many years in prison and scores of foster homes and detention schools. He experienced the club bouncer's words to imply that he was unwanted. Those who are raised in a subculture in which aggressive expression is the only recognized pathway to others, in perceiving a slight—even an unintentional one—swiftly give vent to violent reactions.

In examining Mike's life, I was shown abundant evidence that unacknowledged shame had pervasively taken over his life since he was a mistreated child, impeding him from building feelings of self-esteem. *Unacknowledged shame* refers to suppressed feelings about one's difficulty in becoming the person one seeks to be, which results in the painful sense that one is incapable of establishing a system of shared meanings with others, and therefore, one has lost and may never regain an interpersonal bridge with significant others. In other words, Mike's persistent fear was that he would be alone forever—unnoticed, uncared about, unwanted.

As such, Mike's morbid sense of shame compelled his violent rage; it was the silent, unacknowledged killer in his life, not the death threats from dangerous others.

Choice is predicated on awareness. Because of extremely diminished intelligence, brain disease, or chemical imbalance, people in some instances may be incapable of recognizing options and therefore have little or no freedom of choice. But this extreme incapacity, I believe, is quite rare. Mike was certainly aware of other options in situations in which he became violent.

He told me that it was at times when he felt uncertain about the consequences of trying to act properly that he felt a flood of *despair*. Despite recognizing what he should do to behave properly, acting in an unfamiliar way was too tiring and difficult for him. At those moments his rage and resentment at the injustices done to him filled his consciousness, and he felt unwilling to continue trying to do the right thing. Instead, he decided, he would get even with those who made him who he was—a vicious brute. In short, Mike was cognizant of options other than violence during his destructive episodes, but chose not to follow them because he was so resentful and enraged at other people that he *did not want to act righteously*.

Consequently, it is one matter to maintain that some offenders, due to their incapacities, are unaware of moral options. It is quite another to claim that most offenders lack the capacity for responsible behavior.

Our behavior is a product not only of how we have been treated, but also of the choices we make in dealing with the dilemmas and ordeals in our lives. Victims of trauma and psychological conflict—such as reflected in the primary factors—gradually become transformed into perpetrators of destructiveness by their continual decisions not to consciously address their suppressed grievances and hurt.

As Swiss psychoanalyst Carl Jung (1976) claims, we deny the dark side of ourselves at extreme cost, because that which we don't bring into consciousness appears in our lives as fate. Jung's idea is that a person's past inescapably clings to him or her, and if the shadow of some of its events is too terrifying to examine, the cast of that shadow becomes one's eventual destiny.

Based on the work of sociologist Lonnie H. Athens, who interviewed imprisoned violent criminals, science writer Richard Rhodes (1999) contends that the urges, thoughts, and experiences that impel these individuals to malevolent acts are *common to us all*. Each of us has a dark side: the hurts, angers, and vulnerabilities that result from experiences of shame, humiliation, and the reactive feelings of self-contempt (Simon 1996). What differentiates destructive people like Mike from other people is the unwillingness of destructive people to *examine* their dark side. They need to be able to come to terms with their inner forces in order to prevent their rage from getting displaced and acted out against anyone who has actually hurt them, those who stood by and did nothing to stop the abuse, and even those who did not know but should have known and cared and should have done something to stop the hurt (Goldberg 1997a). The unwillingness to introspect keeps one a prisoner of his own toxic self-contemptuousness. Nothing in the world is as painful and unendurable as severe self-contempt. When other people hate you, it is troubling; when you loathe yourself, it is unbearable. To survive the sufferer must cast these hateful feelings outward. Thus, unexamined self-contempt gets converted into contempt against the world. James Gilligan (1996), on the basis of several decades as a prison psychiatrist, contends that the most awful things that have happened in our world have resulted from intense shame and self-hatred.

But cannot the unwillingness to examine self-hatred be due to the impact that early trauma had on the offender's capacity for volitional behavior? Of course, but, then, there are always impediments to self-knowledge. This is as true of people with fortunate childhoods as those with more traumatic backgrounds. Unfortunately, commonsense notions about the nature of the human mind make extreme distinctions between abnormal and normal behavior. And here lies the problem! Commonsense notions about free will, based on extreme differences between the normal and abnormal mind, equate difficulty with impossibility. They, of course, are not the same. Whereas none of us has absolute free will, there are few who have no freedom of options. It is here that many people either misunderstand or fail to recognize the important distinction between "explaining" behavior as contrasted with "justifying" it.

Explaining behavior helps us understand how these actions came about; it does not by itself remove or excuse a person's responsibility for his behavior. Consequently, there is a crucial difference in the claim that early trauma *predisposes* an individual to act in a certain way and the avowal that childhood factors *determine* adult behavior.

All of the destructive patients I have treated were aware of options but chose to disregard the more humane ones. In accord, Rhodes (1999) indicates that Lonnie Athens's interviewed inmates accepted responsibility for their destructive behavior, insofar as most admitted that at the time of their criminality they were aware of the choices they were making.

Metaphorically, to act malevolently is to ignore, avert, and deny roadsigns along a hazardous highway that inform the driver that he is headed in the wrong direction. For example, each of my malevolent patients knew from similar previous events the consequences of his behavior unless he took decisive action to stop the destructive pattern from continuing. But he didn't stop; consequently, his destructive behavior was an expression of informed decision.

Does this mean that the notion of irresistible urges is fallacious? I believe so. For instance, let's take one of the most dangerous types of destructive behavior—serial killings—and examine this type of behavior in order to assess my thesis. Serial killers are alleged by forensic psychologists to be victims of irresistible urges: their behavior is typified by a highly compulsive set of ritualistic acts in which they select a victim (in accord with the unwitting identification of the victim with the offender's own searing, early trauma), follow and stalk the vulnerable person, and then when the victim is alone and most helpless, abduct and sadistically kill.

The concept of irresistible urges was taken by psychologists from biology. As a biological concept it does make sense: for example, beyond conscious control are attempts to breathe when suffocating and to regurgitate when digestively irritated. But as a psychological explanation the notion is highly suspect. The serial killer is not without choice. Any law enforcement officer who has dealt with these killers can verify this. The officer can testify to situations in which the stalker was at some point in his ritualistic behavior apprehensive about a potential danger to himself: for example, the unexpected arrival of other people, or a forceful fight put up by the victim.

If the serial killer's urge to commit his deadly behavior was actually irresistible, then he would be compelled to continue despite any danger to himself. But that is not what typically happens. In the usual scenario, if the stalker is seriously threatened, he halts, retreats, and comes back to pursue and kill another day. Of course, animals of prey also exhibit similar behavior. But this is probable evidence of animal volition. Like humans, animals have a history in which they develop likes and dislikes. Their cautious behavior involves choices in regard to these preferences rather than to an instinctual reflex of an organism without a brain.

The question, then, is why some people who experienced early trauma are able and willing to make humane choices, while others are not. Sixteenth-century political theorist Niccolò Machiavelli made the remarkably cynical assertion in his *Discourses* that people will always prove bad unless necessity compels them to be virtuous. In contrast, Socrates is shown in Plato's *Protagoras* contending that no one willingly acts malevolently: all virtues are forms of knowledge; the major impediment to moral insight is ignorance. The person who knows what is good will be unable to choose wickedness.

I agree with Socrates, but I will show that it is not intellectual knowledge of good alone that promotes virtue; qualities of personal character that can be developed in adulthood also are required.

THE TASKS AND RESPONSIBILITIES OF VIRTUE

Several months into our clinical work, Mike told me that he had been seeing a psychiatrist privately for seven years when he was outside of institutions, while he continued to drink heavily. Why, I asked, did he stay with the doctor if he wasn't being helped? "By continuing to tell me that I had a serious mental illness and showing me the many ways my childhood caused my illness, he justified my drinking and helped me remain alcoholic."

If ever there was an opportunity to enable Mike to reflect on his *self-deception* this was the moment. Mike had frequently claimed that he was violent because he was a victim of an upbringing that taught him how to protect himself from physical attack by being as vicious as possible. But wasn't he contradicting himself now? By continuing to drink heavily he put himself in a vulnerable position in which violent altercations were far more likely to occur than if he were sober.

I traced with Mike the steps involved in his habitual pattern of violence: he carried around a repository of experiences of shame and injustice, which left him with considerable self-contempt; staying with these feelings was intolerable; he drank to numb these terrible feelings about himself; the drinking energized him in a search for people to hold responsible for the shames and injustices done to him; he felt a heightened excitement in finding a vulnerable candidate, usually someone who unwittingly reminded him of his own hurts. He violated his victim with minimal deliberation, then felt serene and superior to the victim on to whom he had displaced his grievances.

But how, I asked Mike, does his violent displacement cycle enable him to become the person he claims he seeks to be—someone respected for his kind deeds and intelligence, rather than feared for his viciousness? For the first time Mike offered me no facile rationalizations to excuse what he readily admitted was his modus operandi. He asked if I knew what he should do to change his life. I admitted that I didn't. The behavioral sciences would not be of much help. Behavioral scientists have turned their attention far more to psychopathology and destructive behavior than they have to virtuous behavior (Goldberg 1998).

It would be best, I indicated, if we sought out how Mike might redeem his life from the wisdom of those who have openly struggled with good and evil, especially those who had freed themselves from criminal careers.

As I expected Mike to be an equal participant in seeking the best way to change his life, both of us consulted the excellent institution library for books on philosophy, theology, criminology, and literary classics. Great literature offers us inspiration and guidance by describing and dramatizing the ambiguities, paradoxes, and contradictions contained in our various views of virtue and wickedness. We also eagerly sought autobiographies of people who had successfully rehabilitated themselves. Especially helpful was the book *Life Plus 99 Years*, written by Nathan Leopold (1957), who was involved in a crime said to have set the prototype for senseless murder: one of the first cases to show how victims of murder can be chosen at random because these victims as people have no importance to the murderers. Leopold spent thirty-three years in prison.

On the basis of written sources, my experiences working in the community with recovering drug addicts who had lived criminal lives (Goldberg 1997a, chapter 7), and my discussions with Mike, he and I defined *virtue* as any attitude a person exhibits that enables him to be more enlightened, compassionate, and responsible both to himself and others. We arrived at the following responsibilities and tasks required to repair Mike's life: a capacity to learn the language of felt emotion; a concern with fairness and justice for others; the assumption of responsibility for one's own behavior; the possession of moral courage; and the willingness to self-examine. Not surprisingly, these tasks are closely related to my set of primary destructive factors. And while it can be reasonably questioned whether these tasks together are sufficient to restore virtue, I believe that all are necessary. Based on the ideas of Socrates, psychologist James Overholser (1999) recently has proposed a method of promoting virtue in psychotherapy using concepts that correspond with those discussed in the following.

A Capacity to Learn to Speak the Language of Felt Emotion

I was reading Herman Melville's work at the time I treated Mike. Melville's main character in *Billy Budd* explains after he felt compelled to strike and kill an abusive officer, "Could I have used my tongue, I would not have struck him."[4]

Melville enabled me to recognize that Mike's inability to explain the reasons for his actions ironically revealed the very crucible in which his violent outrage was forged. Violence is a kind of language, however primitive and limited. Those who cannot communicate persuasively with their tongues strike out violently from the shame of sensing no effective alternative for verbally defining themselves to others.

Mike required linguistic training in expressing his unacknowledged feelings of shame and hurt to erase the belief that in his essential core he was a brute creature, suffused with only a pretense of civility and sensitivity to others. In short, Mike's language, heavily infused with aggressive, need-oriented words and concepts, reinforced his belief that he had a savage nature. So, whenever he tried to express tender or caring feelings, he generally found at his disposal only crude and emotionally shallow linguistic concepts. In working with Mike I developed Basic Emotional Communication (BEC).

BEC is designed to enhance an ongoing emotional dialogue

between two (and sometimes more) people involved in a significant relationship. The method demonstrates safe and effective ways of sharing hurts, fears, and desires with others without destructive anger. As such, it disarms hurt and anger and leads to personal and relational gain (Goldberg 1991a). I discuss BEC in detail in section C (see Theory and Method Appendix).

A Concern with Fairness and Justice for Others

Wise philosophers and theologians have pointed out that there is a basic question to which each of us must respond in summing up one's life: Has one been idle for the most part, unconcerned with the lives of others, a greedy opportunist, or someone who cared and made a difference?

The eighteenth-century French social philosopher Jean-Jacques Rousseau in his *Social Contract* contends that due to a flawed moral education, many lack the ability to see others' vulnerabilities as something they themselves share. Identification with others, he tells us, is required to promote social justice.

Unfortunately, too many people rationalize their lack of concern for others. Mike was hardly unique in telling himself that his first responsibility was to himself. Preoccupied with his own insecurities, he was rarely attentive to others' needs. I confronted Mike with his lack of concern for others, directing him to the ideas of Aristotle, who pointed out in *The Poetics* that since none of us lives alone, the life lived well is founded in friendship. Virtue, in this sense, is best achieved in helping to foster the conditions that extend concern and compassion to every member of society.

As a powerful presence in the institution, Mike was both feared and respected by other inmates and staff alike. However, as a result of our discussions and his extensive reading, Mike became more verbally articulate and an effective spokesman for the other inmates in dealing with their grievances toward staff and in settling inmate disputes.

Learning to be of help to others, as I indicated earlier, is essential to the redemption of a destructive life. To reiterate this important idea: the so-called emotionally disturbed person has been deprived of equitable and balanced relationships with others. Such relationships serve as a lifeline that sustains and maintains the individual, keeping him alive and well. When a person performs needed social and emotional functions for others and is recognized for his help, he is valued by others and by himself. Concomitantly, he experiences a greater capacity for equity with others.

Assuming Responsibility
for One's Own Behavior

The term "responsibility" is used in everyday parlance to cover a number of distinct but related notions. According to *The Oxford Companion to Philosophy* (Honderich 1995), the most important uses of the term are causal responsibility, legal responsibility, and moral responsibility. To be causally (operatively) responsible for a state of affairs is to bring it about either directly or indirectly. To be legally responsible is to fulfill the requirements for liability under the law. Moral responsibility has to do with assuming accountability for our actions.

If we believe that a person has freedom of choice over his behavior, then all three of these uses are interrelated. On the other hand, many behavioral scientists have argued, if we assume that an individual's capacity to choose in some important sense is diminished, he cannot reasonably assume responsibility for his operative behavior, and we cannot regard him legally responsible for the act, any more than we would hold him accountable for incurring cancer. The eminent psychiatrist Karl Menninger (1968) was a strong advocate of this position. I disagree.

Psychology and morality are integrally related insofar as responsibility for destructive behavior. For example, if one has caused an action that results in harm to another, regardless of one's intent or one's understanding of the behavior, morally one ought to act after the fact in such a way as to do one's best to lessen the harm one has caused.

In our present criminal justice system criminals may go to prison for isolation and punishment, but they are not put in a position that obliges them to confront the consequences of their vicious actions. Moreover, in this impersonal administration of justice, victims and/or their loved ones are left out of the correctional system equation. Their needs, other than primitive vengeance, are not addressed.

The obligation to undo or lessen the harm one has caused, I believe, is the bedrock of moral wisdom—found in the teachings of the Jewish philosopher Martin Buber (1953), who stresses that the violation of a moral law is a lesser sin than the recognition that one has done wrong and yet one does not sincerely try to right that wrong with those harmed. In short, from a moral perspective, lack of conscious intent does not abnegate responsibility for being the operative agent of harm. After all, if we are not responsible for our own behavior, then who is?

Perhaps there are fortunate people in the world today who have been raised by such wise and caring families that in growing up they were not subjected in any decisive way to the destructive psychological experiences I have described in this chapter as the "destructive factors." I personally know few such individuals. The people of strong character I know who live caring, decent, and creative lives are those who have triumphed over adversity. The capacity needed to deal competently with contemporary roles and responsibilities (see section A of Theory and Method Appendix) has to do with a person's persistent willingness and courage to struggle to recognize and overcome the adverse impact of some or even all of the destructive factors in his or her early development.

When I discussed these ideas with Mike he expressed an interest in my finding his victims in the community: he asked me to locate them and have them visit him in the institution. He admitted that while he was anxious about these encounters, he now was in touch with feelings of painful shame; he realized that he couldn't become the person he sought to be without face-to-face meetings with his victims. Only by assuming responsibility for his actions, he recognized, would he be able to actively investigate his own motivations in the events that had caused him trouble.

The administration of the institution would not allow me to bring in Mike's victims. But they did encourage me to set up a group in the institution in which inmates who were more often than not victims and inmates who were predominately perpetrators could come together to encounter and try to understand what it was like to be in the skin of the other. The rationale was that the offender needs to interact responsibly with others who oppose his point of view and who have been harmed by his pernicious behavior. My clinical experience with drug addicts taught me that only by a *gradual openness and empathy* to the **85** unfamiliar feelings and beliefs of others can the destructive person change his way of life.

Moral Courage

Our perception of courage, as of heroes, has shifted radically from past ages. In ancient sagas, courage was seen as fortitude in dealing with external enemies and natural disasters. As we have become more self-aware in our contemporary age, courage has increasingly come to mean psychological bravery, the will to face our divided urges and inner terrors in order to create a vibrant discovered self (Goldberg 1997a).

To act as if he were the person he sought to be rather than the despised self he experienced himself as, Mike had to actively seek out possibility. This requires moral courage because the effects of his possibilities could not be ascertained in advance of "turning toward possibility." Erich Fromm (1963) observed that each person may seek some ideal state of freedom, but people are not equally desirous of enduring anxiety and discomfort in pursuit of psychological freedom. Mike exhibited a courageous attitude by asking to meet his former victims.

A Willingness to Self-examine

Many believe that malefactors refuse to change because they *enjoy* committing wrongful acts. It is true that most destructive people justify their behavior on the basis that they are superior to the rest of us: the pernicious attitude that the victim is so weak, stupid, or incompetent that he or she can be treated as an object rather than someone who deserves decent regard.

A very different picture emerged, however, when I probed beneath the grandiose rationalizations of my malevolent patients. All had suffered deep hurt and shame from the failure to achieve emotional connectedness with their early caretakers. It was during those moments of painful shame in which they poignantly expressed their aching need to be understood and cared about that my clients were willing to examine their behavior thoroughly and make amends for the harm they had done. I make no claim that this was an easy and always successful project. As Leopold's (1957) rehabilitative experience in prison indicates, it can be a long, gradual process of removing compartmentalized vulnerability and hurt, and bringing them into consciousness.

Mike met with me three or four times a week (extra sessions when emergencies arose). In our sessions Mike began to define himself in terms of his desired self and in so doing he was able to discover the "lost voice" of his deeply buried despair about his human limitations. With a more articulate and compassionate "new voice," Mike set goals to make amends for the harm and hurt he caused. On his release from the institution he became a staff member of a halfway house program for offenders who were released into the community.

As mortals we are imperfect. We make mistakes. But no less characteristic of our humanity is our capacity to self-reflect, to experience regret, and to seek redemption for our mistakes. Therefore, we should be held accountable for an awareness of the causes of our actions, as well as for their consequences. No less is required if we are to establish a just and compassionate society.

The next chapter tells of a client who assumed my identity; I was only able to reach him once I began to understand the role self-deception plays in consciousness and memory.

NOTES

1. Recovery ethics refer to the values and mores that are crucial in a criminal offender's overthrowing his antisocial, immoral life.

2. Resistance analysis refers to a subject's examination of the factors that are interfering with his relentless exploration of his motives.

3. When psychologists discuss deprivations in a child's life, they usually are referring to physically absent and/or abusive caretakers. In contrast, in studying the lives of my destructive patients and others discussed in the psychoanalytic and psychological literatures, I have found that many of them were of privileged backgrounds and were not physically abused. However, what they were deprived of—as section B demonstrates—was their caretakers' constructive involvement in their lives.

4. There are some who object to the examination of fictional characters as if they were real people. This criticism, while often valid, is shortsighted in regard to the great literary psychologists, e.g., Shakespeare, Dostoyevsky, Tolstoy, Conrad, Hawthorne, and so forth, who are generally more psychologically insightful than contemporary psychologists. Clearly, Freud held the conviction that fictional characters provided insights for understanding human behavior (Freud 1908).

REFERENCES

Abbott, J. H. 1991. *In the belly of the beast*. New York: Random House.

Ainsworth, M. D. 1964. Patterns of attachment behavior shown by the infant in interaction with his mother. *Merrill-Palmer Quarterly* 10: 51–58.

Bowlby, J. 1953. Some pathological processes set in train by early mother-child separation. *Journal of Mental Sciences* 99: 265–72.

Buber, M. 1953. *Good and evil*. New York: Scribner.

Freud, S. [1908] 1958. The relation of the poet to day-dreaming. In S. Freud, *Creativity and unconscious*, 44–54. Reprint, New York: Harper.

Fromm, E. 1963. *Escape from freedom*. New York: Holt, Rinehart & Winston.

Gilligan, J. 1996. *Violence*. New York: Putnam.

Goldberg, C. 1977. The reality of human will: A concept worth reviving. *Psychiatric Annals* 7: 37–57.

———. 1991a. *On being a psychotherapist*. Northvale, N.J.: Aronson.

———. 1991b. *Understanding shame*. Northvale, N.J.: Aronson.

———. 1992. *The seasoned psychotherapist*. New York: Norton.

———. 1996. Introduction. The approach to positive adult development. In *Clinical Approaches to Adult Development*, edited by M. L. Common, J. Demick, and C. Goldberg, 1–7. Norwood, N.J.: Ablex.

———. 1997a. *Speaking with the devil: Exploring senseless acts of evil*. New York: Penguin.

———. 1997b. The Chautauqua Institution lecture: The responsibilities of virtue. *International Journal of Psychotherapy* 2: 179–91.

———. 1999. Swords into plowshares: Exploring the recovery ethics of destructive lives. *Psychoanalytic Review* 86: 993–1012 .

Honderich, T. 1995. *The Oxford companion to philosophy*. New York: Oxford University Press.

Jung, C. 1976. *The Portable Jung*. New York: Penguin.

Kohut, H. 1959. Introspection, empathy and psychoanalysis. *Journal of the American Psychoanalytic Association* 7: 459–83.

Lapsley, J. N. 1967. The concept of will. In *The Concept of Willing*, edited by J. N. Lapsley. Nashville, Tenn.: Abingdon Press.

Leopold, N. F. 1958. *Life plus 99 years*. Garden City, N.Y.: Doubleday.

Levy, D. M. 1946. The German anti-Nazi: A case study. *American Journal of Orthopsychiatry* 6: 507–15.

Macmurray, J. 1957. *The self as agent*. London: Farber.

McWilliams, N. 1984. The psychology of the altruist. *Psychoanalytic Psychology* 3: 192–213.

Menninger, K. 1968. *The crime of punishment*. New York: Viking.

Midlarsky, E. 1968. Aiding responses: An analysis and review. *Merrill-Palmer Quarterly* 14: 229–60.

Monroe, K.R. 1991. John Donne's people: Explaining differences between rational actors and altruists through cognitive frameworks. *Journal of Politics* 53: 394–433.

Overholser, J. C. 1999. Elements of the socratic method: VI. Promoting virtue in everyday life. *Psychotherapy* 36: 137–45.

Rhodes, R. 1999. *Why they kill*. New York: Knopf.

Silberman, C. E. 1978. *Criminal violence, criminal justice*. New York: Random House.

Simon, R. I. 1996. *Bad men do what good men dream*. Washington, D.C.: American Psychiatric Association Press.

Temerlin, M. 1963. On choice and responsibility in a humanistic psychotherapy. *Humanistic Psychology* 3: 5–48.

4

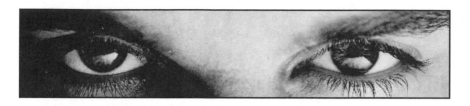

THE CLIENT WHO
ASSUMED HIS
ANALYST'S IDENTITY

A Psychology of Self-deception, Consciousness, and Memory

There is nothing worse than self-deception—when the deceiver is at home and always with you.

—Plato, *Cratylus*

PSYCHOANALYSIS HAS NEITHER A COHERENT THEORY OF CONSCIOUSness and memory nor a nonparadoxical explanation of self-deception (Goldberg 1999). By means of a clinical case, I explore the function of self-deception as a disavowal of consciousness and memory rather than a contradictory state of knowledge, as self-deception traditionally has been viewed.

CASE STUDY

The presenting complaint of a patient whom I shall call "Sydney" involved "strange beds." From time to time he awoke in the bedrooms of women he didn't recall having met. Wrongful behavior, he sensed, must have led him to his newly found, temporary companions; but

Sydney didn't remember and was afraid to inquire about the previous night. Psychoanalysis, he hoped, would help him discover what he had been up to that caused his amnesia.

Sydney was a highly educated, well-spoken forensic pathologist in his early forties. His sessions were spent for the most part berating himself for his career's lack of distinction. I had considerable trouble getting him past feeling sorry for himself. It seemed as if the only insight he had gained in the first few months of treatment was the realization that the compelling motive that directed him toward medical pathology was his sense of helplessness in regard to his own mortality, and how this unrecognized apprehension related both to his serious case of scarlet fever as a child and to his parents' continual accusation that he was selfish.

His European-born parents (he, a schoolteacher; she, a nurse) criticized Sydney's preoccupation with his own needs; they were particularly outraged at catching him as a child playing "doctor" and other such games with several of his younger female cousins and playmates. They encouraged him to think less about himself and more about others. An unaltruistic existence, they repeatedly warned, is an unworthy life. They demanded that he study earnestly so he could help people in a way others could not. As a pathologist, he came to view death as a generic illness that someday would be conquered by science, as had other illness.

Sydney, a clumsy and normally poorly dressed person, began to attend sessions dressed in suits identical to mine and spoke in a similar intonation as I did. When he alluded to conversations he had with some of my colleagues, I anxiously suspected that he might be involved in behavior outside of his sessions that could sully my reputation.

I questioned him. He sheepishly admitted to having spoken with my colleagues in the medical school where he taught. He was considering analytic treatment with me, he told them, and needed information in order to properly make up his mind. Apparently these colleagues foolishly supplied personal data about me. At home Sydney began to wear the same style clothing as I did. After a couple of weeks he would look into a mirror and practice speaking and gesturing as I did. Sydney claimed that his impersonation was something that took over his behavior without his awareness or control. The pattern of his induction of my identity suggests otherwise.

Moments before Sydney put on his "analyst suit," he felt bad about himself. He compared himself with me. He felt deficient and told himself that he needed a couple of whiskeys to stop caring about his failures (knowing, of course, that he would not stop at a few). Then he went to his desk to gather his notes about my personal behavior. After studying them, he went to a special closet where he kept the analytic suits separate from his regular clothing and put one on.

From his closet he moved to the front of his large dresser mirror. Here he practiced his impersonation. Initially, when he did, the face in the mirror stared back at him and recriminated his improper behavior. With considerable effort at first, he refuted the accusation with such rationalizations as: if his analyst was as clever and emotionally resilient as he had been told, then Sydney's behavior would merely serve as a provocative psychological challenge. After a few sessions of talking back, he no longer was aware of any internal resistance to impersonating me. In sum, although his behavior followed the same pattern each time, Sydney chose to ignore the signs of what was to follow. When I angrily insisted that Sydney examine the sources of his destructive behavior toward me, and also figure out what he might have done in misrepresenting me to others, he stormed out of my consulting room coldly telling me that as an experienced analyst I shouldn't get upset so easily.

That evening, after my last therapeutic session, I reflected on my angry reaction to Sydney. To gain some control and a more objective perspective, I asked myself: if I were to match Sydney with a literary character, who would that be? With barely a moment's hesitation, I recognized his resemblance to the depersonalized Henry Jekyll in Robert Louis Stevenson's famous tale, *The Strange Case of Dr. Jekyll and Mr. Hyde*. I have always regarded this short novel as poorly written; at the same time it is a fascinating psychological study of a conflicted personality: the tale of a person with a dual personality—a benevolent, respected physician and scientist by day; at night a stunted, evil man with an insatiable appetite for power and pleasure. Down through the ages, myth and popular belief have suggested that each of us is not a solitary self but consists of at least two distinct personalities in conflict with each other because we delude ourselves about our needs and desires. Stevenson captures this dilemma in Jekyll's inner dialogue: "The pleasures which I made haste to seek in my disguise were . . . undignified. I would scarce use a harder term. But in the hands of Edward Hyde, they soon began to turn toward the monstrous. [I] stood at times aghast before the acts of Edward Hyde; but my situation was apart from ordinary law, and insidiously relaxed the grasp of conscience. It was Hyde, after all, and Hyde alone, that was guilty. [I] was no worse; [I] woke again to [my] good qualities seemingly unimpaired" (86–87). Here Jekyll demonstrates the essence of self-deception: he acts as if Hyde is simultaneously *both he and not he*.

Examining Jekyll's behavior, I recognized my anger as a derivative of my own self-deception: one of the motives for my many years treating seriously destructive patients, I had told myself and colleagues, was a vicarious attempt to reach and emotionally heal Nicky, the close friend of my youth. While in college I visited him in a state hospital for the criminally insane. I offered to help him any way I could. He looked at me with scorn, sprang to his feet, turned around, and quickly left the visitors' meeting room. I never saw him again. But until this moment I had somehow forgotten that a few years later while in graduate school I received a postcard from Nicky. He was no longer in prison; yet I made no attempt to find him.

My shameful feelings about Nicky's contemptuous behavior toward me, I then realized, might have set up an assumption about Sydney's behavior that was invalid. In other words, how certain was I that his impersonation of me was an expression of contempt? Wasn't it as possible that Sydney wished to be like me? Because of my anger I had failed to explore with Sydney the most important question of all: why would he wish to assume my identity in the first place?

Setting aside my practice not to initiate a follow-up call to a non-suicidal patient, I phoned Sydney and asked the question I missed earlier. He mentioned a number of complimentary remarks made by my colleagues about me. I interrupted him and said that he was seeing me in an overly idealized way. In reflecting on why I had become angry at him, I told him, I was forced to recognize that my reaction was due to a self-deception—that a phone conversation was not the place to discuss this. I apologized for my behavior in our last session, and said that he might now wish to reassess his perception of me. I said this because I assumed that if Sydney actually perceived me in the unrealistic way he described, his overidealization of me had not furthered his analysis.

Instead, of course, I could have explored his response to me as a manifestation of transference. I believe, however, that in general we analysts overdepend on transference analysis rather than taking advantage of realistic similarities between us and our clients.

I told Sydney that I suspected that he, too, had been self-deluded about central issues in his life and this might be the cause of his amnesia about his strange evenings. If we met together, I pointed out, we might throw some light on each other's self-deceptions.

He startled me by asking me if I expected him to pay for sessions if we were going to help each other. I wasn't sure for a long moment how I should respond to what ostensibly was a reasonable question. Finally I said, perhaps using an inapt, defensive analogy, "Listen, you learn more about pathology from the corpses you examine than they learn about you. Yet, I haven't heard you say that you are turning over your salary to the families of these people or to a charity. So, since we have agreed to work in a certain way, which includes your paying me a fee for my guiding this process—regardless of who may eventually gain more from the experience—let's continue our arrangement until it is clear to both of us that our contract needs to be renegotiated." Sydney agreed and told me that he would return to sessions the following week.

In the first session after his return, Sydney, no longer wearing my style clothes, described a persistent dream from childhood. He saw his father, tall and nude in the darkened bedroom of his younger sister, slowly approaching her bed. She shouts out, "Sydney." He adds, "She must have been calling out for me as her older brother to protect her. But if I heard her, I must have shut her out; I mean she was saying more than just my name, but I didn't listen."

Sydney was obsessed with the dream for the next several sessions, but could provide no more associations. If Sydney resembled Jekyll, wasn't it possible that his reported dream was not a dream, but a fragment of an actual event in which he, like Jekyll, disavowed his own participation?

I asked him to speak to his sister about the dream. He did so reluctantly. She recoiled, he reported, and with a shudder, told him that she had a similar persistent dream—only differences were that it was *Sydney* (age ten) who approached her (age eight) and that the missing words (from Sydney's dream) were, "Stop! Don't do this, Sydney!"

I recognized at that moment that if I was to help Sydney I needed to understand the nature of self-deception.

SELF-DECEPTION AS A METAPSYCHOLOGICAL PROBLEM

Self-deception is conventionally viewed as a way people try to protect themselves from threatening revelations by ignoring information they possess which contradicts their preferred view of themselves. My clinical experience suggests that self-deception is a form of the "if-only" fantasy which posits that if only people would treat me as I wish they would, with no effort on my part, I would no longer be just an ordinary, rather insignificant person, easily forgotten, quickly replaced. This crippling fantasy I believe lies at the core of all forms of psychopathology and interpersonal conflict.

The crucial importance of self-deception has impressed observers, at least since the oratory of the Greek moral idealist Demosthenes in the third century B.C.E. But it was Sigmund Freud who first developed a comprehensive theory to account for self-deception. Among Freud's most important discoveries is the realization that the underlying cause of psychological disturbance is our fear of self-knowledge: information which when consciously recognized induces us to feel weak, incompetent, ashamed, and unworthy—leading to self-hatred. But because Freud discovered that an awareness of the defenses against self-hatred is crucial to psychological recovery, the basic goal of psychoanalysis, although never explicitly addressed as such, is to identify and trace the motives that lead people to mislead themselves.

It seems reasonable to contend that the problem of self-deception led Freud to the notion of the unconscious. Freud's (1900) original account of mental life claims that because conflicts between the demands of the unconscious mind and the requirements of the conscious mind threaten the psychological well-being of the individual, psychological defenses are erected by the conscious part of the mind to keep itself unaware of threatening urges. In short, in order to hide painful truths about herself, a person imposes blinders on her own awareness.

This explanation raises a plethora of troublesome problems, the most important of which is a paradox: since lying to oneself isn't due to ignorance, misinformation, faulty reasoning, or being duped by someone else, we are faced with a puzzle. How can the same person simultaneously both recognize and fail to detect that she has a forbidden urge? How can she be both deceiver and deceived (Solomon 1977)?

Freud (1923) tried to resolve this paradox by dividing the mind into three realms: one that is unconscious and censors unacceptable thoughts and feelings; the conscious part that is aware of only censored material; and a realm that is unconscious but accessible to consciousness. This system, according to psychoanalyst Roy Schafer (1979), requires an inelegant and anthropomorphic mental apparatus: "As traditional metapsychologists, we seem to imply, though we would not openly avow, that the person is always more than one individual. We imply this multiple of individuals constituting one person in this way: we set up a number of agencies or divisions within the person's so-called mental apparatus, and hold that each of them functions in the manner of an individual in that circumscribed set of objectives, a certain type and amount of energy, and a strategy and influence. Further, we speak of each agency or division as relating to others as one person might relate to other people" (270–71). In short, according to psychoanalytic theory, people lie to themselves in the same way as they do to other people.

The French existentialist Jean-Paul Sartre (1956), in his well-known criticism of Freud's explanation of unconscious defenses—found in his *Being and Nothingness*—depicts psychoanalysis's notion of the unconscious as an absurd attempt to allow people to escape responsibility for their behavior. After all, Sartre points out, if part of the mind is responsible for bringing about the repressed awareness of the other part, and if psychoanalysts are intellectually honest, they must recognize that repression is a *chosen* strategy rather than an unconscious automatic process. In short, according to Sartre, the self-deluded person is someone who *dishonestly refuses* to admit what he knows.

In his later writing Freud (1937) himself recognized that there were problems with his theory of the unconscious and formulated a third theory of the mind. He explains that the ego, that part of the mind that represses threats to the personality by rendering the ideation unconscious, is itself partially unconscious.

THE EVIL WE DO

Logically, two crucial questions remain unanswered in regard to the *what* and *why* of self-deception in psychoanalytic theory:

1. If it is the ego which supervises unconscious defenses, how does it keep itself unaware of what it is doing? Doesn't describing the ego as partially unconscious merely push the role of a "knowing censor" an additional step? This type of secondary level of keeping the first unconscious requires an ad infinitum number of secondary steps. Psychoanalysts Kurt Eissler (1962) and Morton Gill (1963) provide the most substantial attempts to present this logical dilemma as an apparent but not a real problem. Neither succeeds: Eissler's attempt to evade the logical problems by means of an analogy of vision and defense contains dissimilar crucial aspects; Gill's explanation is overly vague about key issues in resolving the problem.

2. From whom does the unconscious try to keep forbidden impulses hidden? Other people? But then this elaborate setup would not be necessary. Is it for the psychic economy of personality? If so, the strategy is ineffective, since the forbidden impulse remains active in the id (the unconscious) and therefore ego defenses must remain continually cognizant of its derivatives if the defense is to succeed. In this regard, Herbert Fingarette (1969) points out: "Defense aims to reduce anxiety, of course, and so long as the main outcome of defense was thought to be a form of self-induced ignorance, it made a certain sense to suppose that 'what you don't know won't worry you.' But once we abandon the notion that defense brings a kind of blissful ignorance to some 'agency' of the mind, the question forces itself upon one: why should anxiety be reduced by defense any more than, better than, or different than would be the case if we merely curbed our impulses and/or deceived others quite consciously?" (116).

The most compelling theory I have found to account for self-deception is that of psychoanalyst and philosopher Herbert Fingarette (1969), quoted above, who begins his explanation by showing that self-deception is quite different from lying to others. He does this by turning the crucial question of how it is possible for defensive activity to remain unconscious upside down. This is to say, "Instead of asking how the defensive action is kept unconscious, we need to ask how it— or *any* mental content—ever is made conscious. Instead of being puzzled by a mental content's not being conscious, we must become puzzled a bit by its becoming conscious" (120).

Psychoanalysts and philosophers, claims Fingarette (1969), by using the wrong set of concepts to try to explain self-deception in a nonparadoxical way, trap themselves in either mechanistic accounts of the phenomenon that require an infinite regression of operations, or they describe it in a such a way that the behavior can no longer be appropriately regarded as self-deception. In other words, "Paradoxes arise in connection with self-deception when we characterize it primarily in terms of belief and knowledge, or in terms of 'perception' language such as 'appear' and 'see.' It is via the 'perception' terms that a bridge is established between belief and knowledge on one hand, and such notions as 'consciousness' and 'awareness' on the other " (34). Instead, Fingarette (1969) proposes "a fundamental change of emphasis. This shift of emphasis consists of divorcing certain of the 'cognitive-perception' terms, and showing, by reinterpretation, that they would be better treated as members of the 'volition-action' family." From this premise, Fingarette next proposes that the model of explicit consciousness be built on the metaphor of a *skill*.

By use of a skill model, "It would follow, of course, that one *can* do some 'such thing' as resolve to become explicitly conscious of something, or refuse to become so, or become so effectively or ineffectively, systematically or haphazardly, for good reasons or bad; and it follows that one becomes explicitly conscious by virtue of learning, even training" (p. 38).

The specific skill Fingarette (1969) has in mind as a model for becoming explicitly conscious of something is the task of articulating what one is experiencing or doing. As such, he proposes "that we not characterize consciousness as a kind of mental mirror, but as the exercise of the [learned] skill of 'spelling-out' some feature of the world as we are engaged in it . . . [T]o spell something out is to make it explicit, to say it in a clear and fully elaborated way, to make it perfectly apparent" (39).

Furthermore, the spelling out by the ego required to make us explicitly conscious of a feeling or activity should not be regarded as a random or automatic process. To become "explicitly conscious requires a quite specific 'mental act,' an act in which the ego selects a particular item from an indefinitely large range of possible items, and highlights this particular item" (121). In other words, consciousness is an act of intentionality: the assertion of a specific skill, induced by a specific purpose, with no overriding reasons not to attend to that activity. **99**

Consequently, "the self-deceiver is one whose life-situation is such that, on the basis of his tacit assessment of his situation, he finds that there is an overriding reason for adopting a policy of not spelling out some engagement of his in the world. . . . [Moreover] he does not stop at refusing to spell out what is so. He is forced to fabricate stories in order to keep his explicit account of things and the way things really are in some kind of harmony such as will make his account of things plausible. However, he does not spell out that he is doing this" (62). In short, in the language of volition, the element of *purposefulness* is necessary for there to be self-deception. "If our subject *persuades* himself to believe contrary to the evidence *in order to evade*, somehow, the unpleasant truth to which he has already seen that the evidence points, then and only then is he clearly a self-deceiver" (28)

INNER SPEECH

There is some empirical evidence to support Fingarette's notion that a lack of spelling out induces self-deception. Although the actual cognitive processes which mediate self-awareness have not been empirically verified, experimental evidence (Morin and Everett 1991; Scheier, Buss, and Buss 1978; Siegrist 1995) suggests that conversation with oneself about oneself—whether silently or outloud—faciliates self-consciousness and discourages self-deception. In other words, the exercise of language enables us to be aware of ourselves. Obviously, not all introspection is constructive: there are patterns of inner speech which contain fallacious assumptions about the subject's personal capacities and those of his social world—patterns that impede him from accurate assessment of his own motives and those of other people. *Constructive inner speech*, therefore, requires the subject to "divide" his consciousness into that of a "speaker" and that of a "listener." The listener applies the rules of internal and external coherence, empirical adequacy, and congruence to the speaker's personal capacities and examines this information in light of the speaker's assumptions about himself and his social world. In other words, in a coherent verbal report there is a logical consistency among the various elements of the story, which fits congruently with well-established information about the subject under discussion. The report also is aesthetically sound: the conclusion ably addresses the problem posed in the story. Finally, the social and moral values espoused in the report are consistent with the speaker's typical attitudes (Polonoff 1987).

If constructive inner speech guards against self-deception, then, were Sydney's incorrect and partial memories of events due to distortions in his inner speech at the time of the events or to defective memory processes? The notion of memory as narrative suggests the former.

MEMORY AS NARRATIVE

Traditionally, psychologists have maintained that experiences are encoded in memory like a motion picture film (except that all the sensory input, not only sight and sound, are captured in memory). Therefore, it is believed, given an appropriate inquiry technique—hypnosism, sodium pentothal free association or whatever—can bring forth faithfully even the most painful and fearful events. This is a fallacious assumption. Memory is not like a movie or videotape, able to capture the event as it actually occurs.

We are language-oriented beings. Our recognition of what we experience, and how we understand these events, depends upon linguistic percepts; conceptualization creates our sense of reality. Memory also depends on words, the story the subject tells himself as the event unfolds, as if the speaker is presenting the experience to a listener not present at the event. Moreover, not only do we try to explain what happens to us by means of stories we creatively construct at the time of the event, but in fact we experience what happens to us as it occurs in terms of a story that has personal meaning for us.

The Italian writer Primo Levi (1993), from his experience in concentration camps, insightfully points out that in extreme (i.e., stressful) situations our language is strained to find words to express our ordeal. Failing to find the right concepts to meaningfully put our felt experiences into the perspective of our own previous experiences or those of others we know of through language (i.e., their stories), we experience

101

what is happening to us as unreal. Lacking adequate linguistic concepts, people revert to defense mechanisms that speak to the "unreality" of that moment. Among these are denial, depersonalization, withdrawal into one's private world of hallucinations, catatonia, autism, and so forth.

But obviously a number of people survived the concentration camp who were not as linguistically skilled as such survivors as Levi, Viktor Frankel (1964), and Elie Wiesel (1989). In addition to the sheer luck to have someone present who helped to get extra food, provided protection, and kept up one's morale, an additional factor was necessary to survive: an ability to deal with the difficult problems of survival by one's capacity to spell out one's situation in practical terms. Accounts by Frankel, Levi, and Wiesel, among others, suggests that the stories the survivors told themselves conceptualized their horrible situation in a way that it could be dealt with adaptively. This is to say, their linguistic skills enabled them to remain reality-related by making meaning of their horrific experience. Prolonged suffering in situations that lack reality for a person induces psychosis. It is important to recognize that one's survival skills are consistent with one's personal identity.

PERSONAL IDENTITY

An individual's *personal identity* is a complex enterprise. It consists not only of the sense of who one is currently, but includes beliefs and desires about who one should be. When there is a congruent fit between what one experiences as the circumstances of one's life with the images, fantasies, and intentions of one's desired self, a feeling of competence and well-being accompanies these experiences (Goldberg 1991a). So, for example, if a child's early experiences of lust and desire are treated in a healthy way by his caretakers, he will have good feelings about himself. But if during his first awakenings of strong desire he is treated with condemnation and shame, as Sydney's account of his critical attention from his parents suggests, the child will be induced with a sense of "badness" (Goldberg 1997).

In order to hide from a sense of painful badness, a child will lie and pretend; deceit makes effective self-examination difficult; consequently, the sense of badness cannot readily be uprooted and replaced with reasonable expectations for oneself. On the contrary, the inculcated hidden feelings of self-contempt gradually stabilize the child's negative personal identity: he becomes convinced that he is helpless and alone in the world. This acute helplessness compels one to hide. Indeed, helpless aloneness can become so painful that it causes episodic amnesia about who one actually is. In attempting to escape from their painful aloneness, people like Sydney, sometimes without conscious awareness, take on someone else's identity— living as if they actually were that person—insatiably consuming those aspects of life that were not possible in their former identity. For this to happen psychological splitting and depersonalization must take place.

Through a process of "Me"/"Not Me" *depersonalization*, Sydney psychologically split into an *observer* (the listener) and *participant* (the speaker) selves. He identified with the observer self, so what happened to the participant self did not register as his own experience. In effect, his observer self acted as if "This isn't happening to me (the observing self). It is happening to the other (the disavowed participant self). I'm just an onlooker." Because his participant self was attributed as belonging to other people, Sydney remembers that it was first his father, then his colleagues, and finally me, who did the wrongful things in the beds in which he strangely awoke.

We are faced here with a crucial treatment dilemma: if the narrative told by the observing self is distorted then it would seem that a more accurate version of an event is not possible—yet, there is sufficient evidence that people do recover crucial parts of "forgotten" experiences. The theory of the dual brain can help understand recovered memories.

DUAL BRAIN THEORY

Neuropsychologists have long known that the human brain is composed of two hemispheres that seem to mirror each other in structure (bicameral). Despite their identical appearance, they have separate neurological functions, and they are regarded as having separate ways of comprehending reality.

THE EVIL WE DO

According to R. Joseph (1993), a neuropsychologist, "[E]ach half of the brain has developed its own strategy for perceiving, processing, and repressing information, as well as specialized neuroanatomical interconnections that assist in mediating these functions" (22). In this view, the left hemisphere is analytic, capable of reasoning and literate communication. The right hemisphere speaks in the language of movement, imaginary, metaphor, and design. Moreover, the two hemispheres seem to have entirely distinct memories and experiences. The differences in functioning are because the left hemisphere of the modern brain has evolved to handle functions such as language and manual dexterity that were absent in our earlier ancestors. As the modality of language, the left brain is also the seat of conscious memory, which is dependent upon the ability to put experiences into words. Since the right brain specializes in experiences that do not require conscious responsiveness, it is regarded as the place where the unconscious resides (Joseph 1993).

A highly controversial psychohistorical account of how the left brain evolved to become the monitor of rational human activity is provided by Princeton University psychologist Julian Jaynes's (1976) notion of the bicameral mind. Jaynes uses the generally agreed upon observation that people seem to possess a *sixth sense*, which relays information to the brain without relying on the senses of sight, hearing, touch, taste, or smell. He suggests that extrasensory perception, which we all possess to a greater or lesser extent, is a throwback to a crucial form of communication of preliterate humankind.

According to Jaynes, the authors of the Jewish Bible, the *Epic of Gilgamesh*, and the *Odyssey*, along with their less literate contemporaries, entirely lacked what we call "self-consciousness." Since their awareness was directed outward, toward the external world, these ancient writers were unable to examine their own motivations and intentions; in short, they were incapable of introspection.

To people of the twenty-first century so accustomed to "looking inside of ourselves" before choosing a course of action, this is a baffling, even nonsensical idea. For one thing, on even the simplest level it is difficult to conceive how a person can make any complex decision without some sort of contemplation.

Jaynes explains that the people of that era were able to deal with the tasks and burdens of their lives by hearing voices telling them what to do, voices that they regarded as divine. He contends that an auditory hallucination, considered to be evidence of a serious emotional disturbance today, is in fact a throwback to the neurological commands of an ancient era of human development.

The "bicameral" period, as Jaynes terms it, began before 10,000 B.C.E., when hallucinations served to orient and guide a humankind not yet intellectually evolved enough to exercise deliberate personal control. In his view, when the ancient hero described in sagas heard the voice of a god telling him what to do, the voice actually originated in the person's right brain and was heard by him in his left brain, as through a transmitter.

In contemporary times, even though our two brains have different mental systems—indeed, "think" differently—they usually work cooperatively to exchange information. However, there are important exceptions: "[L]ack of communication can be intentional—the left brain just does not want to know what is really going on emotionally as the information may be too painful or upsetting to consider consciously" (Joseph 1993, 47).

To treat self-deception, both the reasons for the deception and a more complete narrative must be acquired from the encoded information in the right brain.

TREATMENT

Analysts use themselves as mirrors to help their clients see themselves more clearly. The mirror, however, is reversible; it forces the analyst to perceive himself without guise (Goldberg 1991b). In asking myself why another person would want to assume my identity, I had to closely examine not only my more admirable qualities, but also my dark side. I recognized that Sydney was able to portray me because he was highly attuned to some aspect of my life that I had consciously denied.

What I saw in the countertransferential mirror was the reason for my not wanting to see Nicky again: his sudden, explosive anger that I had witnessed as his teammate in athletic events in school was too close to my own. Even though I had offered to help him, after learning of his destructive violence I did not wish to be reminded that in many ways we were similar.

By spelling out my experiences with Nicky—both positive and negative—that were influential in developing my personal identity as a youth, I was able to consciously examine my suppressed fears about my similarities with Nicky. I did this by free-associating to what I could recall of the sentience in the events of the years I spent in school with Nicky. In other words, I assumed that if experiences are denied consciousness they reside encoded in the available modalities of the right brain—sounds, smells, and propioceptive feedback (sensory feedback that we experience from our movements and bodily positions). To be spelled-out they need to be translated to the literate left brain by free association.

I suggested that Sydney also free-associate to the primodial senses of his "strange bed" experiences. Slowly fragmented images emerged of women's smells, sounds, tactile caresses. In these partial experiential gestalts—that is to say, experiences that strive for completeness—to which he gave voice, Sydney was increasingly less an observer; eventually he became a visceral participant.

I interrupted him from time to time to change his "it" references to "I" and "me." I also drew his attention to his passive language so that he would use more reflective and active terms to capture his encoded experience. Sydney's increased use of dynamic terms and descriptions helped him spell out what he had hidden: not his badness, but fear that he was ordinary. Finding himself in bed with so many attractive women was his attempt to deny that he was just an ordinary person. But the "strategy" didn't work because it violated his parents' values and their insistence that his specialness should consist in his helping other people. Once he no longer needed to deceive himself he was able to recognize that he was not a bad person—mean-spirited or manipulative. Indeed, as a medical scientist he was trying to help people, however indirectly. If only people knew that his work could one day benefit society, he hoped, then he would be properly rewarded for his dedication and hard work. His awareness of what he intended for himself enabled him to start to make firm commitments to other people.

The next chapter concerns another unusual patient—a woman who had put out a "contract" on her husband's life. Nora's case provided insight for me into how psychological defenses are formed.

REFERENCES

Eissler, K. R. 1962. On the metapsychology of the unconscious. *Psychoanalytic Study of the Child* 17: 9–41.

Fingarette, H. 1969. *Self-deception*. London: Routledge & Kegan Paul.

Frankel, V. 1964. *Man's search for meaning*. New York: Washington Square Press.

Freud, S. [1900] 1965. *The interpretation of dreams*. Reprint, New York: Avon.

———. [1923] 1990. The ego and the id. In the *The standard edition of the complete psychological works of Sigmund Freud*, edited by James Strachey, 19: 3–60. Reprint, New York: W. W. Norton.

———. [1937] 1990. Analysis terminable and interminable. *Standard edition*. 23: 209–50.

Gill, M. 1963. Topography and systems in psychoanalytic theory. *Psychological Issues*, Monograph 10.

Goldberg, C. 1991a. *Understanding shame*. Northvale, N.J.: Aronson.

———. 1991b. *On being a psychotherapist*. Northvale, N.J.: Aronson.

———. 1997. *Speaking with the devil: Exploring senseless acts of evil*. New York: Penguin.

———. 1999. The patient who assumed his analyst's identity. *Journal of the American Academy of Psychoanalysis* 27: 177–89.

Jaynes, J. 1976. *The origins of consciousness*. Boston: Houghton Mifflin.

Joseph, R. 1993. *The right brain and the unconscious*. New York: Plenium.

Levi, P. 1993. *Survival in Aschwitz*. New York: Macmillan.

Morin, A., and J. Everett. 1991. Self-awareness and "introspective" private speech in six-year-old children. *Psychological Reports* 68: 1299–1306.

Polonoff, D. 1987. Self-deception. *Social Research* 54: 45–53.

Sartre, J-P. 1956. *Being and nothingness*. New York: Washington Square Press.

Schafer, R. 1979. The idea of resistance. *International Journal of Psycho-Analysis* 54: 259–85.

Scheier, M., A. Buss, and D. Buss. 1978. Self-consciousness, self-report of aggressiveness and aggression. *Journal of Research in Personality* 12: 133–40.

Siegrist, M. 1995. Inner speech as a cognitive process mediating self-consciousness and inhibiting self-deception. *Psychological Reports* 76: 259–65.

THE EVIL WE DO

Solomon, R. C. 1977. *The passions*. Garden City, N.Y.: Doubleday.
Stevenson, R. L. 1985. *Dr. Jekyll and Mr. Hyde*. New York: Bantam.
Wiesel, E. 1989. *Night*. New York: Bantam.

5

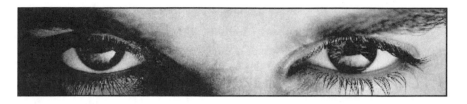

THE CLIENT WHO ARRANGED TO HAVE HER HUSBAND MURDERED

Psychological Defenses as Personal Strategies

Give sorrow words: the grief that does not speak whispers the o'er fraught heart and bids it break.

—William Shakespeare, *Macbeth*

IN MY CLINICAL EXPERIENCE, THE DESTRUCTIVE ACTIONS OF MALE-factors are based on one or both of two pernicious beliefs: (1) The victim is so weak, stupid, or incompetent that he or she can be treated as an object rather than someone who deserves decent consideration; or, (2) the victim is so threatening to the offender's physical or psychological well-being that any destructive action is justified (Goldberg 2000). The case presented here involves the latter belief.

I saw Nora for psychoanalytic treatment shortly after her acrimonious separation from her husband. At the time, Nora was thirty-five, with long reddish hair and a brogue that she brought with her as a child from the Emerald Isle. There her father had been a diplomat and a member of the Parliament. Nora, the eldest of three children, had inherited her father's intellect and early career—she practiced criminal law.

Nora played an audiotape for me during her second session of analysis. During a long-distance car drive, she had taped a conversation between herself and her estranged husband, a notorious gambler and alleged swindler. Their angry discussion focused on the fact that before he had left their home to start a relationship with another woman, he had stolen her confidential files of clients she represented, together with $750,000 of Nora's security bonds. He planned, she told me, to use the money to stage what virtually every boxing promoter at the time (twenty years ago) called "The Heavyweight Fight of the Century," but themselves had been unable to arrange.

During the taped conversation, her husband coolly tells Nora that if she allows him to keep the bonds and accepts an uncontested divorce, he will return the files unread. If not, he will turn them over to those who would take full advantage of the information they contain.

Nora responds with unmitigated contempt in her voice and suggests that he probably already has seen the files. If so, he knows that they include information about those she represents in organized crime. Unless he returns the files, she tells him with the intonation of someone practiced in informing others of the gravity of their injudicious behavior, she will notify these exceedingly volatile men of the incriminating information he holds.

He calls her bluff, telling her that she must realize that her life would be forfeit as well as his if she informed her clients that their lives were no longer confidential.

I asked how she planned to handle the situation. She replied that her husband could keep the files and bonds, or she could have him eliminated and retrieve them—it really made no difference to her. But he had wronged her, and justice demanded that he would have to pay. Toward this end, she had already hired a "hit man" to exterminate her husband.

I expressed concern that despite his treachery, it wasn't worth going to prison for the rest of her life for having her husband removed. She sneered at my caution, a patch of vividly colored skin visible around her neck, as she informed me that professional killers rarely get caught. But even if she should be apprehended, so what! She had *never regretted anything she had ever done.* "Besides," she added, "anything I have ever done that has resulted in hurt to someone else would have been done to me if I gave people the opportunity."

The Client Who Arranged to Have Her Husband Murdered

How should I regard Nora's lack of regret in planning her husband's murder? I wondered at the time. For no matter how enraged any of us might be at the betrayal of someone with whom we have been emotionally intimate, the regret we experience in serving as their executioner will stop most of us from acting lethally on our hurt and angry feelings.

On the other hand, I was fully aware from my clinical experience with clients who had committed serious violent acts (Goldberg 1997) that a lack of regret for their behavior was bonded to their severe early psychological trauma. In other words, exploration of their histories revealed that each of the offenders I treated became violent to inure against some great suffering. How *consciously aware* was Nora, I wondered, of the specific ways her suffering induced her to by-pass feelings of compassion and concern for a person for whom she apparently had once deeply loved—and probably still did?

The extent of our awareness of the motives that shape our behavior is an old and controversial psychological issue (Goldberg 1977). Psychoanalysts differ widely on the extent of freedom of awareness they attribute to people (Fromm 1964). Orthodox analysts contend that the unconscious is a relentless ghostwriter of our lifescript since our behavior, for the most part, is determined by prior events which have been *repressed*: "The exclusion of specific psychological activities or contents from conscious awareness by a process of which the individual is not directly aware" (English and English 1958, 458).

In contrast, humanistic analysts hold that we are capable of recognizing our pressing motives, since for the most part people use *suppression* rather than repression to deal with threatening thoughts and feelings. "Suppression is a preconscious and conscious psychical process, in which ideas and affects are deliberately excluded from consciousness. . . . [T]hey are (as a consequence) recoverable" (Eidelberg 1968, 424).

Oddly, because the crux of the controversy between orthodox and humanistic analysts as to the capacity of people to be aware of their motives rests on the extent that suppression and other consciously controlled defense mechanisms are used by the clients in the cases presented, there are few references to the role of suppression in the psychoanalytic literature (Werman 1983). A review of scholarly discussions about defense mechanisms clearly reveals that Freud's claim that **111** the theory of repression is "the cornerstone upon which the whole structure of psychoanalyis rests" (Freud 1914, 16) still dominates.

Nevertheless, to whatever degree psychoneurotics have access to their own motives, the general agreement among analysts is that destructive people have far less. This is because most analysts seem to accept the commonsense notion, discussed in chapter 3, that due to their severe early trauma, destructive people are compelled to act in large part from deeper, more uncontrollable and unaware parts of the mind than do psychoneurotics (for example, Menninger 1968). I disagree with this view.

In this chapter I examine the defense mechanisms at work in Nora's lack of regret for her destructive urges. I seek to show that the degree of awareness Nora possessed about her pressing motives was predicated on *conscious emotional strategies* she employed in order to deal with anxiety and threat to her feelings of *agency*—the existential sense that she was capable of becoming the person she sought to be. Over time, these strategies, because they are forms of self-deception, gradually limited Nora's self-awareness and freedom of behavior. Consequently, to the extent that Nora's behavior is generalizable, repression and other defense mechanisms that operate at an unconscious level dominate only with the "permission" of the conscious mind. Moreover, this arrangement is not phylogenetically set—innate to human development—as orthodox analysts contend (A. Freud 1936); it is based upon prior "decisions" the individual made in regard to his or her ability to tolerate psychological threat (Fromm 1964). My contention that repression can be arrested by conscious voluntary intentions is consistent with University of Kansas professor of psychology David Holmes's (1974) report on his extensive review of research investigations of repression. He indicates: "[T]here is no consistent research evidence to support the hypothesis derived from the (psychoanalytic) theory of repression. The lack of evidence for the theory is especially notable in view of the wide variety of approaches which have been tried and the persistent effort which has been made during the last half century to find support for the theory. Certainly, the lack of empirical support for the hypothesis derived from the theory of repression cannot be attributed to a lack of research interest in the topic.

"The conclusion that there is no experimental evidence . . . should not be interpreted as suggesting that there is no selectivity in what persons are able to report of their previous experiences. On the contrary, the results of many investigations clearly reveal a selectivity of recall. The important point to recognize, however, is that the patterning of the selectivity is often inconsistent with the predictions derived from the (psychoanalytic) theory of repression, and/or the findings can be better accounted for by process other than repression" (649). In other words, no experimental study has found a systematic way that people recall their past experiences that is consistent with psychoanalytic theories of repression.

NORA'S HISTORY

Nora had been subjected to an unresponsive and disturbed relationship with her mother, a beautiful, vain, and emotionally distant woman who was more concerned with her dashing career-diplomat husband's love affairs—he had fought several pistol duels over women during his service on the Continent during their marriage—than with the care and development of her three children.

For much of her childhood, Nora spent most of her time at home alone in her room: reading, listening to music, daydreaming. Rarely did her mother seek her out or concern herself with Nora's solitary activities.

Starting with her earliest pangs of jealousy at the birth of her baby brother when she was six, Nora frequently was involved in acrimonious arguments—even physical fights—in school with classmates, whom she claimed received preferential treatment from teachers. Recognizing her envy and hurt at the arrival of a brother, but not knowing how to comfort her, Nora's parents chose to emphasize her anger rather than her hurt. Whenever they observed her rage they told her that her feelings were wrong: any other child would gladly change places with her in order to receive the opportunities and possessions she had been given. Consequently, she was a selfish, rotten, and ungrateful child. Accusations of her badness brought on a somatic reaction: blushed skin, from her neck down.

Her parents' admonishments had several adverse effects on her character: Nora was led to believe that her angry feelings to the loss of exclusive intimacy and specialness with her parents meant she was a child with bad judgment, who was incapable of understanding her own feelings. Second, she vowed to herself to live up to her parents' moral judgment of her as a child whose anger compelled her to commit acts abhorrent to conventional morality. To mock the values of the groups in which she was involved, she lied and cheated in games with classmates and in her schoolwork (although she was usually the brightest in her class). These patterns continued into adulthood. Moreover, her contemptuous behavior was continually ignited by still another factor—self-deception. Nora, by claiming that she had never regretted anything, was making the unwitting statement of her ongoing refusal to mourn her inability to have made some significant difference to her parents.

A child's capacity to consciously grieve losses and hurts is a crucial factor in adaptive behavior. In contrast, an inability to mourn is the child's dysfunctional reaction to parents who discourage her from expressing disappointments and grief. Many life experiences turn out to be disheartening to the helpless and dependent child. Parents feeling ashamed in having disappointed their child, and not knowing how to set things right, exert pressure on the child to shed no tears over bitter experiences.

To the extent that the child is unable to consciously acknowledge and give words to her inability to achieve or maintain a desired relationship with her parents, or someone else she regards as important to her, she is condemned to a world of pretense (Farber 1966). Because Nora was unable to express her upset over the lack of control over her life, she felt compelled to find ways of pretending that she was not as helpless as she felt. The more her parents treated Nora's experiences of disappointment and loss as if these experiences didn't matter, the greater was Nora's need—in order to deny her helplessness—to pretend that she could get whatever she wanted, whenever she wanted. Nora's destructive urges, in an important sense, were attempts to show that she had control over her life—she could do whatever she pleased.

Through the capacity of her intellect and her choice of career, Nora found a way in her professional life to thwart her painful parental neglect. Her sense of deprivation and less-than-valued treatment from others made her a tenacious representative for poorly educated but rich and powerful men who operated on the far end of morality and the law.

In turn, although women in power were initially unfamiliar and uncomfortable for these men from a traditional southern European upbringing, her undaunted willingness to win in any way necessary—legal or not—quickly won over their admiration and trust.

On the other hand, her searing hurt found its way into her attempts at friendship and intimacy—where it contaminated her emotions with the fear of betrayal and mistrust. Nora's psychic hurt brought her into analysis.

NORA'S EMOTIONAL STRATEGIES

Nora did not seem cognizant of the ways that she angered people, but she was clearly aware of her *choices* in how she responded to her aggrieved responses to their lack of satisfactory interaction with her. For example, in regard to not wanting to be bothered by the demands of her aging parents: "They are getting what they deserve. They were just too narcissistically involved with their own needs to properly care for me; now I ignore them. Other people might need to keep demanding that their parents love them, not me. Just because they treated me as unlovable doesn't mean that I am. Why do I have to *keep digging into myself* to find out if there was something about me—I did or was—that alienated them from me? *Self-scrutiny is just too depressing!* It is far better that I find the most exciting, sought-after man and show them that I am what men want."

Humanistic psychoanalyst Erich Fromm (1963) observed that each of us may seek some ideal state of freedom, but we are not equally desirous of enduring anxiety and discomfort in pursuit of psychological freedom. People regulate the kind and amount of anxiety they feel able to tolerate in their quest of the goals they seek by means of *emotional strategies*. I refer to them as "strategies" because I believe that each of us undergoes a conscious process in deciding on his or her strategies. I also contend that all of us can be described as holding a set of relatively consistent flexible or inflexible strategies, much in the same way social psychologist Milton Rokeach (1960) has described an open-closed minded continuum of belief systems.

In clinical terms, people with inflexible strategies seem unwilling to withstand high degrees of cognitive disorganization, which are inherent in situations that are emotionally complex, ambiguous, or involve uncertainty of outcome. Because anxiety is easily aroused in these situations, inflexible strategizers seek situations where quick, easy, and certain solutions can be readily anticipated. For example, throughout their marriage Nora insisted that her husband account for his every moment apart from her. She had behaved similarly with a series of previous lovers. Her husband, as did the others, responded to her attempts to dominant with intense anger. Nora blamed the rageful reactions of her lovers on the fact that all men are untrustworthy and don't want to be held accountable. Too uncomfortable to stay with her hurt for very long, Nora was unable to recognize that it was her fear of betrayal that had resulted in her highly controlling behavior toward her husband and other people. Typically, rather than expose her vulnerable feelings to conscious scrutiny, Nora dealt with her emotional concerns as she did legal issues: in a logical way that brought her to a decisive rational solution. For example, situations that raised the possibility that Nora's lack of tolerance for weakness in others was less a product of her high standards for competence and courage than it was fueled by fears about her own limitations were those that induced her to take decisive action to prove her superiority.

Unable to identify the feelings that impelled her impulsive behavior, Nora's intellectual analyses of her problematic issues were often sterile, straitjacketed by rationalized justifications. These rationalizations gave her a pseudosense of competence and courage. Her plan to have her husband murdered was an example of this emotional strategy.

Awareness is a motivational state, directed by one's emotional strategies. Experimental evidence, as I indicated in the last chapter, suggests that inner speech facilitates self-consciousness and discourages self-deception. But of course we will never know ourselves thoroughly; the best we can realistically hope for is to continually gain a more accurate version than we had previously. Consequently, our willingness to stay with introspection provides us, along with dialogue with wise and trusted others, with the best means available for an accurate version of ourselves.

The opportunity for constructive inner speech was curtailed in

Nora by the emotional strategies she had chosen that pressed her to take *immediate*, decisive action about her precipitous urges in order to avoid continued painful threats to her sense of agency. The reason for these emotional strategies is best understood in the context of the roles shame and pride play as monitors of personal identity.

When a child feels she has secured the esteem of others, she develops a sense of positive identity. But if instead she is disregarded and humiliated, as is usually the case with children who cannot satisfy the excessive demands of their parents, she will likely develop a negative personal identity. This depleted sense of self is not passive; its accusatory "narrative voice" continually informs her in painful ways that she is incompetent, inadequate, unwanted, leaving her with a feeling of "badness" and self-contempt (Goldberg 1991a).

It was to her accusatory voice that Nora was saying no in her unwillingness to tolerate continued self-scrutiny: her emotional strategies were designed to deflect criticism from herself by presenting her as a misunderstood and insufficiently appreciated *superior* person. To validate her sense of agency as a superior person, Nora first tried *shamelessness*. For example, she choose to boldly represent vicious mobsters by any means at her disposal. But in the intimate areas of her life, shamelessness alone was insufficient. It was joined by *bravado*: Nora sought to raise her self-esteem by boasting to me (and, I am sure, to others) that she lived by a higher morality than do conventional people. In other words, she tried to convince me that she was providing a social benefit to society: she was willing to actually do, in her own words, "what other people dream and fantasize about doing, but are too 'gutless' and dishonest to admit"; in her case, to kill a thieving, betraying husband. In this sense, Nora was convinced that she was a role model for fearful and disgruntled people, inspiring them to stand up for their authentic wishes and ambitions.

EMOTIONAL STRATEGIES IN DESTRUCTIVE BEHAVIOR IN CAMUS

The close similarity of Nora's emotional strategies with that of Albert Camus's protagonist Meursault in *The Stranger* suggests that Nora's   **117** emotional strategies do not pertain to her alone. Meursault is condemned to execution for having killed a man he had not seen up close until just moments before he shot him. He says in the novel, "I have never regretted anything in all my life. I've always been far too much absorbed in the present moment, or the immediate future to think back," and of the event of the shooting, he recalls, "And just then it crossed my mind that one might fire, or not fire—and it would come to absolutely the same thing."

At Meursault's trial, the most damning charge the prosecutor brings against him is that Meursault's lack of strong emotion and his indifference to social convention are indicative of an insensitivity to others' feelings; and, as such, he is an unredeemable criminal who doesn't deserve to live.

Meursault's lack of affectivity does not initially concern him—he tolerates the demands other people put on his life without question or protest. Believing that life lacks an inherent meaning, his view of existence posits that acting one way rather than another is immaterial. His sole existential principle is to live with as minimal an effort as he can manage. Nora lives materially lavishly; existentially, her emotional strategy, like that of Meursault, is to live as a minimalist.

In the diary Camus used to structure his novel, he refers to Meursault as the man who does not want to explain himself (Lottmann 1980). Unwilling to examine the basis for his personal beliefs is costly to Meursault in terms of getting caught up in a destructive act without knowing how he arrived at that place. As such, he is as much a stranger to himself as he is to others: unaware of what is important to him until it is too late—until he has been condemned to death. For Nora, too, her emotional strategies are ways designed so not to have to explain herself to herself or anyone else.

TREATMENT

When Nora told me that she had hired a "hit man," I became concerned and indignant about the legal and moral dilemma in which she had placed me. Previously in my career, I had treated a number of violent patients in forensic and psychiatric facilities who threatened to kill me or someone else. But the institutional facilities in which I treated them had built-in safeguards against violent acting out. The consulting room in which I saw Nora in my private practice lacked these constraints.

I discussed with Nora my concern about her threat. When she indicated that she was adamant about having her husband eliminated, I responded:

"You know that I simply cannot let you carry out a murder that I am aware you are planning! My conscience wouldn't allow me, neither will my legal responsibility."

"But what about the confidentiality to which I am entitled?" she retorted.

"I don't know the answer to the confidentiality issue. But it seems to me that *we both* have a problem here: you want to kill someone; I don't want you to carry it out; yet, I don't want you locked up, either—it would make my continuing analysis with you very difficult."

Nora stared at me with a menacing gaze, "It seems like all of the above are your problems, not mine." I used my indignant counter-transferential feelings to inform Nora that her potentially destructive behavior was also her problem because it was unacceptable both to me and to the integrity of the analysis. "By endangering me, you are placing at risk the help you sought in coming to see me."

I reminded Nora that she had described her parents as contemptuous in their parental functions. As such, she had been continually a victim of their contempt. Not surprisingly, she had behaved contemptuously in her intimate relations and was doing the same to me by telling me of her plan and not calling it off. Consequently, "Should I continue the pattern as others have in the past and treat you with contempt by terminating analysis? Or should I have you arrested? Or should I vent my indignation by hitting on your vulnerabilities? Or should we start a more constructive new pattern: to find out what are the positive experiences that you seek, but don't seem to know how to reach for, except in hurtful ways—even in regard to those from whom you seek good experiences?" Nora nodded at the last option.

I continued, "Okay, then! If you are willing to hold on to your vulnerable feelings and closely examine them rather than disguise them in rage, then we both may learn something useful for you in getting at the **119** positive things you want in your life. But before we can move on there is still your threat to your husband."

With a shrug of her shoulders, she replied: "I don't know what you want me to say. I do want the files and money back from my husband. Maybe then I will call off the 'contract.' But I don't want you to communicate directly with him. . . . He is very clever. He'll trick you into divulging information about me that is none of his business. Therefore, I can't give you his phone number or his whereabouts."

"I have a solution for your concern about my communicating with your husband."

"Which is?"

"You have a personal attorney, the one who referred you to me. I am going to inform him of the situation and have him talk to your husband." I did. Nora's attorney was concerned but not surprised by my information. He knew, he said, of Nora's threats against her husband in the past when the husband had "stepped out" on her with other women. He had warned the husband of the threats in the past and would again today. He did.

The situation described in this case obviously is not one which an analyst often faces. I recognized that I needed to take a far more active role than analysts normally do. I discussed with Nora the tape I had heard, showing her how her interactions with her husband seemed to be an expression of the resentment she harbored about the failed closeness with her mother. I went on to speculate that, in turn, her husband's betrayal was, at least in part, due to a psychotic rage he may have experienced in the way she had treated him during their marriage—probably reminiscent of a very disturbed relationship with his own mother.

In a subsequent session, I recommended a meeting between her and her husband alone, and supervised her in how to use Basic Emotional Communication[1] with her husband so that he would at least return the files, and she could call off his murder.

She agreed, but only with a proviso: she would set up a meeting with her husband at a local courthouse in order to negotiate the return of her securities and files. If he would not turn them over to her, upon leaving the courthouse, she would signal her hired assassin to carry out his assignment.

In fact, in the courthouse, her husband returned her files. Nora allowed him to keep some of the bonds as compensation for the termination of their marriage.

The story did not end at the courthouse. It had a final, strange twist. Also waiting for Nora outside of the courthouse was her own personal attorney, with whom she had entrusted her files and securities. Following her return home from Europe, after the harrowing experience with her ex-husband, she asked her attorney for her property. He readily handed over the files, but claimed that she had never given him any bonds.

More sessions were required to dissuade Nora from her belief that the world was replete with liars and cheats, and that to eliminate any of these predators was a benevolent service to humankind.

The following chapter discusses the case of Henry, who in his first few sessions with me reported a series of dreams in which, posing as a policeman, he had attempted to rape women whose cars he had pulled over on the highway at night. The details of Henry's dreams closely corresponded with those of a serial rapist who was at large at the time I was treating Henry.

NOTE

1. The pattern of interaction carried out by her parents was built on manipulating others by trying to evoke guilt in the others by focusing on their character faults and inferred moral obligations to them. Nora interacted in a similar way. By doing so, she pushed away even those who cared about her. Once she began to recognize this, she was taught the principles of Basic Emotional Communication (see section C).

REFERENCES

Eidelberg, L. 1968. *The encyclopedia of psychoanalysis*. New York: Free Press.

English, H. B., and A. C. English. 1958. *A comprehensive dictionary of psychological and psychoanalytic terms*. New York: McKay.

Farber, L. 1968. *The ways of the will*. New York: Harper & Row.

Freud, A. [1936] 1966. *The ego and the mechanisms of defense*. Reprint, New York: International Universities Press.

Freud, S. [1914] 1990. On the history of the psychoanalytic movement. In *The standard edition of the complete psychological works of Sigmund Freud*, edited by James Strachey, 14: 3–42. Reprint, New York: W. W. Norton.

Fromm, E. 1963. *Escape from freedom*. New York: Holt, Rinehart & Winston.

— — —. 1964. *From the heart of man*. New York: Harper & Row.

Goldberg, C. 1977. The reality of human will: A concept worth reviving. *Psychiatric Annals* 7: 37–57.

— — —. 1991a. *Understanding shame*. Northvale, N.J.: Aronson.

— — —. 1991b. *On being a psychotherapist*. Northvale, N.J.: Aronson.

— — —. 1997. *Speaking with the devil: Exploring senseless acts of evil*. New York: Penguin.

— — —. 2000. The role of emotional strategies in destructive behavior. *American Journal of Psychoanalysis* 60: 107–18.

Holmes, D. S. 1974. Investigations of repression. *Psychological Bulletin* 81: 632–53.

Lottman, H. 1980. *Albert Camus: A biography*. New York: Braziller.

Menninger, K. 1968. *The crime of punishment*. New York: Viking.

Rokeach, M. 1960. *The open and closed mind*. New York: Basic Books.

Silberman, C. 1978. *Criminal violence, criminal justice*. New York: Random House.

Werman, D. S. 1983. Suppression as a defense. *Journal of the American Psychoanalytic Association*, Supplement 31: 405–15.

6

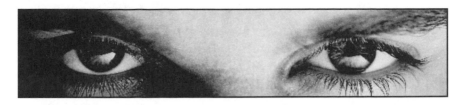

THE CASE OF THE
SUSPECTED RAPIST

An Analyst's Uncertain Knowledge

It isn't the things that you don't know that get you into trouble; it's the things you know for certain which are not so.

—Anonymous

CONVENTIONAL PSYCHOANALYTIC NOTIONS ABOUT KNOWLEDGE and truth are examined in this chapter in regard to their ability to assess a client's actual behavior outside of the therapeutic situation. To this discussion I bring in a little-explored area of knowledge: the analyst's *existential knowledge of the other*, as intersubjectively derived in the analytic situation.

The most comprehensive function of psychoanalysis is the provision of a revolutionary perspective from which to view human history. The psychoanalyst-as-historian claims that few who have ever lived possessed an enlightened understanding of their existence. In the past, a person's recognition of the forces influential in his life story was parochial, politically shaped by the societal myths sanctioned by those who ruled over him. The Freudian revolution afforded a radical change in how history could be understood. It promised (Freud 1914) that each person, persistently curious about his own mental life, is in a position to be his own best historian, provided that he examines his history with a professional guide trained in the pursuit of psychological truth.

A patient in his first few sessions with me reported a series of dreams in which he attempted to rape women. I was alarmed because certain of the details in the dreams corresponded to information I was given by a police officer, whom I also was treating at that time, about a serial rapist then on the loose. Referred to as the "Beltway Rapist" by the local media, for the previous year-and-a-half he had used a police overhead blaring light on his car to stop female motorists traveling alone at night on the highway and then assaulted them. I noticed that the patient's car, parked outside of my office during sessions, fit the description of the car (minus an overhead light) reported in the media as that of the perpetrator. Although the model was a popular one, the similarities in the dreams and to the car with that of the Beltway Rapist were sufficient to suggest the possibility that my patient's reports were not dreams but fragments of actual events that my patient had either intentionally presented in camouflaged version, or from partial amnesia.

It is one sort of matter to be uncertain about the information reported by a psychoneurotic, whose major problem is his inability to translate his wishes into actions, and quite another to be wrong about a patient who is unable or unwilling to stop his harmful behavior toward others. Consequently this case posed a number of serious ethical and personal concerns for me. If my patient was the Beltway Rapist, he was dangerous. But *was* he the Beltway Rapist? How could I be certain if he wanted to mislead me? And if I determined that he had raped, but was not a serial rapist, should I report him—even though I could not be certain that he would rape again? If I should report him, then to whom? But if instead I attempted to treat him, how should I proceed? And what would be the risks to society, to my reputation, and even to the patient himself?

Analytic doctrine cautions that my ethical and personal concerns have no clinical significance in psychoanalytic practice. As countertransferential issues, they can only interfere.[1] The singular matter of importance is a search for the psychological truth about my patients' mental lives.

But what in fact is the nature of the psychological truth the analyst pursues? According to traditional theories of knowledge, only those beliefs that are acquired by reliable methods can be regarded as truthful. Consequently, as an analyst I must be concerned with such questions as: What do I actually know about another person? How well do I know what I assume I know? And how can I accurately assess this information?

Unfortunately, questions that pertain to what we know and the validity of our knowledge have not been squarely addressed by psychoanalysts. Typically, they have responded to epistemological issues by begging the question. In other words, they have evaded the burden of proof which requires the analyst to provide verifiable evidence that he actually has valid information about the patient's mental life, and have offered instead theoretical discussion and clinical vignettes that describe the analyst's trained intuition and interpretive skills at deciphering the unconscious meaning of the patient's verbal statements and behavior.[2] In short, analytic theory presents, without proof, the analyst's intuitive and interpretive skills as enabling the analyst to accurately reconstruct the patient's developmental history.

Psychological reconstruction, according to Freud (1937), is similar to the excavation by an archaeologist who explains lost-to-history events from the artifacts recovered from these events. But, in fact, despite Freud's lip service to seeking the truth, pragmatics rather than verified knowledge guided his theory of clinical practice. Freud treated all psychic experiences—dreams, fantasies, and actual behavioral events—as identical, because he believed that psychic reality, not material reality, is the basis for character development (Goldberg 1989). Thus, while admitting that a clear distinction may be of importance to analytic theorizing, Freud (1925) assumes that for purposes of clinical practice, the difference between what the patient has fantasized and what has actually happened to him is of no significance to the patient's understanding of his own motivation.[3]

But clearly there are clinical situations that cast serious doubt on Freud's clinical assumption. Notably, they include events in which accurate information is crucial to protect the lives of people upon whom a patient may wreak havoc. Whether or not analytic theory can help in these situations is a neglected subject of analytic inquiry.

PSYCHOANALYSIS AS TRUTH-SEEKING

Freud (1914) claims that psychoanalytic inquiry produces psychological truth in that it follows the epistemological requirements of the natural sciences. In fact, his interpretations of clinical data are couched in quite different discourse than those of scientific explanation. He attempts to prove the validity of psychoanalytic methods of inquiry by *analogy* rather than by empirical evidence (Ricoeur 1978). For example, Freud (1913) describes free association as similar to that of a passenger (the analysand) sitting by a window of a train at night, describing the passing scenes (the analysand's stream of consciousness) to another passenger (the analyst), who has no direct access to the window. This analogy, while vivid and clever, is not an apt one—i.e., the train has many windows, which offer different perspectives on the passing scenes. Which window provides the best vantage? And, of course, the best view of what? Moreover, Freud assumes that one set of sensory reports—verbal—can accurately describe another—visual. Indeed, it is a dubious assumption that a visual model best captures the analysand's stream of consciousness.

The philosopher Ludwig Wittgenstein (1966) points out in examining Freud's method of inquiry that it is nearly impossible to explain anything without some use of metaphors. Nevertheless, Wittgenstein indicates, Freud's attempts to account for psychological events as governed by the same principles as biology, chemistry, and physics are not creditable.

It is hardly surprising, then, that a number of influential analytic theorists, most notably Roy Schafer (1976) and Donald Spence (1982), following the lead of George Klein (1973), contend that the nature of the data recovered in an analytic encounter is that of narrative truth rather than historical or factual truth.[4] The notion of narrative truth employed by Schafer and Spence is derived from the skepticism espoused by many contemporary philosophers who contend that attempts to obtain verifiable objective truth is futile. Instead of asking whether an idea is truthful, they prefer to inquire about its *utility*; that is to say, what unique, interesting, or heuristic value does the idea contain?

The notion of narrative truth suggests that Freud's method of inquiry is more akin to the contextual analysis of literary work than that of empirical science. The analyst listens with the poet's ear: usually without conscious intent he seizes upon the patient's narrative to select certain features of the story. His selection is based on the familiarity of the material to his previous clinical cases, classical studies in the psychoanalytic literature—particularly those of Freud and his own mentors—or even from his reading of literary fiction. The analyst then attempts to explicate his patient's character on the basis of the similarities between his selected information and the significant attributes of patients or literary characters he apperceptively (without conscious awareness) has chosen as explanatory models.

If I am correct about the nature of the analyst's knowledge, what does this say about his reputed status as a psychological expert? When we refer to expertise in the analytic situation, it is accurate to speak of it only in a relative sense: if the analyst is regarded as an expert, it is because he is assumed to know more about the nature of psychological discourse and inquiry than does the client. In fact, as long as the focus of the analytic inquiry is to decipher dreams and fantasies, the analyst may be the expert. But if, on the other hand, the nature of the inquiry is that of *actual events*, then the client who has been *a participant of the event* would be the more knowledgeable of the two. This recognition speaks to Freud's (1937) metaphor of the analyst as an archaeologist: the analogy doesn't recognize that it is our acknowledged participation in events that gives us expertise, not our access to explanatory theories of the events.

CASE STUDY

I received a phone call from a man who found my name under "Psychologists" in the telephone classified pages. "Henry," as I shall call him, asked if I was a psychoanalyst. As an adolescent, he told me, he had been caught shoplifting. A juvenile court judge directed his mother to send him to a psychotherapist. For a few months, he spoke weekly with a kindly older man who referred to himself as a psychoanalyst. Henry's recent inquiry indicated that the doctor no longer lived in the area. He had talked with three other therapists whose names he also found in the phone book. He either didn't like their phone voices or found them too concerned with his ability to pay. They probably made the judgment that to select a therapist from a phone book shows extremely bad judgment. Together with meager financial resources, patients with bad judgment don't make for comfortable private therapy cases! I, on the other hand, considered the possibility that Henry's method of selecting a therapist reflected his social isolation. He did not trust anyone sufficiently to ask for a recommendation.

Henry was thirty-five, somewhat taller than average, sturdily built, with dark hair that fell across his forehead. He was well-spoken but circumspect: suspicious of me and how I might use the information he gave me. He payed in cash, used an alias, and would not provide his address or phone number. He told me that he would not accept treatment under any other conditions.

Henry grew up in the Maryland suburbs of Washington. He had few close family members, none of whom he had kept in touch with for the past decade. He had not finished college and was unmarried. Women, he told me with a wink, found him attractive, but he supposed that they were put off by his sudden aloof demeanor in relationships they may have assumed were progressing well. He discussed his male acquaintances with less affect than he had the women: they met for activities such as bowling, ballgames, and beers after work. But there was no one with whom he shared his inner life.

My first impression of Henry was that of someone who was well-guarded and apprehensive of others' motives — probably for most of his life. He was of above-average to superior intelligence; had done well in school, he said; and had started college, but now he was working at a low-level federal government position that was unchallenging and required little interaction with others. I diagnosed him as a "paranoid character" — without delusions. He also was depressed (since childhood, I would later find out). His mood was not so much clinical depression as that of existential malaise: he seemed to have no discernible goals and no sense of purpose in how he lived his life.

Upon hearing Henry's report of his dreams, I felt an urgent need to ascertain whether these reports were of actual events — which might implicate him as the Beltway Rapist. Should I ask him directly? I wondered. Of course not, I reflected: Henry had been evasive about everything I had asked him up until now. If he were a rapist, why would he be straightforward with me? Consequently, what would I gain from his denial of criminal behavior? Moreover, if I acted as a criminal investigator with this paranoid man, he'd flee—which would neither prevent more rapes nor help curb his destructive behavior (which keeping him in treatment might do).

Yet, if it was foolish for me to act as a criminal sleuth, it was highly appropriate for me to behave as a psychological detective. My clinical work with seriously destructive patients (Goldberg 1997) had alerted me to the assumption that all criminal behavior is *intrapsychically reversible* for the perpetrator; that is to say, in the criminal's psyche he is both victim and perpetrator. Criminal behavior, from this perspective, is an *identification denial* (Goldberg 1991) of the perpetrator's unacknowledged *shared weaknesses* and *vulnerabilities* with those of his victims. For example, in the rape scenario, both victim and rapist are psychologically "frozen," unable to escape: the victim's paralyzing fear is that she is powerless and incompetent to handle the perpetrator, rendering her a physical prisoner of the situation; similarly, the perpetrator's apperceptive identification with the weaknesses and vulnerabilities of the victim—which he unwittingly tries to decimate—melds him magnetically in place with the victim.

If my clinical assumption is valid, I thought at the time, I might learn something useful about Henry's possible criminal behavior by obtaining information about his past experiences as a victim. I asked Henry if he had ever been raped. He jolted in his chair and looked startled at me across the analytic space. I qualified my question by indicating that I meant by it whether he had ever been assaulted by someone—physically or even psychologically—in such a way that he experienced his inner being violated.

Henry was emotionally close to his father, he told me, a first-generation Greek-American who was as unscrupulous in business as he was ambitious. He tried to turn every opportunity to his financial advantage, regardless of whom he stepped on, even after acquiring sufficient income to comfortably support his family. As a child Henry had wished to follow his father into business; often he went to work with him on off-school days.

The major turning point in Henry's life occurred during his tenth **129** year. His father was caught in a serious crime which involved shady business deals. Henry was home the day that the police came and led his father away in handcuffs. His father looked weak and defeated as he was dragged out of the house to the patrol car. He was muttering that his own father repeatedly referred to him as a "loser."

For months after the incident Henry felt self-contemptuous, ashamed that he had let himself get close to someone who allowed himself to be treated as humiliatingly as had his father.

Henry's mother was also lost to him after his father's arrest. A sensitive, vulnerable woman, she responded to her husband's disgrace with fits of agitated depression. Several times during the years following her husband's imprisonment she was hospitalized for psychiatric treatment. Henry was as embarrassed and upset by his mother's uncontrolled crying spells as he was by his father's collapse at his arrest. But his fury felt boundless when he found her in bed at various times with deliverymen and local shopkeepers. Following these encounters he ran away from home. On each occasion, the police found him wandering along the side of a highway. He began his shoplifting during this period of his life.

BORROWED SHAME

Familial shame is highly contagious. It can be cast out in such subtle, indirect ways by an unwitting parent that the child, although perceptive and intelligent, is unaware of the painful feelings of humiliation of which he is the recipient. I call this process "borrowing shame" (Goldberg 1991). Very few of us go through life without at some time or other acquiring this unfair burden. We are especially susceptible when a person we care about or closely identify with harbors self-punitive feelings of self-contempt and despair (Goldberg 1999).

Henry's father's continual sense of inadequacy about how he lived his life—that Henry related to me—seemed to have fueled his rogue business practices. As such, it had fostered a destructive bond between him and his son. His mother's unsavory behavior, impelled by her loneliness and anger toward her husband, imbued Henry's feelings toward women with rageful contempt.

Henry was too immature to understand his father's intrapsychic suffering. He interpreted his own bad feelings as indicating that he was the one who had done something wrong. When a child is unable to care for a parent in the way he has been taught he should, he is apt to explain his emotional difficulties as due to something deficient, wrong, or even evil in him. Henry's thefts as a youngster were expressions of his negative personal identity. Unaware of his borrowed shame, he couldn't uproot and replace it with reasonable expectations for himself. On the contrary, he was convinced that he was a social pariah who was helpless and all alone in the world unless he took some radical action to change his personality.

As Henry related his deliberate vow at his father's trial and conviction never to allow himself to be vulnerable to others, the energy with which he related his life story accelerated, as exemplified by his rapidly tapping foot and the pounding of his fist on the side of his chair.

I asked him in what ways did his decision affect how he treated other people. My comment proved to be premature. Henry looked at me for a long while with what appeared to be a sad slight smile. He finally said, "I have nothing more to say for now."

The last few minutes of the session were silent except for a question of mine. What I sensed from Henry was that from this point on I would have to figure out his story without any intentional help from him. I verbalized my impression. He nodded in agreement.

My second assumption, in seeking to ascertain whether Henry was the serial rapist, was that few rapists enter any form of psychological therapy in order to try to understand themselves. In other words, we learn by doing. Opportunities to choose between good and bad occur continually in our daily lives, from the smallest matters. How we respond to earlier choices shapes our moral (and immoral) choices now and in the future. Such extreme behavior as rape, therefore, is usually among the last of many steps along a continuum of unkind, indecent acts. And the rationalizations used to justify cruel behavior by the time someone becomes a rapist are no longer subject to rational and moral scrutiny. Thus, those who reach this stage of personality development are usually unable or unwilling to self-examine the motives for their behavior (Goldberg 1997).

131

If Henry wasn't seeking self-understanding, then why was he in my consulting room? It is the nature of human interaction that people try to influence one another. I assumed by examining how Henry was attempting to influence me that I would be able to recognize why he had come to consult with me. Upon reflection, I became aware that I was feeling annoyed and frustrated by him. Further self-examination revealed that my feelings were due not only to the perplexing personal and ethical dilemma his presence in my consulting room put me in, but also to a subtle paradox in which Henry's subtle manipulation placed me.

My clinical experience suggests that the central motive of patients who have been involved in serious destructive behavior is to restore a sense of agency to their feelings of personal identity by reversing the conditions that imbued them with shame and despair. What I experienced from Henry were concerted efforts to repair his agency by influencing my regard for him in two major ways:

1. *Henry as a superior person.* He brought sports magazines to read in the waiting room prior to sessions, alluded to their content at the beginning of sessions, and mentioned that he had been an excellent high school athlete who had been scouted by the Baltimore Orioles major league baseball team. He also indicated that the women he had dated wished to continue the relationships despite their dismay at his aloof behavior. His implicit message, as I understood it, was that he was a sexual stud. He also alluded to his skill in handling women who teased and promised sex but didn't want to deliver.

Taken together, Henry's implicit messages seemed to be attempts to impress me with his superior masculinity. So if he were a rapist, this need could be interpolated as the conviction that he lived by a higher morality than other men—that is to say, he had the "guts" to do what other men dare only do in fantasy[5]: overpower and take complete possession of women. This "authenticity"—I assumed he believed—gave him a special right that other men, who are afraid to live freely, are not legitimately entitled.

2. *Henry as deserving redemption.* Henry also described in extreme detail the disappointing and pathetic role models his parents were for him. During these recitations, Henry seemed to crave forgiveness for his unspecified faults, deficiencies, and malfeasances because he was

not properly prepared by his parents for responsible behavior. He interspersed his narration of his parent's failings with excessive praise of me as a compassionate and perspicacious listener.

The paradox I experienced with Henry was due to a *contradictory pull on me*. To accomplish my dual tasks the patient must not only elevate my status to that of superior wisdom and benevolence so that I would have the authority to redeem him for his sins, but he must also overwhelm me with his macho presence so that I am readily convinced that he is a superior person who should be allowed to behave any way he wishes. In short, the paradox in which Henry had placed me required me to be simultaneously wise and authoritative, gullible and weak.[6]

CONCLUSION

In my earlier clinical work with destructive patients I was not aware of their two simultaneous needs. By either overly supporting or too strongly confronting some of these patients, I failed to deal effectively with them. I realized from my work with Henry that only by holding their two powerful needs in balance could I lead them to an emotional awareness of the paradox in themselves, which creates the intersubjective "frozenness" in which they and their victims get trapped, i.e., the wish both to impress his victim with his "stud sexuality" and for her to forgive him for his desperate need to impress her.

Unfortunately, I didn't get the opportunity to use my insight in treating Henry. The Beltway Rapist was caught. Henry did not return for his twelfth session. He left a message on my telephone answering machine that he had left town permanently. He had committed a couple of rapes a few years past, he said, and he was afraid that if he stayed in the area he also would get caught—not caught in the act, but for his past behavior.

The following chapter is the story of my encounter with an unfortunate child in South America. Although I have always been deeply attuned to feelings of shame, I had not understood its beneficial effects until this encounter. I explore here the effect this experience had in my work with destructive patients.

THE EVIL WE DO

NOTES

1. Moral and ethical responsibilities are separate here for the analyst. Moral concerns refer to personal and societal codes of behavior. Analytic doctrine claims that the analyst should be morally neutral. While this is arguable (Goldberg 1998), ethical concerns are not. They are unavoidable insofar as they involve professional responsibility. In other words, whether or not an analyst is morally accountable for his patient's behavior, his professional behavior as a physician, psychologist, social worker, or some other discipline is governed by a professional code of ethical conduct that explicitly mandates him to prevent destructive acts he is aware that his patient is likely to commit.

2. A careful examination by a philosopher of the protocols of a course of psychoanalytic treatment suggests that in fact this is not how the analyst actually operates. B. A. Farrell's (1964) examination reveals the absence of evidence that the interpretations of the analyst in question were declarative statements based upon data evident in the patient's statements. Instead, according to Farrell, they seemed to be *transmutive* acts intended to modify the patient's dysfunctional behavior.

3. Psychoanalyst and professor of social thought at the University of Chicago Jonathan Lear (1998) indicates that "a psychoanalysis is not an impartial scientific endeavor, but a therapeutic measure. Its essence is not to prove anything, but to alter something" (113–14). My own clinical experience tends to confirm this view: exploration of the factual nature of the analyst's contention, even to the extent that I assumed it possible to ascertain, was secondary to modifying the behavior the patient was paying me to change.

4. Freud (1933) defines the *truth* that psychoanalysis seeks as a scientific endeavor: "a correspondence with the external world." But insofar as what the analysand tells is shaped by defensive mechanisms, orthodox analytic doctrine contends that it is the analyst's task to use his "intuitive to sense the nature of this distortion and offer the analysand an interpretation which will reinstate factual truth" (Zusman 1976). Humanistic analysts claim that these interpretations are narrative rather than factual truths.

5. Shakespeare's Richard III justifies his villainy thus:

> Conscience is but a word that cowards use,
> Devised at first to keep the strong in awe;
> our strong arms be our conscience, swords our law!

(5.3. 10–14)

6. Psychoanalyst Heinz Kohut (1977) speaks to this issue in regard to lengthy "mirror transference" in the analysis of severely disturbed narcissistic personalities. Psychoanalyst Otto Kernberg's (1972) clinical approach in working with destructive borderline patients seems to be consistent with the approach I used in my clinical work with Henry.

REFERENCES

Farrell, B. A. 1964. The criteria for a psychoanalytic interpretation. In *Essays in philosophical psychology*, edited by D. E. Gustafson, 299–323. Garden City, N.Y.: Doubleday.

Freud, S. [1913] 1990. *On beginning the treatment*. In *The standard edition of the complete psychological works of Sigmund Freud*, edited by James Strachey, 12: 122–44. Reprint, New York: W. W. Norton.

———. [1914] 1990. The history of the psychoanalytic movement. *Standard edition*. 14: 3–42.

———. 1933. *New introductory lectures on psychoanalysis*. New York: Norton.

———. [1925] 1990. *Autobiographic study. Standard edition*. 20: 3–71.

———. [1937] 1990. *Construction in analysis. Standard edition*. 23: 240–65.

Goldberg, C. 1989. The shame of Hamlet and Oedipus. *Psychoanalytic Review* 76: 581–603.

———. 1991. *Understanding shame*. Northvale, N.J.: Aronson.

———. 1997. *Speaking with the devil: Exploring senseless acts of evil*. New York: Penguin.

———. 1999. A psychoanalysis of love: The patient with deadly longings. *American Journal of Psychotherapy* 53: 437–51.

Kohut, H. 1977. *The restoration of the self*. New York: International Universities Press.

Kernberg, O. 1972. Treatment of borderline patients. In *Tactics and techniques in psychoanalytic therapy*, edited by P. L. Giovacchini, 254–90. New York: Science House.

Klein, G. 1973. Two theories or one? *Bulletin of the Menninger Clinic* 37: 102–32.

Lear, J. 1998. *Love and its place in nature*. New Haven: Yale University Press.

Ricoeur, P. 1978. *The philosophy of Paul Ricoeur*, edited by C. E. Reagan and D. Stewart. Boston: Beacon.

Schafer, R. 1976. *A new language for psychoanalysis*. New Haven: Yale University Press.

Spence, D. 1992. *Narrative truth and historical truth*. New York: Norton.

Wittgenstein, L. 1966. Conversations on Freud. In *Lectures and conversations on aesthetics, psychology and religious belief*, edited by C. Barrett. Oxford, England: Blackwell.

Zusman, W. 1976. A discussion on the paper of Ricardo Avenburg and Marcos Guiter on "The content of truth in psychoanalysis." *International Journal of Psychoanalysis* 57: 19–21.

7

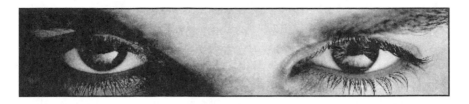

AN ENCOUNTER
WITH AN
UNFORTUNATE CHILD

The Role of Shame
in Constructive Behavior

Shame opens a pathway to ourselves.
—Max Scheler, *The Nature of Sympathy*

WHY A PERSON ACTS HONORABLY IS ONE OF THE MOST PUZZLING issues in the study of morality. Throughout history numerous explanations have been offered, but no consensus of opinion has prevailed. Some believe a person acts properly because he has been instilled early in life with good values. Others claim that direct life experiences are more crucial than childhood teachings; still more point to the presence of exemplary role models as exceeding that which has been taught or personally experienced. And, finally, there are those who maintain that learned factors are of minimal importance in fostering human virtue. After all, they indicate, we expect virtuous behavior from humans, but not animals. Even the most intelligent and best trained animals don't act protectively toward humans from a sense of righteousness, no matter what they are taught, but from a bond of affection and loyalty with those with whom they are familiar. Consequently, it is reasonable to assume, these philosophers claim, that a moral sentiment is a unique, inherent quality of the human mind. In this regard, the eminent eighteenth-century German philosopher Immanuel Kant (1956) postulated that it was the human capacity to reason rather than to respond emotionally that fosters virtue. By this he meant that social and emotional experiences are unnecessary—and often interfere—with the mind's inherent capacity to recognize the superiority of virtue over immorality.

Obviously the explanation we endorse in regard to virtue's mainspring has significant implications for psychology and education: if the capacity for moral behavior is an inherent quality of the human mind, a course of rational training would be the most appropriate way to free malefactors' minds of misconceived assumptions about human existence that have impelled their wrongful and destructive behavior. If, on the other hand, virtue is a psychological induction from direct experience and/or the emulation of exemplary role models, then we must shape those experiences and models that best impress our children with the appropriate moral messages (Goldberg 1997).

The vignette that follows concerns the question why we act virtuously. It suggests that shame may play a crucial role as a guardian of virtuous behavior because of its role in the development of empathy and identification with others (Goldberg 1999). I discuss the status of shame in the psychoanalytic and psychotherapy literature following the vignette.

The story takes place in a distant land. The specific location should not divert our attention from the recognition that the crucial elements of the situation are similar to those with which many of us are routinely confronted.

He was a slight lad of nine or ten. His tan, rough hemp shirt was tattered and his trousers, a couple of sizes too large, held by a length of cord. He may have been wearing shoes, although the impression I have of him was barefoot. What I remember best was his immutable, sad demeanor and that he tightly clutched in his left hand a picture postcard and a small box of plastic-covered matches. The tenacity with which he held these meager items suggested that they were all he materially possessed.

The photo on the postcard was that of the city plaza of Cuzco, Peru—once the sacred city of the Incas—now a teeming South American metropolis, high in the Andes mountain range, visited by tourists for its historical sites and awe-inspiring churches filled with priceless religious relics.

The picture card was carefully wrapped in a piece of clear plastic. The matches were the type manufactured throughout Latin America, purchased in shops for the equivalent of a North American nickel.

The child had approached our table as a female friend and I were dining late one summer evening in a popular Cuzco restaurant. Three musicians, young men of Cacharpayan Indian descent from the Andes, were playing haunting ancient tunes on a small stage in the front of the restaurant. We were captivated by the music, new to us, as it was a number of years before musicians from the Andes would become a ubiquitous feature of North American metropolitan life.

Throughout the evening we had watched small children, in groups of twos and threes, slip into the restaurant and approach the patrons' tables, heavily laden with delicious Peruvian dishes. They were acrimoniously scooted away by the patrons, and then ousted from the establishment by stocky waiters wearing white smocks around their dark suits and no-nonsense grimaces.

A few of these poorly dressed children, first casting furtive glances, returned. Carefully making their way to where the patron families sat, they looked up with their sad child faces at the customers consuming their food with apparent gusto and abandon.

The boy who approached our table stood silently for a long moment. His large brown eyes seemed filled with tears. Or were they mine that countenanced despair? By what quirk of fate was I well-educated and able to travel frequently to South America, while at the same time this small child stood before me impoverished and uneducated? I had no doubt that by his socioeconomic circumstances he was destined to a life of hardship—perhaps not a very long life at that. Were he to live long enough to have children of his own in this land of disadvantage and violent political strife, his unhappy legacy to his offspring would be to have no real hope for better things in life, perhaps not even the necessaries. The pack of cigarettes my friend smoked each day undoubtedly was more costly than the price of food his family, if indeed he had one, could afford him that day.

We spoke to him in Spanish. He told us that his name was Pedro. But it was difficult to ascertain where he lived in the city. Pedro was **139** quite inarticulate in his own native tongue. But conversation was not his immediate interest.

Remaining mute, he thrust his left hand toward me, revealing his postcard and matchbox. I asked if he was selling the items. He slowly nodded. Not speaking, he hadn't stated a price. I assumed that he wanted me to exact the proper value of his items. But I was reluctant to do so. For if he sold the two spare items he held, what besides his shabby clothes would he possess?

Not surprisingly, he looked malnourished. The food on our plates was simple fare, but plentiful and savory. I realized that it would be more reasonable to feed the child than to purchase his only salable holdings.

I invited Pedro to sit at our table. He fretfully looked around at the occupants of the other tables, then vigorously shook his head. In retracing the sweep of Pedro's glance, two things were evident: first, my friend and I were the only foreigners present, and second, if Pedro sat at our table it would be a breach of local customs. The other waifs were standing by the customers' tables, rapidly consuming with their bare hands leftovers from the patrons's dinner plates. Not one child had been invited to sit down at a table.

A look at my companion confirmed my sense that we were too uncomfortable with Pedro standing by our table, eating the scraps from our plates, to respect local mores. I cringed, embarrassed to associate myself with the rich stranger in a white suit, played by the actor John Huston in the 1940s film *The Treasure of the Sierra Madre*, who disdainfully flipped silver coins to the beggars in a shabby Mexican seaport; nor did I wish to act like a feudal lord casting unwanted food from my table to starving peasants. I wanted to respond to Pedro in a humane way. But I didn't know how to proceed.

After a few awkward moments pondering upon my discomfort, my course of action was clear: the climate between Pedro and my companion and myself would not be benevolent unless we were all seated. So I more emphatically repeated my invitation to Pedro to sit down at our table, pulling out a chair for him next to me. With measured movements he complied. We ordered food from a waiter, who disapprovingly kept his eyes on Pedro, as he served him a glass of milk and a plate of food. Pedro consumed the food with rapid thrusts of his right hand; his left held fast his two possessions, as if someone might steal them if he were to loosen his grip on them for even an instant.

When he had finished eating he looked up at us, and then stared ahead with the same unhappy expression as when he had first appeared at our table. I sensed that this inarticulate child was feeling embarrassed sitting with us: not knowing how to thank us; or what he should say or do in taking leave of us.

In recognizing Pedro's distress, I again became aware of my own uneasiness. Although the restaurant was quite cool, my face felt flushed, my hands and throat wet with perspiration. I also was close to tears. The symptoms I was exhibiting, my years of clinical experience suggested, were those of *shame*. But why, I puzzled, was I ashamed? I had not done something wrong. Indeed, I was trying to act decently as best I could.

Then I remembered the words of G. W. F. Hegel. One of the best definitions to help us understand the decisive factors involved in shame was offered by that famous nineteenth-century German philosopher (1892). He tells us that shame is an anger against what *ought not to be*.

Applied to everyday life, Hegel's definition seems exceedingly accurate. We all know of the notorious father who viciously slapped his daughter who had tearfully returned home from having fallen from a tree she was climbing, badly abrading her knees. His angry words and actions imply that she was being punished for having done something wrong. Viewed from the outside, the father as educator was attempting to discipline his daughter to take proper care of herself. The father's anger and the daughter's guilt manifestly seem to be the major emotional players in this allegorical scenario.

However, quite a different psychology ensues from viewing the drama from the psyche of the father. He is the caretaker of his child; he cares deeply about her. Not surprisingly, he became frightened and upset from seeing how vulnerable his child is to injury. Moreover, he not only fears for her, he is ashamed that he has failed as her protector. His fleeting awareness of his inability to shelter his child sufficiently stirs his anger against what ought not to be. In short, the father feels self-recrimination that he is not an adequate father at such times, when he is forced to recognize that he can do little to protect his beloved child from being vulnerable to life's hurts.

To divest himself from his sense of painful impotence, which he nei- **141** ther understands nor knows how to deal with, the father strikes out at his daughter. By blaming her for his uncomfortable feelings (of help-lessness), he unwittingly has transposed his child from a victim of injury to that of a perpetrator of a wrongful act: behaving as an irre-sponsible child (no wonder that the waiters in the restaurant treated the children so badly!). Moreover, by becoming angry at his child, the father insulates himself from his daughter's hurt.

Unfortunately, in the transformation of feeling helpless to blaming the person who arouses one's sense of inadequacy, a destructive inter-personal pattern is established. Emotionally separating himself from people who awaken his sense of vulnerability makes it difficult for the father to be empathically in touch with his daughter's needs, or anyone else's, for that matter (Goldberg 1997).

The allegorical story of the angry father had important implications for me. It was not until my encounter with Pedro that I became suffi-ciently aware of how strongly demonstrations of unfairness and injus-tice affected me. I was angry at the conditions that militated against children like Pedro having the same opportunity as those born more socioeconomically fortunate to survive, to live fully and well.

To ease my shamefulness in having affluence in the face of the dire impoverishment this child represented, I needed some way to bridge the vast cultural gap between the child and myself. In other words, I felt pressed to find a way of indicating to this inarticulate, intellectually lim-ited and seemingly despondent lad that our brief encounter together was mutually beneficial. Do I mean satisfying? Hardly! Indeed, I was only too aware that the time with Pedro was exceedingly difficult for me!

I had started on this trip to South America as a reward for a suc-cessful year of psychoanalytic practice in which I had completed a number of projects that I regarded as insuring my recognition as a well-regarded psychoanalytic writer and practitioner, including a well-received book. However, the experience of shame I felt with Pedro interrupted the placid and unprobed self-satisfaction I was feeling the moment prior to meeting him.

What had disturbed my unexamined satisfaction with myself was a sense of *sadness*. Baruch Spinoza (1949), the excommunicated and exiled Jewish philosopher of the seventeenth century, noted in his *Ethics* that there is sadness that accompanies the uneasy self-consciousness of shame. In his view, shame as sadness expresses the tension between what "is" in one's current existential condition and the "ought" of one's sense of who one is or should be. In other words, we are valuing beings. Our sense of shame, if we allow it, can play a constructive role in recognizing the responsibilities of virtue by reflecting upon the discrepancy between the person we seek to be and who we experience ourselves being at that moment.

I realized that I was still struggling with the need to justify who I was — in this instance someone who cared about the suffering of others: undoubtedly, the emotional component that directed me to a career as a psychologist and psychoanalyst.

My experience with Pedro revealed something of my own inner being in such a way that I was in closer touch with my deeper sensibilities and convictions than I had been prior to our encounter. I came to recognize at that moment that my caring about the separation between myself and some other who was deprived was not an indication of some pallid oversentimentality, but the affirmation of my sense of agency — my striving to be the person I wished to be. It is our sense of agency that leads us to virtue — those attitudes that enable us to be more enlightened, compassionate, and responsible to both self and other.

And, fortunately, I was not helpless against what ought not to be. No, not as long as I recognized my shame as my willingness to care! Consequently, I needed to inform Pedro that he wasn't given food because of our pity for him, but that all three of us had gained something from our shared moment. But how, I wondered, could I convey this idea to him in a way he would understand?

My eye again caught the scenario of Pedro clutching his postcard and matchbox and my friend's pack of cigarettes on the table before her. She routinely lit up a cigarette after a satisfying meal.

The solution suddenly struck me. I asked Pedro if he would allow me to examine his matchbox. He readily handed it over. The cardboard container had a pretty design on it, but the matches had only ignition value. I said to Pedro in carefully chosen Spanish idiom that my friend, as he could see, smoked cigarettes, but she had forgotten her matches back at her hotel. I suggested that we exchange the food we had bought him for his matchbox. He instantly nodded in agreement. It also appeared as if his facial expression had changed following my offer. For **143** a brief moment it seemed as if he was faintly smiling. But I am not certain. In an instant after our negotiation, still gripping his postcard, Pedro had bolted up out of his chair and was through the door of the restaurant into the chilly Pervian night.

The agreement of a swap of goods had freed Pedro, my companion, and myself from an embarrassing moment. But more importantly for me, it provided a means for responding to my sense of agency. It bears repeating: We all have choices about good and bad every day of our lives. How we approach and choose to deal with these daily issues will shape the more difficult moral choices we face later on. If we respond in ways that are indifferent, callous, or contemptuous, we begin to lose the ability to be virtuous, as well. And though we continue to have an opportunity to behave well, to do so becomes more strange—unlike the person we are now experiencing our self to be. In short, our characters are forged by the choices we make. We change as we choose.

A thorough examination of the etiology and clinical implications of shame is a neglected area of psychological investigation. The *Psychological Abstracts*, the yearly compendium of books on psychology subjects and articles contained in psychology and psychiatry journals, does not have a separate subject category for it, placing this elusive affect under the category of guilt. In short, shame and its variants are the most seriously neglected and misunderstood emotions in contemporary society (Goldberg 1991).

Psychoanalysts traditionally have attributed the most complex and difficult cases (which we would now evaluate as impinged with shame and despair) to the agent of guilt rather than the steward of shame. Due to an overabundance of clinical studies of guilt, the emotional workings of shame have only recently received some of the careful psychological attention they deserve.

Admittedly, a recognition of the presence of shame in the therapeutic situation can be a difficult task. Therapists must often actively seek out their clients' shame from a minimum of manifest clues (Robertiello and Gagnier 1990). However, there are several important reasons for us to heed the presence of shame in psychotherapy. First, the very position of being a psychotherapy client is perceived as a humiliating one by many in contemporary society. It implies to them that the client is incapable of living competently without someone else's help. Consequently, many people eschew psychotherapy unless compelled by desperation.

Additionally, the very distressing symptoms that are brought to psychotherapy by clients are deeply implicated with shame. Psychoanalyst and psychotherapy researcher Helen Block Lewis (1987) indicates that closely examining the psychodynamics of shame reveals that it is the key to what Freud (1923) identified as the "archaic" or irrational guilt that breeds neurotic and psychotic symptoms. From her long-standing clinical concern about shame, Lewis (1971) has shown that a protracted empathic immersion into the affective state of all clients in psychotherapy uncovers deep and painful feelings of shame. They are usually difficult to detect because of the protective overlay of defense mechanisms, such as grandiosity, that cover the gripping sense of defeat, failure, and emptiness that fosters shame and despair. Several investigators (Blinder 1970; Crouppon 1977; Harder and Lewis 1987; Hoblitzell 1982; Smith 1972) have shown that shame enacts a greater role in depression than does guilt. Since shame is closely associated with the bitterness and animosity people direct toward themselves when they realize that they are living a futile life, it is small wonder that psychotherapy clients feel ashamed.

Understanding the role that shame plays in human development also enables us to correct inappropriately conceptualized clinical conditions. For example, what we call "pathological guilt," in most instances, is actually toxic shame. Moreover, there is probably no such clinical entity as "survivor's guilt" (Goldberg 1997). In other words, people who suffer from these two so-called syndromes have not done something wrong, at least, not in a way that they have consciously chosen—the requirements for a sense of guilt. Instead, they were powerless to prevent harm to those they cared about—other people and/or themselves—a condition that promotes shame and despair, not guilt.

Moreover, shame plays an especially crucial and often disguised role in the lives of male psychotherapy clients. It probably has an even more dysfunctional role with males than females, because women are usually more in touch with and less threatened by their feelings of shame; and, therefore, have less need to hide these affects from themselves and others. So whereas a woman may seek help for the conditions which **145** foster her shamefulness, a man is more likely to inner negate these feelings, and act angrily to restore his sense of competence as a male.

Psychotherapists, it also should be pointed out, cannot avoid the issue of shame in effective clinical practice because they themselves are subject to being shamed as part and parcel of their daily clinical endeavors. This is because the ashamed client has the proclivity, in turn, to humiliate the therapist. In other words, the caring and concerned practitioner—as my story may suggest—is susceptible to shame to the extent that he cannot meaningfully reach and help to heal his suffering client. The inexorable shaming of the therapeutic encounter awakens unresolved personal concerns and conflicts of the psychotherapist.

Finally, I need to indicate that several influential contemporary social philosophers have fostered a misconception of shame in their social and moral theories because they have failed to recognize that shame has positive, proactive qualities, in addition to its toxic properties.

The modern social philosopher John Rawls (1971) is one of the most articulate and influential of those who claim that shame discourages moral action. In his book *A Theory of Justice*, he describes shame as "the feeling that someone has when he experiences an injury to his self-respect or suffers a blow to his self-esteem" (442). If self-respect is a necessary condition for active participation in moral behavior, Rawls claims, then shame antagonizes constructive behavior insofar as it depletes our vitality and willingness to deal with moral issues. In other words, according to Rawls, shame is painfully dysfunctional because it involves a loss of self-respect, and without self-respect "nothing may seem worth doing, or if some things have value for us, we lack the will to strive for them. All desire and activity becomes empty and vain, and we sink into apathy and cynicism" (440).

How does shame induce apathy and hopelessness? According to Rawls, shame is an emotional reaction realized *after* a wrongful act. As a past event cannot be changed, regret and passivity are shame's unfortunate legacies.

The notion that the ashamed is a captive of some regrettable past event is a crucial misconception of Rawls and other modern moral philosophers. They fail to recognize that shame may be experienced in at least two different ways: one, it may be unacknowledged until after the

event, or two, it may be incurred *during the event*, as my story shows, as an *accentuated sensitivity* to another person's emotional state by means of a *conscious identification* of the other with one's own affective experience.

Rawls's second error is his assumption that self-respect is a constant state—in other words, once attained it will be maintained evermore. Contrary to Rawls's claim, as I have shown in my story, self-respect needs a *continual seeking* of those conditions that foster our pride and self-esteem. These conditions require a sensitive attunement to our social and moral responsibilities. In this regard, shame serves ably as a guide for these responsibilities.

What Rawls and other modern moral philosophers fail to recognize is that shame is a normal part of life. As guardian of a complex cluster of emotions, it comes in a variety of shapes and has a host of functions. And not all experiences of shame are deleterious. Quite the contrary! In different manifestations and contexts, it may be toxic, restraining, or even constructive. Therefore, whereas it is true that toxic shame is the harbinger of hopelessness, healthy shame—the recognition that what we require to feel pride and self-esteem are realistically attainable although not yet achieved—provides a crucible of freedom. In small doses, shame is a prod to self-improvement by providing a means for penetrating self-discovery.

If there is a significant difference between me and the destructive people I have treated, it is in regard to how we have responded to feelings of shame. They have *denied their identification* with people whom they unwittingly sense share similar vulnerabilities and hurts with them—by running away, making intimacy and interpersonal cooperation impossible; or they have treated the vulnerable others they encounter in hurtful and destructive ways. In short, my clients' interpersonal incompetence and destructiveness is derived from their *refusal to stay with* and *self-reflect* on their shameful feelings. When experiencing shame, I, in contrast, have been willing (at least, some of the time) to closely examine the reasons for my feelings, and as a result, I have often been able to constructively respond to those aspects of myself that caused me to feel bad about myself.

In sum, shame may serve admirably as a mark of our humanity (Schneider 1977). In fact, the experience of shame is like a mirror that reflects back to us parts of ourselves that are typically hidden. Shame **147** experiences are vivid and painful because they foster an accentuated and disturbing sense of self-consciousness. These are moments in which we become aware, as I experienced in struggling to examine my feeling of concern for Pedro, of aspects of ourselves—our ambitions, longings, and sentiments—that are both valuable to our sense of who we are and, at the same time, prone to misunderstanding and derision by other people. In the Pedro story I am referring to the disapproving waiters in the restaurant and even the other customers who didn't seem overly concerned about the welfare of the children begging at their tables. At the time, I imagined that they regarded me with scorn for what they viewed as my oversentimental behavior toward Pedro. What they probably didn't realize (even if they cared) was that my reflection on the incident in the restaurant enabled me to recognize that I did not know myself and other people sufficiently to live fully, well, and with pride. I had *hidden from myself* my most basic values: justice and compassion. Accordingly, the French existential philosopher Jean-Paul Sartre (1966) in *Being and Nothingness* admits: "I am ashamed of what I *am*. Shame therefore realizes an intimate relation of myself to myself. Through shame I have discovered an aspect of my being."

The desire for wisdom, like other virtues, has its roots in a sense of shame. It begins with the realization that one does *not* know something that is of importance to living well, and that which is not known is knowable and *should* be known. Shame is positive if it enables us to chose and act. In short, shame becomes constructive upon a reflection on my ignorance and my resolve to learn that which until now I have failed to recognize as important to how I intend to live my life.

REFERENCES

Blinder, J. 1970. The relative proneness to shame and guilt as a dimension of character style. Ph.D. diss. University of Michigan, Ann Arbor.

Crouppon, G. A. 1970. Field-dependent-independence in depressive and normal males as an indicator of relative proneness to shame or guilt and ego-functioning. *Dissertation Abstracts International* 37: 4669B-4670B (University Microfilms No. 776292).

148 Freud, S. [1923] 1990. *The ego and the id*. In *The standard edition of the complete psy-*

chological works of Sigmund Freud, edited by James Strachey, 19: 3–63. Reprint, New York: W. W. Norton.

Goldberg, C. 1991. *Understanding shame*. Northvale, N.J.: Jason Aronson.

———. 1997. *Speaking with the devil: Exploring senseless acts of evil*. New York: Penguin.

———. 1999. The role of shame in constructive behavior. *Journal of Contemporary Psychotherapy* 29: 253–61.

Harder, D. W., and S. J. Lewis. 1987. The assessment of shame guilt. In *Advances in Personality Assessment*, vol. 6, edited by J. N. Burcher and C. D. Spielberger, 89–114. Hillsdale, N.J.: Lawrence Erlbaum.

Hegel, G. 1892. *The logic of Hegel*, translated from *The encyclopedia of philosophical sciences* by William Wallace. Oxford, England.

Hoblitzelle, W. 1982. Developing a measure of shame and guilt and the role of shame in depression. Unpublished predissertation, Yale University.

Kant, I. [1781] 1956. *Critique of pure reason*. Reprint, New York: Liberal Arts Press.

Lewis, H. B. 1971. *Shame and guilt in neurosis*. New York: International Universities Press.

———. 1987. The role of shame in depression over the life span. In *The role of shame in symptom formation*, edited by H. B. Lewis, 29–50. New York: Lawrence Erlbaum.

Rawls, J. 1971. *A theory of justice*. Cambridge, Mass.: Harvard University Press.

Robertiello, R. C., and T. T. Gagnier. 1990. Shame, shame. *Journal of Contemporary Psychotherapy* 20: 117–21.

Sartre, J-P. [1943] 1966. *Being and nothingness*. Reprint, New York: Washington Square Press.

Schneider, C. 1977. *Shame, exposure, and privacy*. Boston: Beacon Press.

Smith, R. L. 1972. The relative proneness to shame or guilt as an indicator of defensive style. Ph.D. diss., Northwestern University.

Spinoza, B. [1677] 1949. *The ethics*. Reprint, New York: Hafner Press.

8

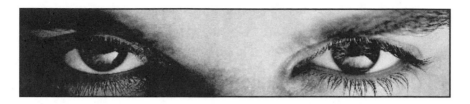

THE CLIENT WITH A
DEADLY SECRET

Learning to Listen to Oneself

Nothing is as oppressive as a secret.
—Jean de La Fontaine, *Fables*

THE EARLY WINTER RAIN DESCENDED UPON THE WINDOWS OF MY CON-
sulting room with a rhapsodic resound. At the same time, the intense
resentment I was experiencing toward Vincent, my client on the analytic
couch, was more than a match for the outdoor cascades of precipitation.

The prolonged downpour had been predicted. The weather report
had forecast that we would be bound by several days of showers. My
inner displeasure with Vincent, on the other hand, was unexpected,
unfathomable, and unsettling.

I was a beginning psychoanalyst, but well trained and clinically
experienced as a psychologist. I was not supposed to lose composure
with clients. Yet, I recognized with concern that wintry day with Vincent that I was barely managing to keep my fitful mood to myself.

Because of this strong, unusual reaction to my client I assumed that
he and I shared a secret. Our mutual concealment, an envelope, contained the key to understanding him.

I will start at the beginning. Something curious was happening in Vincent's session that morning. But I was not aware of how remarkably this analytic hour would unfold until moments before the session ended. At the outset I was aware that Vincent, a fluent speaker, was taking longer than usual to begin.

He was a handsome man, tall and slender of stature. His wavy gray hair, wire-framed glasses, and neatly groomed beard gave him a distinguished presence. On the other hand, his typical attire of ascots and ill-fitting, casual suit vests, and slacks presented Vincent with the admixed sartorial presence of a man of a past world, unsure of the present. Actually, he was quite mindful of how people perceived him, however uncertain he was of how to influence their positive regard.

I constructed a synopsis of Vincent's history to refamiliarize myself with the troubling person lying on the couch only a foot from my chair.

Vincent's father scorned humanitarian pursuits. He was a free-spending, dashing character: a compulsive gambler and womanizer who deserted Vincent and his mother when Vincent was nine years of age. Vincent saw his father only occasionally. Unexpectedly, he would ring the doorbell and lead Vincent to an expensive imported roadster. Vincent never saw the same car twice. Sitting in the backseat, enrobed in furs, would be a smiling, overdressed woman. The same woman never reappeared. The days they spent together were magical. They went to lavish restaurants, and in the afternoon sat in a private box at the racetrack. Young Vincent was introduced to an array of men with long cigars and expensive suits. His father would lean over and whisper that one of these men and he were on the verge of finalizing an important business deal, which would make him financially secure: enabling him to take Vincent to live with him. This was always the most precious moment of all for Vincent.

Nevertheless, during the time he spent with his father, Vincent felt it necessary to conceal his fears and insecurities. He sensed it unsafe to put any demands on his father. He later realized that he had never felt free to be emotionally close with him.

The big business deal apparently never came off. His mother tried to hearten Vincent by telling him that his father really loved him and would be very proud of him when Vincent became an eminent person.

Hope had been Vincent's innocence. As long as he believed his mother's words about his father's intentions, he was inspired and self-confident. When his father died he felt abandoned to the mercies of an angry, embittered mother who continually blamed his father for her miserable life.

In our sessions, Vincent and I had reconstructed the notion that his refusal to give in to the physical pains and illnesses that typify early childhood and preadolescence was an unrecognized attempt to impress his father. Vincent had always tried to be as different as he could from his mother, to whom his father had referred as a hypochondriac.

I found in my working with him that when Vincent began to converse, he did so with an almost inaudible cough, revealing his shyness. His persistent lack of self-assuredness seemed ironic. Vincent once had been a world-famous radio commentator and an international correspondent, covering among other events the Spanish Civil War and World War II. His lack of good taste in choosing clothes was offset by the natural grace and simple dignity of his speech. He spoke in a deep, musical voice, trained by the love of operatic harmony. It was, of course, the warm, reassuring baritone of his radio voice, rather than his appearance, by which he was known to countless listeners of my parents' generation as they waited anxiously at home for good news about their beleaguered sons and husbands serving in the war across the sea.

In the session I describe here, Vincent finally began to speak by relating a memory from long past. He spoke of sitting in his mother's living room. It was only hours before he was to catch an army transport flight with a select cadre of correspondents to report the battles of North Africa.

His mother was at that time of life, he realized, that he might never see her again. The room in which they sat had been his childhood bedroom. It was filled with the relics of seven thousand nights of uneasiness and insecurity. They were listening to a recording of Puccini's *La Bohème*. Vincent had heard this particular operatic rendition in childhood many times before, and once more he was flooded with bittersweet feelings.

His first thought was that if anyone could compose music of such beauty then there must be some reason to live. He then recalled the many evenings of listening to opera while simultaneously casting his plans for the future—which almost always involved a reunion with his father. **153**

His mother, he recalled, was showing him a tattered album of cracked, old photos. One of the pictures was of a striking, joyful-looking young woman. He learned that she was his father's favorite sister. Although his father was the eldest child, she had been the radiant hope of the family. His aunt had been on the onset of a promising concert and theatrical career. Vincent's grandmother would not allow her carefree young daughter to be out alone at night, going to and from the theater and parties she was expected to attend. Vincent's father had been her constant escort. But he had not been able to keep her from harm.

Due to a failed love affair a few years before Vincent was born, his aunt had committed suicide. His father had never spoken to his son of his beloved sister. Indeed, until being shown the album and having his mother speak of her, Vincent had not known of her existence.

Tears filled Vincent's eyes, sliding down his cheeks, as he said that "I knew at that moment in my mother's home that my life's ambition to be a successful journalist and, at the same time, a man with close friends and a loving family would never be realized."

I inquired about his despondent premonition. He did not respond. During the session he had yet to acknowledge my presence. I have learned that when I interrupt a client early in the session and receive no direct reply it usually indicates that it is still too soon to involve myself in the client's narrative. I must, for the time being, allow the client to tell his story in his own way.

Vincent moved restlessly on the couch. He said in a low voice, "Before I left my mother's house for the flight to North Africa I learned that with my aunt's death the sense of well-being left my father's family. My grandfather stopped working. He remained in idle seclusion until his death in his ninth decade. My father's brothers and sisters had to drop out of school to support the family . . . finding whatever jobs they could. A shared depression settled over the family. It lasted the lifetime of all its members. Each of my aunts and uncles died tragically young." Vincent raised his voice a bit to add, "The sense of the tragic is a legacy that I also bear."

His mother's family had not offered him solace, either. They were unsuccessful in hiding their fears. From an early age Vincent had been aware of the tense, hushed conversations of his maternal relatives. The

worst moments for Vincent at home was when the telephone rang: "My mother acted as if each incoming call was a harbinger of still another family misfortune."

His father, in contrast, kept his feelings private. He cloaked his sadness with merriment and good cheer.

Family secrets are frightening for children. This is not simply due to the factual information one fears that a secret holds. Often, more devastating to developing a sense of self-adequacy are the reasons the child imagines that he has not been trusted with a secret.

Even prior to learning about his aunt's suicide, Vincent's father's unwillingness to share any of his private life with him indicated to Vincent that he was regarded as incapable of handling the burden of significant information. Vincent, in turn, came to view himself as weak and fearful.

There is a close relationship between family dynamics and vocational pursuits. Vincent's choice of career as an investigative reporter was related ironically to his exclusion as a child from family secrets. As a friend and, frequently, a confidante to generals, presidents, and prime ministers, Vincent was the person who frequently broke important news stories. Throughout his career Vincent was bound by his word to some powerful authority figure not to reveal these secrets. But he could never set aside his dreadful fear that some day he would mishandle vital information, causing misfortune to many people.

By any fair measure Vincent would have been regarded by most people as brave. He had been imprisoned and tortured by more than one political regime. This had not deterred him from taking on other dangerous assignments. Yet Vincent's self-depreciation resisted disconfirmation.

Once after he had told an audience of businessmen of a hair-raising mission, one member of the assembly stood up and commented to Vincent, "With all the exciting intrigues you have been caught up in, haven't you sometimes felt like James Bond?"

Vincent told me that he had fixed his gaze on the questioner and quietly replied, "Hardly, sir. I would be hard put to recall any such incident during which I was not badly frightened."

As Vincent spoke of his sense of personal cowardice I was aware that the room in which we were meeting had become less comfortable than before Vincent's session started. Inexplicably, his clothes looked **155** more threadbare than usual. I wondered if the rainstorm was inter-fering with the lighting. The room seemed darker than earlier in the session; its various hues of color were verging into a somber gray. I was uncertain at that moment what the actual texture was of the walls and furniture of this consulting room I had long occupied.

My concern with the depressing climate of the session alerted me to some danger imminent, but yet unspoken. I still was unaware of why I was fearful. Some vulnerable part of my psyche, I assumed, was trying to keep me from following my intuitions.

With exerted effort I returned my attention to Vincent for further clues. Having watched him closely for the past twelve months, I was aware of particular patterns in his behavior. From the very beginning of our work together Vincent desperately sought my approval. The fact that he did not try to draw me into his monologue was at odds with his usual style of relating. It seemed this morning he needed my presence but, at the same time, required that I not enter into his narrative. The position in which I was placed had an alarming knell. He was relating to me like a guilty parishioner to his priest to hear an incriminating secret he was compelled to confess. As a confessor, I was required to listen ritualistically: without personal feelings or subjective judgment.

The concept of secrets, as I have already suggested, has special rel-evance to the analytic situation. Behind many disturbed lives resides a painful mystery. The victim intuitively knows that unless his secret is revealed and understood by someone caring and wise, his life will be lived out in constriction and despair. Ironically, as desirous as he is to confess and rid himself of his painful burden, no less urgent is his need to retain his shameful secret. There are inordinately powerful agents requiring his silence; that is to say, he feels bound by loyalties to people from the past to protect them from disclosure of their early shameful and incriminating involvements in his life.

I adhere to the requirements of confidentiality as do priests. But of course I don't give absolution—that is to say, I cannot free my patients from their shameful fraternity with dreaded people of the past by uttering ritualistic words. My task is to enable the victim of the painful secret to question his loyalties to people whom the client feels require him to suffer his mystery alone. What I mean by this is that the client's narrative, containing hidden guilts and shames, is an unfinished story.

I must help him rewrite his narrative, and in the process find a more hopeful and viable way to live.

And as important as are the contents of the secret, no less vital is the climate of the encounters in which these powerful and painful stories are probed in psychoanalysis. The fostering of new and healthier loyalties and relationships can only take place in an atmosphere of caring and trust. Most analysts, therefore, would take cautious note of an analysand, such as Vincent, keeping them at bay. Vincent's efforts to exclude me from a dialogue with him required me to draw his attention to his lack of involvement with me.

I asked if he had any awareness of my presence. Vincent turned in my direction for the first time. He spoke as if from a disturbing dream, "It is odd that I, who have known all the vanities of the world, am asked this question!"

Vincent's statement was a strange response, of course. But I had recognized from the beginning of our work together that because he was not readily in touch with his feelings, Vincent's statements often were difficult to comprehend. When severely stressed, he became momentarily confused and unable to judge appropriately what was happening to him. For example, Vincent was unaware at times that he was angry, whereas anyone in his presence could clearly observe his rage.

Despite the difficulty of deciphering the communication of clients like Vincent, to understand a person analytically means that I am able to explain the client's acts and motives even so far as these behaviors defy common sense. In other words, my clinical understanding needs to account for why people like Vincent act in ways that seem pernicious to their own best interests. Consequently I find it necessary to assume that all communications—no matter how egregious—contain within them understandable information about what is going on in the psyche of that person.

As an analyst, it is of considerable help to have a serious and continuing interest in the arts and the humanities. As such, I recognized the words Vincent had used in his strange statement as taken from the Italian opera *Don Carlo*. I did not remember much of the plot. But, then, it mattered little to my psychological inquiry about the actual story line—more significant was Vincent's conception of the opera.

I asked, "Would you tell me what the story of *Don Carlo* is about?" **157**

"It concerns a mad king who kills his own son and is condemned to live forever as his son might have lived. He finds the requirement impossible. Since he has never given himself the opportunity to know his son, he is unable to find out who his child might have become, and who he would have been in relation to him."

Upon hearing Vincent's words I was aware that soft tremors of anxiety were impeding my usual analytic curiosity. At moments like this in analysis I intuitively know that a secret will follow that involves me in some uncomfortable way. I turned away from my subjective reaction and to the material Vincent was presenting. I was certain that clues to his secret were contained in the protagonist's predicament in *Don Carlo*.

"What does *Don Carlo* have to do with the story of your life?"

"My son died without having given me the chance of knowing him," he responded flatly.

Vincent had not mentioned having children in the year in which I had worked with him. In fact, I remembered quite distinctly that in the first few sessions—a time in which I extensively questioned Vincent about family and other relationships—he had eschewed any mention of marriage.

I looked outside the window as if I expected to find the mystery of how his son died in the muddy field below my window.

It had been raining for the past three days. The mud had formed deep funnels of water, giving the impression of canals of wet clay. As I searched the mud in idle thought, I imagined that a continuous downpour on the decaying leaves and vegetation would cause the canals to flow with odious debris. It also occurred to me that every secret has its own real or imagined odor. I suspected that this had to do with the association of secrets with dank and forbidden places of the psyche. Also, each home has its familiar smell.

I asked Vincent what odor he associated with his mother's home. "The smell of foreboding and despair. It followed me throughout the war and every day afterward. It overwhelms me. I have never known if I will be able to elude it before it finally suffocates me," he emitted with a deep sigh of resignation.

The sound of his words conveyed the same feeling that I visually experienced moments before in regard to the climate of the room. I felt annoyed that Vincent had somehow depressingly transformed my office.

Damn it! I am feeling resentful toward him, I thought, finally identifying my surging emotions. I was able to control their untoward expression only by repeating to myself some basic principles of psychological interviewing.

"Tell me about your son and what happened to him," I heard my voice as it may have sounded in my first year of clinical training as a psychologist.

Vincent's words no longer carried any surprise. Yet the absence of emotion with which he spoke was harrowing.

"I think I killed him. I never found out how he actually died. I suspect that I knew but was afraid to really know. He was just an infant. My wife was away from the house on an errand. I was trying to meet a deadline on a news story. The writing was not going very well. He kept crying. I raised my voice, shouting at him to shut up. He was too young to understand. I immediately realized that yelling at him would only make things worse. I went over to his crib and tried to soothe him. Soon he became quiet. But he stared up at me like he felt abandoned by me. Then I went back to my desk and soon forgot about him. The story I was working on started to fall into place. When my wife came home she looked in on him. Then, I heard the most anguished scream I've ever experienced. Nothing I've ever heard sounded so indignant [What a strange word to use here, I thought]. I went over to her and looked at the child. I instantly knew that he wasn't breathing. I also realized that I must have killed him. But I didn't know how or why. But, then, it would not have mattered whether or not I intended it. My son's death was like a horrible nightmare—the inevitable unfolding of my fate. I had until that moment been able to keep my despondency from overwhelming me. But when he died it was unavoidable to conclude that my ability to feel adequate and good about myself would always elude me. My fate long before my birth had destined that I would never have a confidante and friend. My father never spoke to me of his sister's death or the other painful griefs in his life. I have come to suspect that he caused his sister's death by trying to break up her affair. Oscar Wilde wrote, 'Each man kills the thing he loves.' [What Vincent should have added, but didn't fully recognize, was that he only kills what he loves when he believes he does not deserve it.] I became ashamed of a man I had always so highly admired. What I regarded as my father's dashing **159** ways I now realize was cowardice. I guess I am loyal to my father's character that way. I was never the son he wanted. I, too, have been denied a son with whom I can share the painful episodes of my life. There will never be anyone to understand me, or anyone who even would care to try!"

As I listened, my agitation with Vincent became alarming to me. Clinically, I recognized that this disturbed man was revealing his painful suffering. My proper task was not to play police detective to determine what actually happened to his child, and least of all to assume the role of magistrate in adjudging Vincent's guilt. Nevertheless, I kept focusing on his bland and controlled manner and, especially, his seeming lack of compassion for his child.

Why was I reacting so critically to Vincent? I puzzled. As a psychologist, I had treated vicious criminals. Several of them had brutally raped and murdered. I did not, of course, admire or respect them, but neither did I regard them with the intense resentment I felt toward Vincent at that moment.

A second thought kept intruding upon me. It seemed to feed on my need to justify my resentment. I felt unwilling to let go of the realization that Vincent had largely ignored and excluded me during the session. It was unlike me to be so egocentric in a therapeutic session. Yet I self-righteously reviewed in flashbacks the many occasions when I had made myself available to Vincent within a few hours of his request—times he incurred some particularly stressful event—sometimes at considerable inconvenience to myself. I recalled the occasions Vincent had the police call me after he was arrested for creating a public disturbance. Usually they involved trying to get to see a public official whom Vincent knew from his successful days, and whom he believed owed him a favor. Vincent would calm down within a few minutes after we began to discuss his agitation. Now I kept asking myself how could he treat me this way, effacing all my hard work in trying to understand him!

During the last few minutes of the session I sat in self-contained silence, afraid to speak, for fear my unreasonable resentment might erupt. If I permitted this to happen, it would embarrass me, harm Vincent's precarious self-esteem, and irretrievably contaminate our working relationship.

160 Because the intense resentment I was experiencing toward Vincent was not my usual feeling toward him, I assumed that my own unre-solved conflicts were somehow involved. Consequently, I needed time to figure out what conflicts I was bringing in from my own past before I would be able to work appropriately with him.

Vincent called my answering service very early the next morning to cancel that day's appointment. He had never absented himself from a session before. Although I was concerned about his reasons for not attending, I was more relieved in not having to see him.

I spent his scheduled hour sitting alone in my consulting room, looking out again into the mud. The rain finally had stopped. The tranquility of the morning after the rain served me with an awareness that the mud had special meaning for me. I found out why a few minutes later.

Each analyst has a favorite, trusted medium for exploring the hidden meanings of his client's communications. Many practitioners share with Sigmund Freud the conviction that the interpreted dream provides the golden road to analytic understanding.

For me, on the other hand, it has always been the cadence and resonance of spoken words that convey meanings that transcend their literal connotations. Just as Vincent was trained and comforted by operatic harmony, poetry is a form of expression to which I have always been drawn. I trust it, without reservation, for the evocation of hidden truths about the human psyche. Expanding on the images and moods offered in a verse has provided me with invaluable clues to the riddles posed by the disturbed lives of many of my clients.

Sitting in my consulting room, visually probing the mud from afar, the words of a poem came to my mind with a profusion of disturbing emotion. The precise words were as follows:

> The wind is still now after the tempest of the night;
> Yet I cannot set aside my fear;
> For I have been driven into the burial place of my soul;
> The rain falls now, slow and cold;
> The mud is thick and red;
> How gray is the sky and the sea beyond still grayer fields;
> How come I see the fields as gray
> When I know they should be green?
> I fear the rewake of the wind;
> It serenely ushers a call to my tomb.

Upon recitation, I understood why I had seen the room as dark and the walls as gray in the previous day's session. Vincent's story had untapped some depressing events in my own life. Accordingly, I realized that properly I should revise the last line of the poem to read, "I fear the rewake of the wind; It serenely ushers a call to my father's grave and my own tomb."

I wrote the poem the day of my father's funeral, a year before. Apparently, some communication Vincent had conveyed about the death of his son and the loss of hope of their companionship had joined in my own psyche with the resentment I harbored toward my father for not understanding me and, thereby, not accepting me as a person. He left me with the feeling, similar to Vincent's father, that I was incapable of dealing with important matters.

A progressive understanding of my clinical work over the years has taught me that I frequently encounter unfinished aspects of myself in a therapeutic impasse with a client as I was having with Vincent.

That Vincent excluded me in the session had reopened a psychic wound. The ire I felt toward him was shaped by my animosity against my father for viewing me as a person who will not leave his footprints in the sands of time.

Of course, there is a natural tendency for all of us to identify emotionally with the people with whom we are closely involved. These identifications, however, are generally suppressed when we become threatened by a subliminal sense that we share certain unacceptable traits, or are struggling unsuccessfully with similar issues as the other person. Moreover, in these situations most people can avoid those who evoke uncomfortable reactions in them.

In contrast, the analyst can ill afford to ignore annoying feelings about his clients. His reactions, both those of which he is readily aware and those which he has suppressed, are the tools of his trade. We never truly understand another person except in a recognition of how the other's behavior resonates with our own experiences. So if I am unable to find and examine my own suppressed similarities with a client like Vincent, I will be too fearful, blinded, and limited to be present, active, and available to help.

To decipher Vincent's disturbing impact on me required finding a viable perspective for examining both Vincent's unfinished business with his father and my relationship with my own.

It occurred to me during my session with myself that no one, certainly not my psychoanalytic mentors (who were prone to obscure their ideas by using mechanistic language), has better captured the sense of hopelessness for living fully and well that issues from unfinished business with one's father than the Czech writer Franz Kafka.

Kafka's novel *The Trial* concerns an orderly, industrious bank clerk, Joseph K. On the morning of his thirtieth birthday he is arrested without warning for some unspecified crime. He is compelled for the rest of his life (which is actually only one long day) to try to defend himself from an accusation never explicitly stated by his persecutors.

Kafka's symbolic tale suggests to me that the charges are actually unknown by Joseph K.'s persecutors because it is Joseph K. himself who is unwittingly accusing himself of moral turpitude. In other words, in *The Trial* Joseph K. is both accused and accuser, victim and, at least psychologically, executioner.

What is the moral transgression of which Joseph K. accuses himself? To properly answer this question we need to examine the life of Franz Kafka.

Normally it is unwise to interpret a work of fiction through the spectacles of the author's biography. However, the writer Max Brod, a close friend and confidante of Kafka, insists in his preface to the 1926 edition of *The Trial* that Kafka's work, unlike other European writers, is not best understood in the larger context of European literary history, but almost exclusively in the microcontext of Kafka's own life. And the overriding theme in Franz Kafka's life, according to Max Brod, was Kafka's inability to please his father.

It occurred to me in comparing Joseph K. and Vincent that their inability to please their fathers lay not in what they have wrongly done (the basis of a sense of guilt), but what they *are* (or *are not*) —the basis of a sense of profound private *shame*.

On close examination, Vincent's sense of moral transgression, like that of Joseph K., derives from his devastatingly shameful feelings that his father regarded him as *inadequate*.

But inadequate in what capacity? Neither from Kafka's novel nor Vincent's self-report do we get a clear indication. Why not? Because both Joseph K. and Vincent accuse themselves of moral transgression without understanding the basis of their accusation.

It was an insight into my own unfinished business with my father during the session with myself from which I finally began to decipher the origins of Vincent's profound sense of inadequacy. I experienced my father, as had Vincent and Franz Kafka theirs, as strong and resourceful. As long as I could remember, my father worked six or six-and-a-half days a week, often working fifteen-hour shifts, at the most difficult and unsatisfying types of labor.

Until my father's last breath, I waited for him to be the able, caring father I needed. I had cherished the fantasy that someday we would finally have that cozy chat and, as if by magic, an everlasting camaraderie would follow. But he was gone. Standing on the edge of my father's grave at his funeral, a feeling of futility overtook me. I experienced my father's death as my own epitaph; it signified the end of all hope of ever feeling like a confident and loved son.

During my despondency, my clinical and observational skills did not desert me. As I might search the face of a patient in the assessment period of a new clinical case to appraise what the situation might hold, I looked around the gravesite. There were a few men with shovels in their hands and a rabbi reciting the Kaddish, the Jewish prayer of mourning.

The rabbi had been hired hastily to recite the service. He had not met or even heard of my father before this day. Except for my mother, a few of her relatives, and me, there was no one at the gravesite who knew my father. I realized that my father did not have any close friends. He, like Vincent's father, undoubtedly regarded himself as a prisoner of his life situation. His emotional pain was expected to be borne alone — silently and unflinchingly.

Apparently, also similar to Vincent's father, mine had been adept at concealment; he created the false impression that he was all right when he wasn't. He was probably too ashamed to let anyone, especially me, know that he needed their help.

Yet, clearly something was still amiss in how I understood my relationship with my psychological father. And this factor, I suspected, contained an important clue to Vincent's shameful sense of inadequacy.

Vincent's strange use of the word "indignant" flashed into my mind, together with the intense resentment I had felt in being left out in my efforts to help Vincent during our last session. Powerful words are keys to unlocking painful secrets. From the following set of clinical deductions the phoenix of self-understanding emerged from the ashes of my self-recrimination.

My prior understanding of human relations, shaped by analytic theory, was one-sided. Analytic explanations of disturbed father-son relationships, I came to realize, focus almost exclusively on the child as abused or neglected by a psychologically unavailable father.

In recalling Vincent's sadness in his lack of access to comfort his father, I asked myself, what about the son's shared responsibility with his father for the lack of emotional closeness between them?

Of course, as a child I didn't have the wherewithal to be a real friend to my father. Yet, as an adult, and especially as an analyst, I should have recognized my father as a man who was too proud and unskilled in reaching out for his own emotional needs to allow me to know that he required my understanding. Was my father indignant and resentful that I hadn't permitted myself to recognize him as a lonely and hurt person? Vincent's ostensibly emotionless descriptions of his son's death had brought back disturbing memories of my father's piercing gray eyes sweeping across my path with unspoken hurt and anger.

As my self-scrutiny continued, I became aware that my identification with Vincent consisted of anger at myself for suspending my analytic acumen by continuing to regard my father as the all-powerful person he never was.

Shamefully, I was aware that I had denied an important part of myself—the opportunity to be a friend to my own father. In identifying my shame I recognized that a large part of my motivation for becoming an analyst was to help people with their misery in ways that as a child I had neither the knowledge nor the skill to accomplish with my parents' suffering.

I ended my session with myself with the thought that to overcome his despair over his shameful inadequacy, Vincent, too, required a way to be of help to others, and in return to receive their appreciation.

I met with Vincent regularly, three times a week. Not having heard from him for a full week, it was important that I contact him. He reported having felt extremely humiliated in telling me of the circumstances of his son's death. He said he was unable to face me and return to analysis. I reminded him that he would be lying on the couch and we **165** wouldn't be looking at each other. "This does not matter," he indicated, "because your physical presence is like a mirror for me." By way of explanation, he reported that he had stopped brushing his hair and trimming his beard—seeing his image in the mirror was intolerable.

Although he didn't want to be in my presence, he also didn't seem to want to get off the phone. He told me that after the death of their child his wife had implored him for weeks on end to speak about their loss. He sensed that complying with her request might be wise. If he could have confessed to her his role in the infant's death they might have found some solace together—perhaps even the intimacy that had eluded their marriage. Yet some perplexing force compelled him to hold onto his secret. Despite his intellect and verbal fluency, he seemed to lack the words to tell her, "I have had flashbacks of a shadowy figure, who resembles my father . . . vigorously shaking . . . I mean violently shaking the sobbing child . . . as if he didn't know how to comfort the infant. . . . The child's eyes appeared like daggers . . . daggers of accusation, stabbing at my father's inadequacy as a parent . . . as a human being."

"Was it you or your father you saw in the dream?"

"What a demented dream! I don't really know if it was me or my father. But in fact, my father had been long gone at the time of the child's demise."

Taking a deep breathe, he continued, "After the child's tragedy my depression began to feed on itself . . . eroding my last remnants of self-regard, until there was no pride and self-esteem left. I'm sure my despair . . . my need for protective solitude also . . . drove my wife away and, finally, the last of my friends as well."

"Did you recognize what was happening at the time?"

"Sure, I saw what was happening. . . . I even came across something I once wrote down from an interview with an elderly statesman . . . but felt powerless to act on his sage recognition that 'those who will not share their painful secrets with others suffer their terrors alone.'"

Vincent's career held together a while longer than his personal life: "I have always been able to control my voice: conveying an image of assuredness as a reporter. I did recognize that I had been living a colossal lie for twenty-five years. Still I continued to believe that if somehow I could 'screw my courage to a sticking place,' and confess my guilty deed to someone uncritical and caring, I could finally rid myself of my painful suffering [similar sentiments were uttered by Joseph K. in *The Trial*]. But my last session with you ripped away the cloak of pretense, revealing my humiliating duplicity. My confession wasn't sufficient. Indeed, I felt worse after confessing than I had for the twenty-five years I had held onto my guilty secret."

I was quite puzzled by Vincent's intense distress during the last session. It was evident that the assignment of guilt as the cause of his suffering wasn't accurate. If it were, then Vincent's confession to me should have relieved much of his despondency. Instead, his confession seemed to augment his bad feelings. Moreover, his description of himself—his dread lost sense of self, the feeling that his personality had crumbled away without any personal protection from how others saw him, which led to a restricted life, experiencing social isolation, regarding himself as discredited, and believing himself to be unwelcome to others—was not indicative of someone suffering a guilt reaction, but that of a person inflicted with deep shame.

It is reasonable to infer that throughout his life Vincent had been ashamed of his bouts of depression and despair. He had difficulty believing that other people would want to develop a close friendship with him because he assumed that they, like his father, regarded him as a coward. The feeling that other people disrespected him had persistently contaminated his life.

By continuing to struggle with the feeling that other people disrespected him, he managed to survive on the margin of life. However, the feeling of inadequately caring for his son, if not actually killing him, so pervasively undermined his self-regard that after the tragedy he could no longer function appropriately even in the areas in which he once held consummate skill. Over the years he had become more and more of a recluse.

In the previous two-and-a-half decades he had consulted several therapists. None, he believed, had the slightest notion of how to reach him. He compulsively attended psychotherapy sessions without hope, regarding them as a just punishment for his failure to become a competent person. When he heard me speak in a public forum about the psychological trauma that ensues from guilt, he regarded his attendance at my talk as a fortunate omen.

But why, you may ask, couldn't Vincent confess his shameful sense **167** of himself, just as he finally did his suppressed guilt? Yes, there is agreed-upon language to express one's guilt, which enables the sufferer to speak about his deed and to begin to find ways of making amends for the harm he has caused. This process enables the guilty person to find some solace for his hidden terrors. But the same cannot be said of the experience of deep shame. Human experience futilely cries out for ways of articulating our sense of shame and humiliation. For those like Vincent, shame is experienced as impossible to communicate and to share with another human being.

Unfortunately, there is a deadly link between unrecognized shame and destructive behavior. The destructive act is a shameful protest against the misplaced confidence one has harbored in the qualities of love, trust, happiness, or a desired response from a beloved person.

My clinical experience treating people who have committed serious destructive acts suggests that all of his life Vincent wanted to be consoled and reassured that he is safe and cared about—and in this way he could regain trust in the social order so that he could pursue his life fully and well. But by the time of his child's tragedy, it was too late. He was too hurt, frightened, and cynical to trust anything or anyone again. His destructive act—his self-absorption in his career at the cost of his young child's life—was a frantic effort to be seen, heard, and responded to by those who had disregarded him in his career and in his personal life. His desperate and inarticulate cry exclaimed in effect: "You cannot so easily get rid of me!"

But because the destructive act sullied his moral conscience, it had a dreamlike quality, leaving Vincent uncertain of its actual reality. As a result, he had not until our last session accepted his destructive behavior toward his child as actually having occurred.

During our telephone conversation I searched for a long while for a way to best reach Vincent and to deal compassionately with his suffering. I realized that because his feelings of inadequacy had closeted him from other people over such a long time, what Vincent needed from me was for me to speak to him from my own experiences in such a way that he would no longer need to feel unresponded to in his shame and loneliness.

It was from the realization of my failure to be a friend to my own father that I could give voice to Vincent's plight. In our prolonged telephone conversation I told Vincent, "I am not sure I can help you because I have become aware in listening to you that I share some of your issues." He did not reply. I added, "But I can say this: I recognize the need and the permission in myself to feel compassion for myself during those moments in which I feel inadequate and don't know what to do. Why shouldn't you have the right to do the same for yourself?"

I continued by telling him that I cared about his struggle and what would come of it. "However," I said, "if the only way you can protest your unfair punishment of yourself and your legacy of despair is by not returning to analysis, temporarily or permanently, you have my permission if you need it."

Letting my statement sink in, I continued, "But if you want someone to struggle with you who doesn't have all the answers and can't guarantee you success, I am here."

Vincent then spoke, having said nothing for several minutes: "I am not quite sure what you are saying to me. But I would like to think about it. I will call you back."

Vincent did call back some days later, telling me that he had appreciated that I had spoken to him from a struggle with my own demons. He had never experienced any significant person in his life, he indicated, who had rendered himself vulnerable on his behalf. He conveyed his hope that he had found a friend with a shared mission, and as a result, he was experiencing the awakening of a willingness to explore freely his inner being. He ended the phone conversation by saying that he was ready to return to analysis.

An inherent problem with psychoanalysis, as I pointed out in chapter 1, is that the extraordinary emphasis given to the patient's concerns frequently results in the magnification of self-importance. Vincent needed to offer his friendship to others requiring his guidance and compassion. In other words, for Vincent to come to terms with his morbid destiny, he must become involved with other peoples's suffering, not only his own. He must learn by direct experience that the world does not begin and end with him. Equity theory, discussed in chapter 1, indicates that by recognizing that he can do much to help others, Vincent could learn **169** how to help himself: earning in his mind the right to ask others to assist him when he needs their help.

Vincent had always been a man of strong humanitarian sentiments. His social and emotional withdrawal in recent years had prevented him from compassionately touching the lives of others. In the sessions after his return to analysis, I suggested that he find some way of helping other people. After some investigation, he provided companionship and guidance through a Big-Brother program to a fourteen-year-old African American lad from the inner city named Junior, who lacked a male mentor in his life.

Vincent's time with Junior proved gratifying. Vincent's face seemed more relaxed, and his choice of clothes reflected a more liberated sense of himself which provided him with more confidence in reentering the world he had fled after his child's tragedy.

At the beginning of a session several months later, Vincent excitedly informed me, "I have the best news of all today. You remember my telling you that a public lecture agency I contacted some time ago had asked me to pull together my best news stories and clippings? Well, last night they finally called to inquire if I would consider letting them arrange a lecture tour for me. I surprised myself telling them without any hesitation that I would be delighted if they did. I think I've abandoned my myth of destined suffering."

Our sessions ended soon afterward. Vincent's lecture tours were taking him all over the world.

In the next chapter, based on a clinical case, I attempt to formulate a radical psychoanalytic theory of love, one based on intimacy and mutuality rather than infantile longings.

9

THE CLIENT WITH DESTRUCTIVE LONGING

A Psychoanalytic Theory of Love

Love does not consist of gazing at each other, but in looking outward together in the same direction.
— Rainer Maria Rilke, *Letters to a Young Poet*

THE EARLIEST, MOST BASIC AIM OF SOCIAL BEHAVIOR IS A STRIVING for intimate relations with a caring other. In its mature form intimacy is difficult for most people to achieve. Few suffer well a lack of emotional fulfillment. The sense of living well is dependent upon being desired, appreciated, understood by others. Failure to evoke care from others leads directly to feelings of loss of self-esteem, inadequacy, depression, intense loneliness, and destructive urges (Goldberg 1997).

Adult attempts at intimate relations, claims Freud (1905), fail because they are driven by desperate efforts to secure satisfactions native to the infant-mother bonding; as adult strivings, they result in inevitable narcissistic hurt and depression. I contend that Freud's invective against adult intimacy is misconceived (Goldberg 1999). I seek to show here that failures in adult intimacy are due *not* to inherent infantile patterns, but to lack of knowledge and skill in negotiating equitable and balanced relationships.

171

PSYCHOANALYTIC THEORY OF LOVE

As the most comprehensive theory of human relations, some find it odd that psychoanalysis provides limited assistance in the clarification of the conditions necessary for mature love (Person 1988) or that Freud failed to integrate his asunder views on love into a coherent theory (Bergman 1980). Of course, it would beg the question to fault analysts for failure to tell us how to achieve mature love. Freud's forty years of scattered writings on love inform us that adult intimacy cannot take place because affection and sexuality are split in humans. As discussed previously, Freud (1921) dismisses mature love as a desperate pretense at affection because men cannot experience genuine affection for those women toward whom society legitimizes sexual relations. And women are no more fortunate than men in this regard (Freud 1918).

The split between the subject's affection and sexuality, according to Freud (1905), is unconsciously experienced; therefore, to defend against punitive parental introjects—the internalized rebuke of one's parents for behavior that violates their values—which are awakened by the experience of a new desired object in a sexually similar way as the subject felt toward the desired parent in childhood, the subject develops one or both of two specific self-protective unconscious defenses:

The first is an *ascetic* attitude toward desired objects in which the defense mechanisms of humiliation and disgust are subliminally employed to thwart self-expansive, romantic urges. The second psychological defense is a *moral masochistic* (guilt) reaction in the wake of desire. The subject unwittingly assumes that yearnings for new objects of desire are acts of disloyalty to parental introjects. To avoid this primal sin, the subject, without awareness, seeks to evoke rejecting responses from the desired object. Interpersonal hurt disrupts the transfer of incestuous impulses from a parental introject onto the new object—that is to say, disappointments in love are regarded by analytic theory as messages from one's unconscious that one is receiving punishment for seeking affection from a stranger in the same way one sought love from family (Goldberg 1989). According to Freud (1905), to defend against additional infantile patterns—seductive, repressive, magical, selfish longings for the "lost" object of the mother-infant bonding—asceticism and moral masochism work together, alternating in dominance. Based on this gloomy explanation of attempts at mature love, psychoanalysis has become a theory of emotional effervescence and turbulence distinguished by its lack of delineation of positive, tender affects. It is not surprising, then, that theoretical discussions of love in the psychoanalytic literature for the most part examine sexual strivings rather than discussing the processes toward the attainment of mature emotional intimacy (Reik 1967).

Freud's explanation that mature love fails because the subjects' unconscious guilt for harboring incestuous wishes results in adult attempts at love being simply repetitive editions of infantile reactions should not be taken uncritically; it contains numerous misconceptions. I will address four.

First, what does Freud actually mean by mature love? Because he regarded all forms of love as derived from the same infantile longing, he did not differentiate among the various kinds of love even in terms of their phenotypes—their observable characteristics. I will show later in this chapter that there are two distinct forms of passionate love that differ in the values and the expectations that guide the participants' activities. I call these two types of passionate love "Romantic Love" and "Intimate Love."

Second, Freud (1912) assumes that there is a single universal model for love: the mother-infant bonding in the context of the patriarchal family system. What Freud held as possible both in mature love and in the treatment situation was predicated on the patriarchal model. However, contradicting Freud's assumption, there is considerable anthropological evidence, Bronislaw Malinowski's (1926) studies are but one source, that indicate that the patriarchal system is neither inevitable nor preferable among the array of models of caretaking and intimacy found worldwide.

Third, apparently Freud did not recognize that there is a natural process of evolution in parent-child relationships. Granted that this progression is thwarted in dysfunctional families; nevertheless, common observation makes clear that whereas at first the parents are sovereign and the infant completely dependent upon them, this arrangement changes over time in healthier families: upon reaching adulthood the offspring may form an equalitarian friendship with either **173** or both parents; and as the parent(s) ages, the child may become a care-taker (parent) to the parent(s).

Fourth, unconscious guilt is not the underlying cause of conflict in love relationships. Because Freud fails to clearly differentiate guilt from disgust and shame (Yorke et al. 1990), he did not realize that most of what he attributes to guilt are actually manifestations of shame (Goldberg 1991b). In the following case I present clinical data to show how a better understanding of the role shame plays in intimate relations provides a proactive, optimistic theory of love and intimacy.

CASE STUDY

While I was in analytic practice in the nation's capital, Alex, a dashing but troubled young man with a promising future in the U. S. State Department, was referred to me. Unlike most of his colleagues at the upper echelon of government, Alex had grown up in a working-class family. As long as Alex could remember, his father was rarely at home; he was away on his truck hauling freight—a business that he and Alex's uncles inherited from their father. Since the father's earnings were insufficient to support the family, his mother also worked. As a private secretary to a business tycoon, she made considerably more money than his father, and she never let his father forget it.

In school, Alex—a tall, dark, slim young man who moved with the natural grace of a well-coordinated athlete—was a diligent student and vicious fighter, who at any accusation of wrongdoing reacted by pounding male adversaries to a pulp and verbally scourging female complainants. A talented athlete, Alex had won an athletic scholarship to an Ivy League university. During his sophomore year he met Alice, a quiet, studious young woman also from a working-class family. She became devoted to Alex, and they spent three years together. Shortly before graduation, Alice became pregnant. This was an era in which being pregnant and unmarried was looked upon with strong disapproval. She wanted to marry immediately. A man who kept his own counsel, Alex had not informed Alice about his future plans. Without an affluent or influential family, he believed that only marriage with a woman from a well-placed family could repair what he lacked in birthright. Marriage to Alice was a foreclosure of his ambitions for a career in the government foreign service.

While in a state of despondency about how to handle his dilemma, Alex was invited to a classmate's home in northern Virginia; while there he accompanied his friend George to a party at the home of George's uncle, a prominent official in the State Department. At the party he met George's beautiful cousin Elaine. Alex immediately recognized her as the object of desire he had sought from his first awakenings of an interest in girls. Her social status intensified his attraction to her.

Alex took considerable pride that he was not like other men with whom he was acquainted—lawyers and government officials who talked incessantly about their self-importance. Unlike them, Alex could recite facilely by memory the poetry of Shakespeare, Byron, Shelley, Auden, even Millay and Cummings. Most of the women he met within minutes yielded to his words and tender caresses; swept off their feet, they confessed that Alex was the most seductive man they had ever met.

During their stroll at dusk into the garden at the party, Alex recited poetry to Elaine. She was as taken by Alex as he was with her: she was the answer to his desires no less than his ambitions. But Alice's pregnancy stood in the way. So Alex went back and told Alice that if she had an abortion, he would marry her after they both had found employment and could support a family. But, instead, after her abortion, he announced his engagement to Elaine. This engagement, as with all his subsequent relationships, was immediate, passionate, and quickly exhausted. Each woman with whom he became involved soon found him manipulative and disingenuous.

ALEX'S PRESENTING COMPLAINT

Alex came to see me because of persistent feelings of guilt about his deceitful manipulation of Alice. "I assure you," he told me, "I don't feel particularly bad because of the fetus. I'm not religious and I didn't regard it as a human being. My continual bad dreams have to do with Alice. At night in the midst of my preoccupation with betrayal, my throat closes up, and for a long moment I'm not able to swallow or breathe. I have tried talking with a minister—but it didn't help. Even my confession to a priest didn't change anything. What I did to Alice is the only thing I have ever done about which I feel truly sorry."

I sensed that there was something odd about Alex's admission of guilt. As an aggressively ambitious young man who had made it to the high echelon of government, he must have stepped on many toes on the way up—indeed, injured some. So, why was he speaking only of his guilt in regard to a girlfriend? On sharing my reflection I was told:

"I don't deceive myself: in my heart I don't believe that I am really a decent guy."

"Are you saying that you have done other rotten things?"

"Plenty! For example, I have been told that one or two of my colleagues took their own lives because of what I did to their careers."

"What did you do to them?"

"Listen, Doc! I don't buy this crap about the reverence of life. . . . I mean the nonsense that everyone has an eternal soul or something and is unique and valuable. Actually, I believe there are just two kinds of people in this world —'hammers' and 'nails'; and obviously it is far better to hammer than be nailed."

"So, how did you nail those colleagues?"

"They received what they deserved. They wanted advancement and so did I. If someone gets a particularly good embassy assignment that means everyone else is left out in the cold. So, on occasion, when necessary, I have passed on incriminating information about colleagues— that they are homosexual, take drugs, imbibe too much alcohol, dig young kids sexually, or all the above. . . . I have some acquaintances in the press, people who appreciate my information and are willing to keep the source confidential."

"Were the leaks you provided true?"

"Sometimes they are true; sometimes partially true; occasionally, mostly not true. I don't remember anymore what it was with the guy who jumped out of the window, or with the other one who did it with a shotgun after I leaked scandalous information about them. But none of this stuff bothers me like betraying Alice. I mean, hell! I just went and confessed to a minister about what I did to those guys and I was able to get that stuff off my chest."

The more I was learning about Alex, the less I understood him:

admittedly, his manipulation of Alice was despicable; and granted, he had a closer relationship with her than with his colleagues. But most of us would agree that someone who is the cause of the death of one or more lives is more malevolent than the betrayer of a lover. So what happened to the bad feelings we would expect Alex to harbor because of his wrongful behavior toward his colleagues? It was from an exploration of Alex's family dynamics that I gained some insight into his otherwise inexplicable lack of guilt toward his colleagues.

FAMILY ROMANCE

From his preadolescence on, Alex's mother related to him as a surrogate husband: he was her constant companion; she took him everywhere—her shopping trips, medical appointments, tea with female friends, even rendezvous with men. She also confided to him the most intimate details of her life—i.e., complaints about his father's inadequacy as a husband and a lover; even the details of her love affairs. At first, Alex was proud that she regarded him as mature and important enough to tell him her secrets, but when he tried to separate from her and make friends of his own, especially girlfriends, she criticized him for selfishness, for his lack of loyalty to the person who loved him most. There would never be anyone who would cherish him as she did, she told him. Who would take care of him as lovingly as she?

"But if you love me so much," he would complain when he reached adolescence, "how come you ignore what I *want*?" With deep sobs and wet cheeks, she would reply, "I don't mean to hurt you. Maybe I just don't know how to do the right thing. But I love you so much! Just tell me the right thing to do!" But whenever he did, she simply ignored his wishes and continued to treat him as before.

FATHER-SON BONDING

Alex had a more comfortable relationship with his father than with his mother. His father, a powerfully built man, had the street smarts of **177** somebody who had to fend early for himself. He had grown up in an immigrant family with a tyrannical, narcissistic father whose needs always came first. Alex's father and his six siblings were compelled to structure their lives so as not to infringe on their father's self-indulgence when at home from his trucking business.

With Alex, his father was usually supportive and encouraging (especially in regard to sports and schoolwork), not critical or manipulative like his mother. Yet, two things about his father greatly perturbed Alex. First, in looking back, he could swear that his father was a coconspirator in his mother's seduction of him. He encouraged Alex to please her, never to leave her unhappy. The second matter concerned the movies and ballgames his father took him to on his days off. Following these excursions, he and his father went to the neighborhood ice cream parlor for a malted and a bacon, lettuce, and tomato sandwich. So far, so good! But then he would inevitably spoil everything by cupping his hands to his mouth and whispering the caution that Alex should not let his mother, a health-food enthusiast, know what they ate away from home. Alex, accustomed to reducing all matters of consequence to physical equations, could not fathom his father's cowering to his mother—after all, he wondered, what could a petite woman like his mother do to a big, powerful man like his father?

THE ANALYST'S COUNTERTRANSFERENCE

Traditionally, psychoanalytic training and doctrine has stressed emotional neutrality, which means that the analyst must guard against allowing his own emotional history—particularly, his unresolved issues—to be stirred up by what happens between him and his client. Analytic theory contends that the reawakening of the analyst's emotional history, called "countertransference," can lead to a reduction in the analyst's ability to understand the client and communicate his comprehension.

In recent years, some influential analysts (Winnicott 1956; Greenson 1971; Racker 1972; Searles 1975, for example) have seriously questioned the negative connotations given to the analyst's affective responses to the client. They have insisted that it is necessary for the analyst to remain vulnerable—open to all feelings—in order to be most available and responsive to the other's communications (Goldberg 1991a). In currency with the importance of not prejudging the ultimate value of any of the broad range of the analyst's experiences in the analytic encounter, I use the term "countertransference" here to include all of the analyst's responses to his client: conscious and unwitting, verbal and silent, helpful and deleterious.

On listening to Alex's account of his relationship with his parents, I was startled to recognize that one of the most important ingredients necessary for healthy psychological development—the one that was missing in Alex's relationship with his parents—linked his growing up with that of mine. I will explain with a short vignette.

My own personal analysis in my twenties was interrupted because I was attending graduate school a couple of thousand miles from my analyst (whom I will call Dr. Miller). I planned to marry my girlfriend Harriet during the winter recess from school. My mother strongly disapproved of her. When I returned home at Thanksgiving to plan the wedding, my mother informed me that she had spoken with Dr. Miller, and he had told her that he wanted to meet Harriet. Our conjoint session with him was uneventful. But afterwards my mother told me that Miller was convinced that Harriet was the wrong person for me. When I confronted him on the phone and asked what he had said about Harriet to my mother, he repeatedly ignored my concern; instead, he put the blame on me for my naiveté in believing my mother's words.

In listening to Alex's story I relived the anger and hurt I felt toward Miller for his refusal to tell me just what his feelings about Harriet and me were: more precisely, missing from Miller was a truthful personal statement of where he stood in terms of me. A *personal statement* is a verbal and/or nonverbal communication in which the informant conveys his perceptions and judgments in a direct and undisguised way. These statements convey the composite of the communicator's regard for the other. They are authentic insofar as they are products of the informant's struggle to self-examine and not deny aspects of his/her conscious and preconscious totality as a person. Those individuals who avoid thorough self-examination are not capable of personal statements, as I operationally define here the concept of personal statement. **179**

GUILT AND SHAME

In the throes of my countertransference to Alex I recognized that he was an especially vulnerable victim of the *absence* of truthful personal statements in his family—except to the extent that his parents' moodiness and temper were personal statements. What Alex required from them was the admission from his mother that she was dishonest and hurtful in trying to manipulate him to please her by repeatedly telling him that he was a selfish and ungrateful son. In a truthful personal statement she would need to admit that she tenaciously held onto him because she was lonely and afraid of the sexual demands of an intimate adult relationship. From his father he needed the confession that he had pushed Alex to please his mother because he was not courageous enough to deal with his wife's excessive demands and criticism.

I understood then that Alex's expression of guilt seemed inexplicable to me because it camouflaged his real feelings—emotions with which Alex was not in touch. What he suffered from was not guilt, but *shame*. He was exquisitely sensitized to shame by his mother. She repeatedly informed him that unless he behaved exactly as she wanted, she would abandon him, leaving him unwanted and alone.

Alex's crucible of shame was further shaped by his unwitting identification with his father's feeling of incompetence as a person. Shame is a subtle and contagious emotion—certainly, far more than guilt. It can be discharged in such an indirect way, as I indicated earlier, that the person (especially a child) who is inflicted with the painful feelings of humiliation and shame is unaware of the reception of the unwanted feelings. A sensitive and vulnerable person assuming someone else's shameful feelings is said to "borrow their shame." To reiterate: Very few people go through life without acquiring at some time or other this unfair burden. We are especially susceptible to borrowed shame when a person with whom we closely identify and care about harbors painful self-punitive shame, e.g., feelings of self-contempt for one's failure as a husband and the ordinariness of one's lifestyle. Alex cared about his father, but he was too young to understand why his father was afraid of his mother and to help him with his impacted self-doubts. Understandably, it left young Alex feeling helpless and upset in his father's presence. He felt that he had done something wrong because he did not realize that his bad feelings—the choked-up feeling in his throat that he had experienced since childhood—came from his assumption of his father's sense of failure as a husband and provider. It plagued all of Alex's relationships—it was the source of his sadness, fear, and rage—but he could not identify it for what it was.

Freud's (1905) colossal error in trying to explain the barriers against mature love was to implicate guilt and to ignore shame. Freud, as I have already indicated, confused the dynamics of guilt with those of shame. Guilt, in contrast to shame, is a relatively easy emotion to recognize (because it is cognitive, whereas shame is difficult to identify since it is experienced as physiological discomfort and pain), and to control (because there are societally recognized ways to exculpate guilt's pangs, but there are none for shame). To expunge one's guilt for wrongful behavior a person confesses, requests forgiveness, undergoes repentance, and is then given redemption and accepted back into society. The goal of guilt is the *avoidance* of again doing wrong. Nevertheless, it doesn't teach us how to receive the appreciation and love of those we desire.

What Freud failed to recognize—unlike the psychoanalyst Karen Horney (1950)—is that there is *pride* in guilt even if this attribute is perverse. This is because the attribute of guilt implies that one has the *power* to do wrong or even evil. If the person is punished by self or other, it is because of the realization that he is a person to be reckoned with and requires restraint. This is to say, in guilt one *did* the deed (translation: it is socially and personally recognized that the person has the power to do it).

In shame reactions, in contrast, the person experiences the absence of personal power. How can one confess to shame, even when one can identify its presence? That is to say, how does one confess that he or she is merely mortal—prone to the frailties, limitations, and vulnerabilities that are heir to being human?

In unwittingly identifying with his inarticulate and ashamed father who felt very ordinary, Alex carried the narcissistic seeds of destruction for all of his relationships—the compulsion to lie and manipulate because he felt at a disadvantage with those from more fortunate families in which parents were well educated, reasonable, and true friends **181** and mentors to their children. From his disadvantage, Alex harbored an underlying feeling of lacking protection from the ravages of hurt and disappointment that come from a sense of the lack of legitimate entitlement to that which his more advantaged classmates and colleagues acquired as their birthright. Thus, Alex felt worse (shameful) about his incompetence in establishing an enduring intimate relationship than in being wrong (guilty) for his participation in his colleagues' destruction.

ROMANTIC LOVE AND INTIMATE LOVE

Love relationships are *not inevitably* mired in infantile patterns. Freud was not able to see this from his pessimistic and reductionistic perspective because of his relationship with his own parents. His father died when Freud was still young; and although his mother lived into her nineties, Freud was never able to deal with her narcissistic control over him. Psychologist Ruth Abraham (1982–83) writes that Freud's inability to analyze and come to terms with his extremely complex and ambivalent relationship with his own mother was the major source of his misconceived ideas about the oedipal situation. In a letter to Karl Abraham, Freud wrote: "So I have really reached the age of sixty-two, still unable to achieve that quiet resignation. . . . My prevailing mood is powerless embitterment or embitterment at my powerlessness" (Freud and Abraham 1965, 275). Abraham (1982–83) points out that this statement was made in regard to Mrs. Freud's controlling presence in his life. Sensitive to shame and unable to properly recognize its impact, Freud emphasized in most instances of human conflict an emotion with which he was more comfortable—guilt.

Freud did not recognize (due to his own family dynamics and/or because his observations were primarily based on the families of his patients as reported to him) that only in disturbed families are difficulties with intimacy due to the subject's fear of disloyalty to cruel introjects. In more healthy families, one's caretakers are essentially compassionate and caring—encouraging one to form intimate bonds with loving others. As a result, those from caring and compassionate families seek—with a sense of legitimate entitlement—other compassionate and caring people with whom to become intimately involved. In short, there is something proactive in the human phylogenetic spirit that strives for intimate relationships with a desired other that is not reducible to infantile longings and concern with parental disapproval. It is this propensity for transcendental personal and interpersonal development, based on the importance of equity and balance in human relationships, that strives for mature intimate love with others.

I have now come to a place where I can be more specific about what I mean by "intimacy." Intimacy is a unique personal experience, operationally defined here as the experience of being recognized and emotionally touched in the way the subject desires, such that the subject experiences the other as accurately mirroring his desires for caring and closeness. The other in the intimate encounter is the medium for how the subject wishes to be related to and regarded. The event of intimacy requires a bond between the partners in which each "feels into" the other, as well as an openness with oneself that permits the other to contact typically hidden aspects of oneself. Therefore, unlike romantic love, based on fantasy, intimacy involves the authentic presence of the partners because their exchanges are personal statements.

And unlike its often associated state, a desire for privacy—which is a reaction to the other's encroachment into the subject's experience of time and space—the experience of intimacy has no sense of time. It is experienced as a flow of tactile sensation that requires no actual physical touch (although tender physical touch can accentuate the exquisiteness of intimate relating). The experience is analogous to the reception of evocative music, in which the vibrations of the distal stimulus (the musical instruments) touch the proximal stimulus (the sense receptors), causing a bodily sensation that is neurologically transformed into deeply pleasurable emotion.

Intimacy, grounded in the immediacy of the present moment, is located in space, not time. Indeed, only one's orientation toward the past or future has a sense of time. Consequently, intimacy leads to an accentuated awareness of how each partner in the bonding is using the space between them.

Intimate love also differs markedly from romantic love in that romantic love creates a craving for timelessness—contained in such "if- **183** only" fantasies as: "If only I could retain this (overidealized) image of myself in the eyes of my beloved, time would stop and stand on end, and I would be joyous forever." In contrast, each of the partners in intimate relations consciously recognizes that the perception that this moment can go on forever is an illusion insofar as intimate love is comprised both of elation and sadness: each is fortunate to be so blessed to have found a compassionate and caring other; yet, each has a sense of limitation—the time lost prior to this encounter will never be restored.

I have described what personal statements are, but not how they are constructively employed in mature intimacy. Caring is essential to the encouragement of constructive personal statements. Intimate caring is a demonstration of respect for the other's growth and mystery. It is the willingness to be there for the other rather than to do for the other; this is exemplified in a capacity to listen responsibly to the other rather than to render value judgments and problem-solve for the other. Love, at its most intimate level, is a creative and caring expression of mutuality (Wren 1968). When the other is in distress, the partner's caring concern is that the other's struggles to examine the assumptions she makes about her being-in-the-world will be worthy enough to enable her to be as she intends rather than how the partner or anyone wants her to be.

Mutuality is expressed very differently in romantic love. The courtiers, Denis de Rougemont (1983) indicates, "love one another, but each loves the other *from the standpoint of self and not from the other's standpoint*" (52). In this type of relationship, the problem of love "is primarily that of *being loved*, rather than that of *loving*, of one's capacity to love" (Fromm 1956, 1).

In intimate love, mutuality is expressed as balance and equity. The need for *balance* in intimate relating requires that what I give of myself is at least as important as what I receive. Therefore, I require good enough judgment to chose another as an intimate partner who brings out the best in me—who inspires me to want to give my best—not someone who demands it or depends on it, as in romantic love. The *equity* dimension in intimacy involves an *investment*; that is to say, other people can only give me what they themselves possess. To gain for myself from others, therefore, I need to help them develop their own desirable attributes.

Both intimate and romantic love require *mirroring* to sustain passion. In romantic love each partner holds the mirror not to the face of the other, but in front of one's own face. In this sense, the courtiers are not partners in cooperative personal and interpersonal development, but coconspirators in reinforcing the other's narcissism. As a result, in a romantic relationship, each of the partners harbors a host of implicit expectations and demands he or she anticipates a loving relationship will fulfill. These expectations are seldom articulated. As romantics, the courtiers communicate with phrases and declarations lifted almost directly from overly idealized films, novels, and television dramas. They rarely communicate precisely what they expect from each other until they are thrown into a serious dilemma, and sometimes not even then. In crisis situations, as in the normal course of their relationship, they find themselves ill-equipped to work together as partners. Instead, they berate each other for their inadequacies, declaring that they are furious that the other has not measured up to their standards, expectations they have not previously communicated clearly. So frequently after the breakup of a romantic relationship one exclaims to the other, "I never knew what you expected of me!" (Goldberg 1975).

In intimate relating, in contrast, each partner is willing to face the mirror squarely and to use it to look probingly in search of one's behaviors that contradict one's desire for agency. Shame, if we allow it, may serve admirably as a realistic mirror to detect that which we have neglected in our relationship with ourselves and with others, and to enable us to rectify these neglects. Shame, because it is built on relations with compassionate and caring caretakers, can guide the subject to those ways of being that please those we love rather than concern itself with inciting those we fear, as with guilt. I will explain, using Alex's story as an example.

While in my analytic training, I again reflected on my upset with Dr. Miller's refusal to render me a personal statement during our phone conversation. Although I recognized that his behavior was an expression of his failed analytic wisdom, it nevertheless struck a raw nerve in me. My apprehension as a child was that I, like my father, would turn out to be merely an ordinary person. Reflecting on the patients I was treating during my apprenticeship, my clinical observations suggested that this fear concerned most, if not all, of them as well.

When I asked Alex what about his father he would be the most ashamed to discover that they shared in common, he said, with scarcely a moment's thought, "I need to believe that I'm special, not just another plain face in the crowd. I mean, there were some commendable things about my father, but, hell, he was just another working stiff!"

"Can you, somehow, apply this information to your feelings of guilt about Alice?"

"Yes, of course," he replied after some thought. "It is unbelievable that I haven't recognized this before! I mean, I wasn't really guilty about what I did to Alice, but what I did *to myself*."

"Go on!"

"Well, it just occurred to me that I have been guilty, ashamed, angry, or whatever, or all the above—I don't know which—at myself, because from the beginning I knew—but didn't allow myself to know—that she was the right person for me. I mean, I have never been as comfortable or intimate with anyone—woman or man—as with her."

"So, why did you dump her?"

"Because she was just Alice: She is pretty, but not stunning; intelligent, but not exceptional; socially gracious, but not charismatic. I always believed that I needed someone who stood out—so I could stand out. I can, of course, sweep a woman off her feet the first time I'm with her; I can impress or intimidate any man. But it is only temporary. It quickly wears off, and I'm again just an ordinary guy like my father was. When my dazzle wears off, I feel naked and ashamed of who I am. I have to ruin relationships because I can't stand the strain of trying to be special when I'm not." With this important information in his conscious possession, Alex was ready to learn how to develop constructive intimate relationships. All he needed was an appropriate partner. Soon thereafter, Alex found her and started a relationship that was not quickly exhausted.

CONCLUSION

Although I have contrasted romantic love unfavorably with intimate love, admittedly, romantic passion sometimes serves to inspire the courtiers in favorable ways. Insofar as romantic passion involves a reodering of values and priorities (Person 1988)—e.g., the lovers are willing to take emotional risks and attempt behaviors that they ordinarily eschew—it can, in certain situations, inspire courageous and constructive behavior as well as personality change (Goldberg 1989, 1996). Moreover, intimate relationships, as I have described them here, may begin as romantic passion and, through a willingness to struggle with personal statements, evolve into an equitable, balanced, and enduring partnership.

The final chapter provides recommendations for the modification of psychoanalytic theory and practice.

REFERENCES

Abraham, R. 1982–83. Freud's mother's conflict and the formulation of the oedipal father. *Psychoanalytic Review* 69: 441–53.

Bergman, M. S. 1980. On the intrapsychic function of falling in love. *Psychoanalytic Quarterly* 49: 56–77.

De Rougemont, D. 1983. *Love in the Western world*. Princeton, N.J.: Princeton University Press.

Freud, S. [1905] 1990. Three essays on the theory of sexuality. In *The standard edition of the complete psychological works of Sigmund Freud*, edited by James Strachey, 7: 123–245. Reprint, New York: W. W. Norton.

———. [1912] 1990. On the universal tendency to debasement in the sphere of love (Contributions to the Psychology of Love II). *Standard edition*. 11: 177–90.

———. [1918] 1977. The taboo of virginity. In *Sigmund Freud: Sexuality and the psychology of love*, edited by P. Rieff. New York: Simon & Schuster.

———. [1921] 1989. *Group psychology and the analysis of the ego*. New York: Norton.

Freud, S., and K. Abraham. [1907–1926] 1965. *The letters of Sigmund Freud and Karl Abraham*. New York: Basic Books.

Fromm, E. 1956. *The art of loving*. New York: Harper & Row.

Goldberg, C. 1975. Courtship contract in marital therapy. *Journal of Family Counseling* 3: 40–45.

———. 1989. The role of passion in the transformation of anti-heroes. *Journal of Evolutionary Psychology* 9: 2–16.

Goldberg, C. 1991a. *On being a psychotherapist*. Northvale, N.J.: Jason Aronson.

———. 1991b. *Understanding shame*. Northvale, N.J.: Jason Aronson.

———. 1996. The role of antihero in a theory of courage. In *Clinical approaches to adult development*, edited by M. Commons, J. Demick, and C. Goldberg, 73–93. Norwood, N.J.: Ablex.

———. 1997. *Speaking with the devil: Exploring senseless acts of evil*. New York: Penguin.

———. 1999. A psychoanalysis of love: The patient with deadly longing. *American Journal of Psychotherapy* 53: 437–51.

Greenson, R. R. 1971. The "real" relationship between the patient and psychoanalyst. In *The unconscious today*, edited by M. Kanzer, 213–32. New York: International Universities Press.

Horney, K. 1950. *Neurosis and human growth*. New York: Norton.

Malinowski, B. 1926. *Crime and custom in savage society*. New York: Harcourt, Brace & World.

Person, E. 1988. *Dreams of love and fateful encounters*. New York: Penguin.

Racker, H. 1972. The meanings and uses of countertransference. *Psychoanalytic Quarterly* 41: 487–506.

Reik, T. 1967. *Of love and lust*. New York: Bantam Books.

Searles, H. F. 1975. The patient as therapist to his analyst. In *Tactics and techniques in psychoanalysis today*, edited by P. Giovacchini, 95–151. New York: Jason Aronson.

Winnicott, D. H. 1956. On transference. *International Journal of Psycho-analysis* 37: 386–88.

Wren, J. 1968. Love's coming of age. In *Psychoanalysis observed*, edited by C. Rycroft, 83–117. Baltimore, Md.: Penguin.

Yorke, C., T. Balogh, and P. Cohen. 1990. The development and functioning of the sense of shame. *Psychoanalytic Study of the Child* 45: 377–409.

10

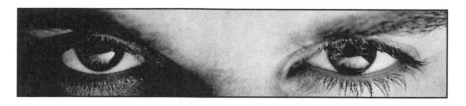

PSYCHOANALYSIS AS HOPE, COMPASSION, AND RESPONSIBILITY

A friend is a person with whom I may be sincere. Before him I may think aloud.

— Ralph Waldo Emerson, *Essays* ("Friendship")

IN THIS CONCLUDING CHAPTER I SPELL OUT WHAT I REGARD AS THE modifications in theory and practice required for psychoanalysis to become a hopeful, compassionate, and responsible psychology.

During the last four decades my clinical experiences have reinforced the conviction I held during my analytic apprenticeship (e.g., Sally's case in chapter 1) that psychoanalysis cannot meaningfully survive in a moral vacuum. Psychological inquiry that does not support constructive human values, because its practitioners believe that they should not influence their clients, is not only unrealistic, but shallow and rootless as well. Most life situations contain moral issues — whether or not we recognize or attend to them. Clinical situations are extensions of this reality. Moral concerns are essential to the well-examined life because they are attempts to find principles and rationales for how to deal with the complex and difficult dilemmas that confront human dignity and purpose.

Psychoanalytic theorists who regard relational and existential issues as no less significant than that of intrapsychic issues are those who have written most extensively about social and moral values in the analytic situation. I include Carl Jung, Harry Stack Sullivan, Karen Horney, Alfred Adler, Erich Fromm, Erik Erikson, Stephen Mitchell, and Jay Greenberg most notably in this group. However, except for Erikson, these theorists focus more on the analysis (examination) of patient dysfunction than they do on proposing ways to *rebuild* lives. Only Erikson gives attention in his writings to the client's social and moral responsibilities to others—which, as I have attempted to show in the cases I have presented, is essential to rebuilding lives.

As a hopeful, compassionate, and responsible psychology, psychoanalytic theory and practice requires an orientation that regards the client's reports as a life story that must be retold as a *better story*—a story that includes developmentally appropriate responses to the existential, social, and moral issues that the client heretofore has not recognized or has ignored. In other words, the analyst enables the client to address denied conflicts in her life story—conflicts that have prevented her from responding authentically (directly) to such questions as:

1. What am I actually experiencing?
2. What does my experience mean in terms of the person I intend to become—that is to say, what is the relation of my experiences to my core values?
3. What fears and conditions are interfering with my ability to experience my existence authentically?
4. How can I reexperience my experience, bringing it into fuller and more authentic awareness—that is, what insights, experiments, exercises, and ways of being will help me complete my experiences?
5. Having reexperienced and completed my experiences, I should have a more lucid conception of who I intend to be. How do I put these values into action—in terms of myself and in terms of others?

Psychoanalysis as Hope, Compassion, and Responsibility

What differentiates the analyst—as I propose here—from other significant people in the client's life is not only the analyst's trained intuition in interpreting the client's intentionality but, as importantly, his willingness to make truthful personal statements of how he experiences the analysand trying to influence him in telling her story. By means of *personal statements*, the analyst conveys his perceptions and judgments in a direct and nondisguised way. These statements provide the composite of the analyst's regard for the client. They are authentic insofar as they are products of his struggle to self-examine and not to deny aspects of his conscious and preconscious harboring of thoughts and feelings about the client. These statements must include the analyst's counter-transference—i.e, specifically how the analyst may have unwittingly "encouraged" the client to respond in the ways she did, as well as the feelings of positive regard he experiences toward the client; otherwise these statements can seem to the client to be narrow and overly critical. In sum, without personal statements, psychoanalysis consists only of a probing process devoid of a constructive intentionality.

Institutionally, to facilitate psychoanalysis as a depth-psychology that rebuilds lives, I propose the following modifications in current analytic theory, practice, and attitude:

1. *Psychoanalysts must recruit the most able practitioners*. Many who enter the profession of analysis seem to believe that an above-average intelligence, an interest in psychological issues, and a desire to help others is sufficient for proficiency. They are mistaken. There is abundant empirical evidence to show that there are many analytic practitioners who are bright, well trained, and professionally adroit, but at the same time are ineffective healers.[1]

If the practitioner has not lived fully, what can she offer those who seek a guide to life but an inane and illusory expertise? One does not respond wisely to the dilemmas and opportunities in another's life simply by possessing theoretical and factual knowledge about the reasons the other became fearful and why his yearnings have gone unsatisfied. The able analyst guides others by the maturity of her own tested self, in so doing, teaching the other how to temper the hard realities of life with passionate and romantic dreams.

Analysts are not only listeners of their clients' tales; they must live **191** in the same world. It is the analyst's enlightened presence in their shared world that gives hope for a more optimistic life for the client. I believe that genuine healing requires more than knowledgeable understanding; the analyst must extend to her client as well the goodwill and friendship that are derived from her firm place in the world outside the consulting room. In short, one ably guides over similar terrain. Those who have cowered in the underbrush of their own personal journeys have neither a compass for the brave nor a sturdy walking stick to bolster the unsteady gait of the fearful.

2. *Competent analytic practice requires skill in self-analysis.* Traditionally, the mandate for understanding the sufferer's problems came from the healer's insight into his or her own suffering. From earliest times healing practitioners have created systems for those they treat in terms of the meanings they have made of their own suffering and life crises. Healers could be of assistance to others only to the extent that they were fellow sufferers. With this recognition in mind, Freud (1912) regarded self-examination to be indispensable to the most profound understanding of any problem, and recommended that the analyst continue a regular process of self-analysis after the practitioner's personal analysis was completed.

Yet, despite its crucial importance in ongoing analytic training, psychoanalyst Richard Chessick (1990) indicates in his review of the literature that the issue of continuing self-analysis after one's training analysis is much more complicated than was originally thought. So difficult, Chessick adds, that no analyst writing about self-analysis has been able to accurately describe the process in terms of the interminable and multimotivational sources of the uncovered material. In other words, the trained analyst seems no better able to remove the barriers that interfere with understanding his own psyche without the guidance of another analyst than is the client.

If self-analysis is actually an indispensable, but poorly understood, professional and personal guide of the analyst, then more attention needs to be given to it in the practitioner's training. Self-analysis must become a prominent component of the analyst's personal analysis, and integral to supervision and coursework.

3. *The reductionistic and pessimistic attributes in psychoanalysis must be eliminated.* We have not yet formulated an influential model of human

development that emphasizes the values of sharing and cooperating. Current psychoanalytic theories place an inordinate stress on loss and psychopathology to explain how people live their lives. Contrary to this position, common wisdom indicates that the central need of human existence is the individual's striving for personal identity, significance, and unification. In short, people can be best understood as acting in such a way as to make their experiences meaningful to them in the context of what they regard as their place in the world.

To move away from pessimistic analytic models requires the recognition that there are many different types of human attachment and development, not the single model Freud (1914) claimed as universal. This change of view would enable analysts to formulate theories of human behavior that are culturally sophisticated, are responsive to female development as well as male, and regard psychological growth as continuous and responsive throughout the life span with the psychological development of significant others.

The language of psychoanalysis must also be reworked. It is not sufficient to change static metapsychological concepts into action language, as psychoanalyst Roy Schafer (1976) suggests, although this is clearly required. Whether or not it was the intention of Freud's translators to disguise his humanistic sentiments by restating his poetic language into scientific-appearing terms, as psychoanalyst Bruno Bettelheim (1983) charges, psychoanalytic discourse today is overly abstract—the actual meanings of many of its concepts are quite obscure.

Analytic concepts are also the language of human foreclosure; that is to say, they are pessimistic about the human capacity for realistic hope, compassion, and responsibility. Current analytic language is a more apt description of inanimate objects than of the motivations of people. Analysts who conceptualize those they treat in dehumanizing ways are likely to treat them accordingly.

4. *Psychoanalysis must be turned toward crucial social and moral problems.* Psychoanalysts have been reluctant to tackle the crucial social issues that most threaten society. That is why Alfred Adler, Harry Stack Sullivan, Karen Horney, Clara Thompson, and other influential analysts became alienated with orthodox theory and practice, and started their own schools of psychoanalysis.

In an ever-increasing progression, psychoanalytic reasoning has **193** been used to evade personal responsibility for harmful acts against others by people of all classes. But in fact it is the affluent and privileged who most benefit from psychoanalytic defenses. For it is they who have the money and wherewithal to hire the most psychologically sophisticated attorneys and obtain the services of leading experts in depth-psychology.

Psychoanalysis has a deserved reputation for the skill of its practitioners in establishing the conditions for a person's lack of responsibility for criminal behavior, with far less skill and attention directed toward uncovering the conditions conducive to a person behaving responsibly. Psychoanalysis will not fulfill its promise until analysts stop promoting a deterministic position that provides an ever-proliferating host of excuses for why people should not be held responsible for their actions.

5. *Psychoanalysis should be returned to all socioeconomic classes.* Psychoanalysts have shown great interest and ingenuity in using analytic reasoning to provide multilayered contexts to works of literature, drama, and culture. They have shown far less interest in the problems of hatred, prejudice, and intolerance that infuse all of our serious social problems. And of course the audience for these sophisticated creative works are the privileged and well educated (Goldberg 2000).

We, as analysts, can no longer allow ourselves to be captive of special interests: a regime in which the best-trained and experienced analysts treat the most affluent and least-disturbed patients, while the most difficult patients are attended to by the least-experienced practitioners. Psychoanalysis must become a torchlight of hope, compassion, and responsibility for all of society.

NOTE

1. Three decades ago, two prominent psychotherapy researchers, C. B. Truax and R. R. Carkhuff (1964), in examining the extensive literature on psychoanalysis and psychotherapy outcome, concluded that the evidence from a large number of empirical studies strongly suggests that on an average, psychoanalysis and psychotherapy "may be as harmful as often as helpful, with an average effect comparable to receiving no help."

Other highly regarded researchers, such as Allen Bergin (1963), Hans Strupp (1963), and Paul Mehl (1972), agree that most analysts and psychotherapists aren't competent. They estimate that only about 20 percent of those who practice are skilled practitioners. As a result, about one patient in ten is a victim of psychonoxious treatment. Many of these toxic practitioners are highly experienced and prestigious members of their profession. Despite the knowledge that these practitioners consistently harm their patients, their reputations are protected by colleagues.

REFERENCES

Bergin, A. 1963. The effects of psychotherapy: Negative effects revisited. *Journal of Counseling Psychotherapy* 10: 244–50.

Bettelheim, B. 1983. *Freud and man's soul.* New York: Knopf.

Chessick, R. D. 1990. Self-analysis: A fool for a patient? *Psychoanalytic Review* 40: 311–40.

Freud, S. [1912] 1990. Recommendations to physicians practising psychoanalysis. In *The standard edition of the complete psychological works of Sigmund Freud*, edited by James Strachey, 12: 109–20. Reprint, New York: W. W. Norton.

— — —. [1914] 1990. On the history of the psycho-analytic movement. *Standard edition.* 14: 7–61.

Goldberg, C. 2000. A humanistic psychology for the new millennium. *Journal of Psychology* (November).

Mehl, P. 1972. Testing the feasibility of major collaborative efforts. In *Changing frontiers in the science of psychotherapy*, edited by A. E. Bergin and H. H. Strupp, 197–208. Chicago: Atherton.

Schafer, R. 1976. *A new language for psychoanalysis.* New Haven, Conn.: Yale University Press.

Strupp, H. 1963. The outcome problem in psychotherapy revisited. *Psychotherapy* 1: 1–11.

Truax, C. B., and and R. R. Carkhuff. 1964. For better or worse: The process of psychotherapeutic personality change. In *Recent advances in the study of behavior change*, edited by C. B. Truax and R. R. Carkhuff, 118–63. Montreal: McGill University Press.

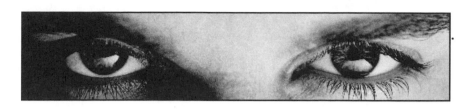

THEORY AND METHOD

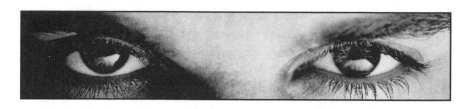

A.
THE DILEMMAS OF
AMERICAN SOCIETY

IN 1895, OXFORD UNIVERSITY PROFESSOR DAVID HARVEY (1989) indicates in *The Conditions of Postmodernity*, people enthusiastically looked ahead to the budding new century, graced with the flowering of the arts, and springing forth with dynamic new scientific inventions: the promise of the good life available to everyone. A century later, most of us anticipate the new millennium with dread.

We live in distrustful and troubled times: disturbed by the unceasing rampage of firearm violence; overwhelmed by daily media reports of child and spousal abuse; tired of paying exorbitant prices in mark-up to organized crime; outraged at the corruption and moral indifference of our public officials; dismayed at continually tripping over the homeless and destitute, who blanket our cities and towns, and imbue our public places with the stench of a soiled, bankrupted, shamed nation. But most of all, we are appalled by the foreclosure of our once optimistic future as a civilization as we enter the new millennium.

Most of us in the United States seem to feel "beaten down" by "the system" in which our society permits our social ills to gain strength and recur. With repetition comes resignation. And from resignation, we too frequently have remained immobilized as a society: we tell ourselves that our societal problems are too complex to solve.

In short, what has largely contributed to our incapacity to deal effectively with our social ills are three issues: an inability to understand a world that is becoming more unfamiliar to us; a lack of vitality to engage this complex world; and the absence of an exemplary societal leader to inspire us for constructive social action by helping us understand what needs to be done.

It is not surprising, then, that when young adults, such as college students, are asked to name their heroes, many say that they can't think of any they would actually regard as a hero.

The loss of constructive societal heroes results from *cynicism* about proper behavior: an adverse reaction to societal permissiveness, a lack of firm values, and an absence of commitment to anyone or anything—except the pursuit of dilettante aims. Cynical people, habitually bored, their inner life unattended, look outside of themselves for revitalization. When we become cynical, we are drawn to self-indulgent others. We are especially fascinated by those who know how to beat the system. We identify with them because secretly we wish to possess this capacity ourselves. We hope that they can serve us as guides and role models for finding the good life: an existence that the three pillars of modern society—religion, science, and education—have not been able to provide.

CYNICISM ABOUT SOCIETAL MORAL VALUES

A willingness to take an active and constructive role in an orderly society is based upon an implicit *social contract*, with the expectation that others will act prudently in accordance with accepted rules of behavior. In other words, if we treat others decently, we expect that they will behave accordingly. However, the Holocaust invalidated our notion of a social contract by radically altering our sense of humanity. The Age of Enlightenment, with its hubristic concept of a superior Western culture, confident of its values and its future, ended with the onset of the

Age of the Holocaust. In short, Nazi Germany gave humanity a shattering moral blow by cynically divesting us of our naive belief that the world in which we live is a just place in which individuals are protected because human life is respected. As a result of the Holocaust, personal innocence that comes from a trust in other people has been lost and the human species desanctified (Nozick 1989).

The pillars of modern society, in failing to explain—let alone prevent—the Nazi genocide and the countless other holocausts and atrocities of the modern era, have effected a serious societal crisis in values. These societal institutions are no longer viewed with the enthusiasm and promise they were accorded at the beginning of the modern era. As such, their ability to establish firm values and constructive goals for living seems limited, if not bankrupted.

However, one may well ask: If what I am stating is valid, how do I explain the fact that whereas in the post–World War II era—the period in which postmodernity began—we still had scores of heroes with virtue and courage as models to emulate, now we have superficial, cynical celebrities?

Our deep cynicism about virtue, I contend, comes from two postmodern factors. The first was the gradual recognition that as terrible as was the slaughter and suffering of the Holocaust, the worst aspect of this horrible tragedy is that it made *no moral difference*; this is to say, humanity has gone on to continue perpetrating atrocities, as if we have learned nothing from the Holocaust. For example, despite the high principles espoused at the Nuremberg war trials, national leaders throughout the world continue to slaughter others—following similar ethnic cleansing practices as those carried out in modernity by the Nazis and the Japanese.

The second factor concerns psychology. For the last several decades, psychology has replaced the former pillars of society as the sine qua non application in all matters in which human endeavor is involved. But, as I indicated previously, the general public *no longer* regards psychoanalysis and psychology as the panaceas they were touted as for decades.

As a result of the factors I have described above, we have little faith in our pillaring societal institutions, psychology, or our fellow humans, and the values derived from them.

Disillusionment with society's moral values has resulted in a *decon-* **201** *struction of reality* for most of us: this is to say, each event we experience is unique—no longer tied into other peoples' experience, or to an overarching system of meanings. Emotionally and morally, many of us experience ourselves alone, unrelated to others. In short, the payoff for our behavior is no longer clear.

In the past certain goals and values were assumed without question to be the basis of the good life: making an adequate living, having a good reputation, receiving the regard and caring of significant people in our lives. For many who are advantaged economically and educationally, the first is too easily obtained, the other two viewed as tired and passé.

As a psychoanalyst, I have treated many young people, for example, young stockbrokers. They were told during their youth that getting into the right schools and making as much money as they could grab in order to acquire all that they desired was the appropriate way to structure their lives. And they did become wealthy, some incredibly affluent, by the time they were thirty, or even earlier. They also were depressed, addicted to hard drugs, and many contemplated suicide.

For still more, despite the sincerity of their efforts, the good life remained elusive. Trying to live the virtuous life in what they experience to be a corrupt and unjust society has resulted in an inability to gain a feeling of well-being.

Under conditions of disillusionment and cynicism, everything is allowable; nothing is too wrong to perpetrate—especially if it amuses us—after all, what other dependable standard do cynical and disillusioned people have than amusement!

THE RESPONSIBILITIES OF PSYCHOANALYSIS

Have I painted too dismal a picture of the moral condition of our postmodern society? Perhaps! However, as a psychoanalyst and social theorist, I believe that psychoanalysis has the potential to provide penetrating insights to advance constructive human behavior which will enable us to formulate the conditions that best foster virtue in our society. At the same time, speaking about virtue has negligible practical import if we lack recognition of constructive options.

My primary assumption in working with clients is that a person's capacity to recognize the constructive options available to live fully and well rests on a sense of competence in fulfilling the roles and responsibilities he has assumed in relationship to significant people in his life. This notion speaks directly to the complexity of postmodern society.

Our contemporary social problems represent the growing difficulty increasing numbers of Americans, following the Second World War, have had in mastering the necessary intellectual, emotional, and interpersonal skills required for competent postmodern functioning. Dealing competently with the changes and intricacies of *historical dislocation*, in which the roles and obligations that bind people together in cooperative relationships in society have lost their traditional meaning, requires a level of psychological understanding that many psychologists, such as Robert Kegan of Harvard University Graduate School of Education, believe few people, even the well educated, possess.

In his book *In Over Our Heads*, Kegan (1994) points out that there is a mismatch between the way most people ordinarily know the world and themselves, and the way that it is necessary to function in order to deal competently with the complexities of postmodernity. It is not simply a matter of competence or incompetence, of course, but of the level and degree of competence required for successful functioning in conjunction with others with whom one is significantly involved. For example, men's roles are more complicated than they were in the past. They have to incorporate into their relationships many of the tasks and expectations previously regarded as women's responsibilities: child rearing and domestic duties, as well as empathy, compassion, and support. Correspondingly, women's roles have become more complicated as women have become an integral part of the business and professional worlds.

The postmodern complexity of both male and female roles cuts across all socioeconomic classes and levels of education. Indeed, although many people can function highly competently in one or more areas of required endeavor, e.g., professionally and/or socially, they are dismal failures in some other important area, say, for example, intimacy. The O. J. Simpson story seems to vividly illustrate this problem in regard to the discrepancy in skill between Simpson's professional and **203** social facilities on the one hand, and his ineptness in relating in an emotionally appropriate way with spouses. Along the same lines, Pablo Picasso, in the film *Surviving Picasso*, is shown as an outstanding genius in his artistic profession, an astute businessman, and a fascinating social companion. At the same time, his fears of intimacy resulted in his infantilizing lovers and wives — creating havoc in all of their lives.

What has caused the need for greater role complexity? In every age of history prior to modernity, only a small cadre of individuals were given access to the wisdom and the resources of their society. They were for the most part the offspring of the social and political elite. Their families ruled every echelon of society. In those periods of history, the demand for personal development for ordinary people was moderate. The Age of Enlightenment, which brought on modernity, however, forged a liberating social contract between the rulers and the ruled. Their compact affirmed that every member of society was entitled to his or her full development as a person. With permission comes responsibility. Those who fail to achieve society's definition of competence are shamed. For example, the role of spouse and that of parent have changed substantially over the past several decades. Adults who have considerable difficulty in assuming postmodern attitudes and responsibilities generally gain little satisfaction from marriage and raise children who themselves are troubled. The use of drugs and guns and the violence they cause are reactions to feelings of shameful incompetence in achieving mature development as defined by cultural standards.

People who are living destructive and/or disturbed lives, according to my clinical experience, have a marked incapacity for intimacy and caring together with a linguistic inability to put felt experience into words required for intimate relating. At times they may be able to identify with others, but then only in transient and restricted ways. In fact, as I have already shown, a person's incapacity for intimacy not only impedes attitudes and responses of compassion and caring, producing a taboo against commiseration with the suffering of others; as importantly, it causes difficulties in *cooperative endeavors* with others that are crucial to the amelioration of many, if not all, of our social problems.

In other words, failing to achieve genuine intimacy, people characteristically try to manipulate and control others. This results in hurt, anger, and counterdefensive reactions. It is ironic but true: a considerable number of people hurt, injure, and even kill those they claim to love. My clinical experience has shown that beneath the vicious persona of violent and destructive people is a great deal of inarticulate hurt with the fear of still further emotional injury.

In short, the liberation of the individual to find his or her full development as a person has accentuated the importance of mature and gratifying human relationships.

To understand how fulfilling relationships are achieved, it is first necessary to recognize that intimate bonding is the basis for all human encounters. I discuss this notion extensively in section C. What I seek to stress here is that we have failed to find solutions to our serious social problems, I believe, because we have tended to focus the problems on the disadvantaged: the underclass, the poor, the deprived, the uneducated, and the deviant—individuals who could not assimilate themselves within societal latitudes of acceptable functioning. The limitation of this position is that, unlike the past, in contemporary society privileged and ordinary citizens are a large part of the problem, as are deviants and the disadvantaged. In short, the people involved in destructive behavior, sociological studies show (Harris et al. 1968; Newton and Zimring 1969), come from all walks of life. It is not surprising, then, as the American sociologists Stark and McEvoy (1970) indicate: physical violence occurs equally as frequently among all income groups and levels of education despite the common assumption that the poor and less educated are more likely to resort to physical forms of aggression to vent frustrations about their failure to achieve a desired emotional life. Correspondingly, of all the destructive people whose case studies I present in this book, only one was a career criminal; most of the others were highly educated professionals.

In sum, the serious problems of our society—violence, drug addiction, family disintegration, and destructive relationships—are pervasive across all socioeconomic and educational strata, perpetrated by those who cannot competently meet postmodern expectations and demands.

REFERENCES

Harris, L., et al. 1969. *Survey by the National Commission on the Cause and Prevention of Violence*, no. PR36,8: v81/J98/2. Washington, D.C.: Government Printing Office.

Harvey, D. 1989. *The conditions of postmodernity*. Cambridge, Mass.: Blackwell.

Kegan, R. 1994. *In over our heads*. Cambridge, Mass.: Harvard University Press.

Newton, G. D., and F. E. Zimring. 1969. *Firearm violence in American life*, no. PR36,8: v81/51. Washington, D.C.: Government Printing Office.

Nozick, R. 1989. *The examined life*. New York: Simon & Schuster.

Stark, R., and J. McEvoy. 1970. Middle-class violence. *Psychology Today* 4: 52–54, 110–12.

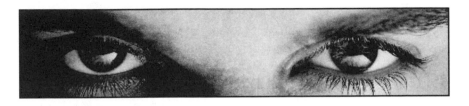

B.
THE EVIL WE DO

The Primary and Secondary Factors
that Promote Destructive Behavior

WHEN WE HEAR ABOUT THE HORRORS COMMITTED BY SERIAL AND mass murderers, we ask why these disturbed people couldn't be detected and helped before they began their heinous careers. Children can be reached by pathways unavailable to us when they are more set in their ways as adults.

Unfortunately, the causes of destructiveness—despite the pervasiveness of violence in American society (Goldberg 1997)—have been poorly understood. Charles Silberman (1978), in his sociohistorical account of crime in the United States, indicates that most of what people believe about destructive behavior is either false or irrelevant, a reference to the knowledge of both behavioral scientists and the general public. Psychologists who study the moral development of children typically have confined their investigations of aberrant behavior to why children lie and steal. Virtually no important studies have been made about the psychological development of children who become involved in serious violence. As a result, psychologists and criminologists cannot accurately point to those youngsters or even adults who are the most prone to violence. This is confirmed by a study reported in the June 1993 *Journal of the American*

Medical Association. Psychiatrists working in the emergency rooms of seven hospitals predicted that 357 patients who were brought in emotionally agitated would become violent within six months. They were right only slightly better than predictions based on chance—53 percent of the cases. Moreover, among a group of patients for whom they predicted no violence during the next six months, 36 percent became involved in destructive acts (Lidz, Mulvey, and Gardner, 1993).

Despite the current state of psychological prediction, it is my contention that the factors that predispose children toward violence are available, but only if we know where to look. Every violent act is driven by compelling forces. No act of violence is senseless, if senseless is meant to imply that the behavior is without understandable motives. Violent acts seem unexplainable only to the extent that we fail to recognize the vicious influences that bear upon children in contemporary society and how children react to these threats. There is something terribly wrong with a nation that has lost track of the needs of its children. Violence by juveniles is a product of our social and domestic conflicts and failures. We live in a society which despite the lavish attention given to children's entertainment largely ignores their basic emotional needs. No less importantly, society often responds ineffectively to those who are caretakers of children.

MURDER BY JUVENILES

Murder is our most fundamental social taboo. It is a sanction forged by the finality of death. Most wrongful actions in life can be corrected; homicide cannot be changed.

A murder committed by a child is even more shocking than one carried out by an adult. The young killer, despite the current commonplace of juvenile homicide, is still viewed as a startling aspect of a murder case. People have conventionally accepted stereotypes from films and television of what a killer should look like. The image of a frightened, withdrawn child in an austere courtroom facing a charge of cold-blooded murder contradicts our cherished beliefs about children.

We claim to be a child-oriented society: children are our hope for the future; childhood is a time of carefree, innocent play, sheltered from the dark side of life. No one wants to believe that an innocent child can turn into a vicious killer. The awareness that children are capable of murder has a dimming effect on the way we view our future as a society.

Until recently murder committed by youth was an anomaly. This has changed radically. Almost every day in some part of the country a juvenile commits a murder; some days several take place. The United States Department of Justice in 1992 reported that the number of homicides in this country by youngsters eighteen years of age or younger had increased 300 percent during the past three decades (DiIulio 1995). In terms of actual numbers, 2,625 murders were committed by juveniles in 1998, according to the Federal Bureau of Investigation (1999). The number of killings of a parent by a juvenile alone averages three hundred a year (Heide 1992). Of course, these numbers do not represent the full extent of the problem. Many serious juvenile offenses are unreported or treated as accidents. And often in the case of younger children who have committed murder, the child is remanded by the juvenile court to a treatment center rather than arrested.

SIGNIFICANT DIFFERENCES AMONG YOUTHFUL MURDERERS

It is important to recognize that juvenile homicide is a social and legal concept, not a scientific one. Any attempt to explain *all* murders committed by youngsters on the basis of a limited number of influences must be rejected as naive. Since there is no single type of child who commits murder, one or a few factors cannot accurately explain murder.

Yet sociological explanations like the widespread watching of television, which glorifies violence, or living under adverse socioeconomic conditions that breed frustration, anger, and susceptibility to drugs, guns, and gang activity have commonly been used by behavioral scientists to account for the sharply rising rate of violence among youngsters.

Behavioral scientists who offer these explanations should know **209** better. Sociological concepts alone cannot accurately account for the motivation that promotes an act of murder.

Simply stated, sociological concepts indicate that the presence of specific social factors in the culture are the causes of violence in that society. But any adequate explanation must pass a rigorous test of validity that consists of three parts. First, it must explain why children who didn't live under these "adverse" social influences—such as, before the advent of television—committed murder. Second, it requires a plausible account of the steps between watching television and committing a violent act. Third, it must provide good reasons why many more children who live under the same social and cultural influences as the perpetrators of murder do *not* commit murder than those who do. Sociological explanations fail all three parts of this test of validity.

On the other hand, even the psychological reasons psychologists offer—the presence of psychosis or severe emotional disturbance, being a victim of sexual and/or physical abuse, having suffered neurological injury, possessing poor intellectual capacity, and so forth—do not provide sufficient understanding of the forces that compel murder. In other words, there are far more unfortunate children who have all of these psychological disabilities yet don't commit murder, while there are youngsters who have only one or a few of these attributes and do commit murder (Benedek and Cornell 1989).

Let us apply this reasoning to the profiles of juvenile murderers. According to the explanations provided by behavioral scientists, most crimes of murder, although deplorable, should be readily understandable. Manifestly many do appear easy to comprehend. For example, certainly some murders are committed by children who have been sexually and/or severely physically abused, or who have watched many hours of television and films imbued with violence. Others were influenced by deviant peers and street gangs who have ready access to firearms, drugs, and other stimulants. And still other juvenile killers have clear signs of brain disease, mental retardation, or serious emotional disturbance.

The problem with this standard profile is that a considerable number of murders committed by youngsters cannot be explained by these criteria (Cornell 1989; Ewing 1990; Reinhardt 1970; Stearns 1957). This is to say, these youthful murderers are not psychotic, do not show apparent signs of serious emotional problems, have no significant physical impairments, are not members of gangs or addicted to drugs, and have not been physically abused or suffered debilitating socioeconomic conditions. Furthermore, they have above-average to superior intellectual capacities. And perhaps most surprising, they have no prior juvenile arrests, no violent history, and no disciplinary problems. In fact, these youths are usually described by people who knew them prior to their murderous act as "sensitive, decent, and polite."

In short, following current scientific formulations we can *only* understand the tensions that compel murder by a rageful child who has been brutalized, deprived, terrified, and pushed by others into crime. In contrast, we are *unable* by these measures to fathom what happens in the depths of the psyches of children who lack the standard psychological and sociological profiles of violent people. The motives of the latter seem *obscure*. This is especially striking when the reasons offered by a youngster of superior intelligence who has murdered are obvious afterthoughts, lacking in insight and plausibility. Furthermore, these crimes are not committed for reasons of material profit, lust, or protection from an immediate physical attack. It is not surprising then that the clinicians and the officers of the court who examine these murderous youngsters with obscure motivation have referred to their crimes as "senseless."

Consequently, when we study the motives of violent children whose actions are not obscured by the veneer of "obvious" reasons — for example, material gain — we are in a propitious position to recognize the deeper reasons behind all acts of violence. Only then can clinicians and society together deal competently with the conditions that give rise to serious violence.

THE THEORY

The concepts I discuss here are based in part on my thirty years of experience as a psychologist who has treated violent youngsters and has supervised other psychotherapists working with disturbed children. My formulation of these concepts also is influenced by discussions with colleagues who have treated children who have murdered, as well as from an examination of the psychological literature. At the time of my investigation there were about a hundred professional publications dating back to the 1930s on children who murdered. But very few were empirical studies. For the most part these reports consist of case studies with an attempt to psychiatrically diagnose the precise disorder which the child suffers. Those studies that do attempt to explain the reasons for the murderous act provide only a solitary motive to account for the child's destructiveness.

My clinical work with children (together with other information discussed above) suggests that there are a number of specific toxic factors in raising children which, when found together, adequately explain why as adults they fail to develop a capacity for emotional connectedness and mutuality with others. Instead, they become involved in destructive behavior:

- Shame vulnerability;
- Benign neglect;
- Inability to mourn;
- Linguistic difficulties expressing feelings; and
- Witnessing significant people who behave as if rageful anger is a legitimate means for dealing with frustration and conflict.

To illustrate these dynamic factors I provide a clinical example for each. These brief anecdotes are not meant to serve as full explanations of a particular murder, but to illustrate a particular primary or secondary factor in the development of the destructive personality. As common sense should suggest, the more prominent the presence of all these factors, the greater will be their impact on a child, and the more likely that the child will commit murderous violence. Moreover, all of the people discussed in the examples, but one, experienced all of the conditions I contend are crucial in the development of a destructive personality, including these primary factors that explain serious violence.

THE PRIMARY FACTORS THAT EXPLAIN SERIOUS VIOLENCE

Shame Vulnerability

The media have given considerable attention to physical and sexual abuse in families. But no less important is the devastating effect of the shameful and humiliating ways many parents, who would be horrified to be called abusive, speak to and treat their children. Verbal shaming of a child consists of words spoken to the child in his presence that undermine the youngster's sense of competence and self-esteem. Humiliating actions are those that treat the child with contempt.

Early and relentless shaming evokes a sense of *badness* in the child. The conviction that she is someway "bad" will be strengthened when others continually inform her—verbally or through their actions—that she is flawed and unwanted. The chronic shame that children suffer prevents them from defining themselves favorably to others, leaving them vulnerable to further neglect and abuse. Prolonged shame invokes self-contempt, which in turn fosters contemptuousness toward others. Family researchers at the University of New Hampshire Yvone Vissing and Murray Straus (1991), in a national representative sample of 3,346 American parents with a child under eighteen living at home, found that 63 percent reported one or more instances of verbal aggression such as swearing and insulting the child. The more verbal aggression used by the parents, the greater was the probability of the child's aggression, delinquency, and interpersonal problems.

A capacity for self-scrutiny mitigates against destructive behavior. However, the more negative a person's sense of self, as a product of a regimen of shame and betrayal, the more painful and less wont a child will be to probe his inner being. Psychologists Blair Justice and Roger Birkman (1972) conducted a study of 173 white inmates of the Texas Department of Corrections to ascertain the factors that differentiated violent from nonviolent inmates. The nonviolent inmates were found to be more prone to self-criticism when their feelings were aggrieved, the violent inmates expressed hostility toward other people rather than self-scrutiny.

THE EVIL WE DO

When Roy was five years old his father deserted the family. Starting at age seven, Roy spent half of his life in psychiatric and forensic institutions. Most of the incidents that led to his detentions involved the sadistic intimidation of women, stopping just short of rape. During psychotherapy with me, he recalled that as a young child he always looked forward to seeing his mother; he felt safe with her. But she died when he was seven, and his sense of security vanished with her. Forever after, Roy felt severely shaken—alone without guidance. Naively, like most children, he had believed that his mother could keep his world safe, just so long as he returned her love with unquestioned devotion. When she died, he felt bitter and betrayed—by her and indeed the entire world.

Trust in ourselves usually develops together with the feeling that we are secure in the world in the hands of significant people in our lives. If our assumption is incorrect, we lose trust—often permanently—not only in other people, but in our own judgment as well. Thus, Roy's sense of well-being and self-worth were overthrown when he realized that his confidence in his mother's capacity to protect him from life's vicissitudes and hurts was misplaced. He underwent feelings that he could neither fathom nor identify. To me it was evident that Roy, like other children thrown on their own too prematurely, had experienced painful shame and fear from the recognition that his fate depended upon others and there was no one he could reliably trust.

Roy's story suggests that often in our lives the shame we experience does not arise from someone's intentional cruelty, indifference, or even ill wishes. Ironically, Roy's shame had its origins in his mother's love; for the more fervently we believe in the benevolent qualities of love and care, the more grievous are the pangs of despair when we are deeply disappointed. Roy's mother tried to shield him by keeping her illness a secret. As she lay dying, he was not allowed to see her or help her in even the small but important ways available to young children. Roy took her unavailability to him as an indication that she lacked confidence in his ability to care for her. His rageful behavior as an adult was a continuous and unsuccessful attempt to expunge the morbid impotence he felt as a child about what he had regarded as her lack of trust in him.

Benign Neglect

This concept refers to the emotional unavailability of parents and caretakers to appropriately respond to the child's needs. It was aptly captured by the television reminder a few years ago that stated: "It is 10 P.M. Do you know where your children are?"

A study in 1994 tried to separate the effects of five kinds of maltreatment: sexual abuse, physical abuse, verbal abuse, emotional neglect, and physical neglect. The finding indicated that the most damaging is emotional neglect (Acocella 1994).

Although the family-of-origin is not the sole agent for socializing children, traditionally it has been regarded as the major influence in personality development.

Benign neglect can be metaphorically described as giving a child a pretty toy rather than a warm and caring embrace. Often it thinly conceals the parents' ambivalence toward their role as parents and adults as well as marked rage and hostility toward each other. Shaming is added to disappointment in not having an available parent: when the child is told that the neglect is in his or her best interest, it will enable the child, for example, to be more self-reliant.

Life is not always reasonable and fair. In each child's life there inevitably will be disappointments and misunderstandings. Nevertheless, the child should be protected from experiencing too frequent and too prolonged emotional pain. On the other hand, if there is too little stimulation in the child's life because he has been thrown on his own when he is still too immature to care for himself, he may acquire an unrelenting hunger for excitement.

Children who develop a precocious restlessness, fed by a craving for stimulation, rarely develop appropriate sensitivity to the subtleties and nuances of life. They can see life only in bold black and white dimensions. These youngsters are directed by an enduring obsession: "I've been cheated, I won't stand for it! I must have my own way! Others won't have their way with me again!" Obviously, these individuals have difficulty empathizing with the pain and suffering of others. Unable to read competently the feelings of those around them, they stumble into conflict which their emotionally more intelligent peers are able to avoid.

Jeffrey Dahmer, the infamous cannibalistic serial killer, is a tragic example of benign neglect. He was a lost child who searched continually for approval and affection, and was never able to secure a sense of emotional security. His parents were professional and well educated. He was never beaten and rarely criticized. He had all of his material and educational needs met. On the other hand, his parents related poorly to each other and their children. His father, a respected chemist, preoccupied himself with research projects to shield himself from his domestic troubles. His severely depressed mother took to her bed for most of the day, and was rarely involved with her two children. After his son's trial, Dr. Dahmer wrote a book which revealed that he and his wife missed what was going on with their son. They didn't seem aware of how tormented he felt (Masters 1993).

Lacking parents as protectors against the unusually many shames and humiliations he experienced as a child, Jeffrey Dahmer couldn't use them as compassionate guides for understanding the world or as models of proper behavior. When young children have to create their own morality, because their parents have left them to their own devices, the result is usually a child who is out of control.

I have stated previously that a considerable number of the murders by youth are committed by those with no past history of violence or extreme behavior. This statement is only apparently accurate. When we carefully investigate the lives of youngsters who are accused of senseless violence, we often find not only a preponderance of the primary destructive factors in their backgrounds, but no less importantly, a series of earlier acts of insensitivity and unkindness. Dahmer's life history supports my contention. From early childhood, he experimented with cruelties he inflicted on small animals. Later he continued his cruel inflictions on other children—until finally, he graduated to sadistic rape, torture, murder, and cannibalism. Because of the lack of monitoring—benign neglect—by his parents and other caretakers, these destructive behaviors went unnoticed or unresponded to by the adults in his upbringing. It is similar with many other destructive youths. William Pollack, a renowned child psychologist who participated with me on a panel on men and violence, remarked at the time, "Boys are in a silent crisis. The only time we notice them is when they pull the trigger."

Inability to Mourn

The brilliant literary psychologist Joseph Conrad, according to his biographer (Meyer 1967), was a secretive man who was reluctant to discuss, even with those closest to him, the painful events of his past. Especially excruciating was the loss of his parents when he was at a tender age. Their absence and the loss of other close caretakers, and his inability to grieve these major hurts, may have prevented Conrad from feeling trust and hopefulness with other people. It compelled him to a world of fantasy in which he was able to control the destinies of those in his psychic world in ways he couldn't with real people (Goldberg 2000).

In other words, children who learn during their age of belief—four to eight, the developmental period in which they are most vulnerable to violations of trust—that they cannot depend upon their caretakers for compassion and security, decide at that early point in their lives that they can survive only by not becoming overly dependent upon others. To rationalize for the loss of caring and concerned others, they decide that they are already very special and don't need anyone else. And they make no efforts to establish mutually satisfying interpersonal relations. Their subsequent behavior, characteristically boastful and expansive, belies their fearful, shamed inner life (Goldberg 1997).

Although Conrad in his personal life was a man who manipulatively demanded the attention of others for his care (Meyer 1967), the protagonists of his novels go to considerable efforts to prove their ability to survive alone. Their endeavors frequently result in disastrous events, as poignantly shown in such novels as *The Heart of Darkness* and *Lord Jim*.

I make no claim that Conrad himself was a violent or destructive person. And if he wasn't, this information is consistent with my theory. This is to say, Meyer's (1967) biography of Conrad strongly suggests that he suffered from four of the five factors that I claim foster a destructive personality. As his novels clearly show, he was capable of expressing the language of felt experience. It well might have been that this capacity saved Conrad from becoming personally destructive, as well as impelled his creative genius. But this is an assumption best reserved for a literary forum.

THE EVIL WE DO

Linguistic Difficulties in Expressing Feelings

Psychologists Blair Justice and Roger Birkman (1972), working in a Texas prison, found that the nonviolent inmates exceeded the violent in expressing "more self-consciousness, which seemed to act as a restraining influence on drastic behavior." But it is crucial to recognize that it is the lack of access to *felt experience*, rather than deficient language skills itself, which is crucial to the personality of destructive people. As children who were made to feel ashamed of having "unacceptable" feelings, their access to the verbal expression of these experiences was impeded. As adults they frequently are pushed toward rage by finding themselves in interpersonal situations in which their psychic vulnerability is painfully exposed in their subliminal sense of a similar vulnerability in another person present in the situation. Unable to express a caring identification with the other because of a deficiency of emotional fluency, they strike out to silence their resurrected hurt.

In 1924 Nathan Leopold and Richard Loeb kidnapped and murdered Bobby Frank, a thirteen-year-old neighbor, the son of a business acquaintance of both their fathers. The media at the time called their heinous deed "The Crime of the Century." No doubt they were referring to the crime as a prototype of senseless murder. The Bobby Frank murder trial, according to the writer Meyer Levin (1956), who covered the proceedings for a Chicago newspaper, was the first to show how victims of murder can be chosen at random: as people, these victims have no importance to the killers.

Nathan Leopold was a brilliant, immensely wealthy eighteen-year-old graduate of one of the finest colleges in the nation. He had been accepted for graduate work at Harvard Law School for the autumn of that year. The wealth of the defendants, from two of the most affluent families in Chicago, and the inexplicable motive for murder, resulted in the most extensive psychiatric investigation of any murder defendants in United States court history up to that time (Weinberg 1989).

Repeatedly asked why he committed the crime, precociously intellectual and articulate Leopold could never provide a reasonable answer. He denied any feelings of remorse. He had done nothing seriously wrong, he claimed. In so doing, Leopold made the tragic assumption that being wealthy and intellectually superior made Loeb and him supermen; everyone, therefore, had to play by their rules.

Few people can live without the support of a social structure that legitimizes their behavior. For Leopold, as for countless other conflicted youngsters, the belief that he was a superior being justified his socially destructive behavior and resulted in the ruin of his brilliant intellectual talent.

Leopold (1958), in his book *Life Plus 99 Years*, indicates that belief in his supremacy was validated by Friedrich Nietzsche's "Superman" theory that was hotly debated by college students of his day. As Leopold interpreted Nietzsche, a superman is a person who is able to maintain such mastery of his feelings that he can murder another person without feeling guilt or regret. Leopold strove to achieve this cold-blooded ideal.

The privilege our society affords the wealthy camouflaged Leopold and Loeb's disturbed psychological dispositions. Emotionally, the psychiatrists who examined them found them to be—despite Leopold and Loeb's high intellect—operating at a six- or seven-year level of emotional maturity. In fact, Loeb still talked to his teddy bear, which he was allowed to keep in his jail cell while awaiting trial (Levin 1956).

It also is ironic that although Leopold was materially and educationally overindulged, he was emotionally deprived by his parents. He was given pretty toys, lavish parties, and introductions to the most influential people in Chicago, but only limited parental contact. He was raised by a governess who waited daily to take him home from school, even as a college freshman. His adoption of a supremacy philosophy was his misbegotten attempt to find a way to figure out how to live his life, using abstract intellectual ideas to substitute for the values of warm, loving caretakers.

Not surprising then, although he was a genius in learning languages (he was supposed to have been able to read and converse in fourteen languages), he lacked the capacity to express articulately his vulnerable feelings. This served to isolate him from his peers. He had been teased and shunned by children his own age for his precocious knowledge and awkward shyness. He had disciplined himself when younger to suppress his feelings.

Witnessing Significant People Who Behave as if Rageful Anger Were a Legitimate Means for Dealing with Frustration and Conflict

In 1960 Dr. Leonard D. Eron, a Yale University psychology professor, embarked on a study to identify the causes of aggressiveness in children. Ten years later he went back and, to his surprise, found that the best predictors of aggressiveness and the likelihood of committing a crime among boys then in their teens had nothing to do with how their parents treated them. It was the amount of television violence they had been exposed to a decade earlier.

Eron's research (1963, 1983) raises an important question about the relationship between aggression and the witnessing of violence in the media: Why after decades of research has no one been able to explain why television adversely affects some people and not others? Eron's findings fail to offer a plausible explanation. However, answers to the following questions should provide a credible explanation: Why in the world would anyone want to watch all the hours of violent television that behavioral scientists like Eron claim youth who commit violent crimes have been exposed to? Are there no other stimulating alternatives in their lives? Where are their parents and caretakers during all the hours they are watching television? And, most importantly, what kinds of relationships do children who have committed violent acts and have logged many hours of watching violent media have with their parents?

I have clinical evidence to respond to the last question. For many of the destructive people I treated, *hypocrisy* was a significant factor in their relationship with parental caretakers. Nora, her story given in chapter 5, told me that she experienced infuriating double standards when her parents punished her for fights at school; she knew of her father's deadly duels to protect his honor. Nora, understandably, was shown that angry outrage is actually acceptable.

In the absence of parental models that encourage compassion and concern for others, youngsters can be profoundly influenced by popular media. Children spend more time watching television than any other part of their day, except sleep (Rubenstein et al. 1972). Eron (1983) found that there is for most children a vulnerable period in their

220

development in which the effect of TV can be especially influential. It is during this period that TV teaches the child that life must be exciting to be worthwhile. For these children, violence-imbued media becomes a habitual means of entertainment that is easily obtained. More importantly, it serves as an untoward guide in making sense of the world in the absence of available constructive caretakers.

The children Eron studied probably were those who were neglected by their caretakers. Children who have caring and available caretakers and stimulating lives don't have the time or the desire for excessive television whether or not the programs are violent. In other words, it is the deprived child who turns to the media for companionship. And if their lives lack stimulation, violent programs provide excitement and modeling. As such, the lack of parental models who demonstrate caring and compassion is one of the five crucial factors in developing a destructive personality.

A woman, who I will refer to as Mrs. Wilma Gibbs, abused and neglected her two sons. She also loathed her wealthy parents, who had disinherited her for marrying an irresponsible man. In turn she instructed her then adolescent sons to steal from her aggressive father and behave abusively toward her passive mother. One of her sons, Peter, who spent most of his time outside of school playing video games in the shopping mall or at home watching television, fatally gunned down his grandmother after she accused him of stealing money from them. The psychiatrist who examined Peter didn't believe that Wilma Gibbs ever directly asked her sons to commit murder. However, her sons were well aware of her feelings toward her parents. The psychiatrist indicated that he believed that Peter committed the murder because he was afraid of losing his seductive relationship with his mother if he didn't give her what she wanted. The other son, George, an assertive young man who had friendships outside of the family, could not be so easily controlled as his older brother. He was not involved in the murder.

Unfortunately, parents increasingly have turned away from their responsibilities as role models and allowed the popular media to assume this critical parental function. Studies conducted by the U.S. Department of Health, Education, and Welfare (Rubenstein et al. 1972) have shown that if a child doesn't obtain good values from his parents, he is unlikely to acquire them from the media.

SECONDARY FACTORS

In many cases in which a child or adolescent commits a serious violent act, in addition to the primary factors discussed above, one or more secondary conditions also contribute to the outrage. These conditions are:

- Parental seduction;
- Heavy exposure to media violence;
- Identification with a philosophy of superiority;
- Conceptual inability to understand death as a permanent event; and
- Family conspiracy.

Parental Seduction

This concept refers to emotional incest (even when no sexual activity actually takes place); it occurs when a mother relates to her son as if he were a spouse. These children are expected to take care of the parent, which includes the role of confidante—discussing adult problems, such as the parent's intimate and sexual relations with other adults. The seduced child has been taught that his emotional needs, often even his basic survival, is dependent upon the seductive parent's demands first being satisfied, as shown in Alex's case in chapter 9.

The "locked-in" child (predominately boys), who has not the social and financial wherewithal to escape, is forced into a dependent, compliant position with the mother; at the same time, significant relationships with other people—in the family and outside—are discouraged.

Typically, fathers or stepfathers of these boys remain relatively uninvolved in family life. In fact, many of them seem implicitly to encourage the intense mother-son relationship since they have trouble meeting the needs of an excessively demanding wife.

The majority of these youngsters are polite, passive, and well behaved. They keep their feelings to themselves and accept the role of surrogate spouse because it seems like the only sure way of receiving adult approval and affection. In other words, they are so interlocked **222** with their parents' psychopathology that nothing seems wrong with them. But their suppressed anger will take a destructive form when combined with the primary factors.

Heavy Exposure to Media Violence

I have already discussed the role of violent media, showing it is of importance only to the extent that parents turn away from their child-care responsibilities, allowing the popular media to usurp their rightful function. Under these circumstance, more than three thousand scholarly studies have demonstrated a direct causal relationship between excessive television watching (and other media viewing) and the development of aggression in viewers. This violent medium is supported by a fallacious myth: Hollywood puts out violent movies which its producers claim is what its youthful audience wants to watch. Actually, children are drawn to action media; films don't have to be violent to hold their attention.

What most importantly needs to be recognized in assessing the effect of media violence on aggressiveness is that young children—especially ages eight to ten—regard what they see on TV as real. As such, they imitate what they see in the media, and will use these shows as role models in how to conduct their lives to the extent that their caretakers fail to monitor what the children see or don't help them separate fiction from reality in these programs.

Identification with a Superiority Philosophy

Many children who grow up under conditions of benign neglect (or in brutal and abusive settings, of course) acquire a supremacy philosophy which purports to reveal the truth about how the social order operates. For the insecure, frightened youngster, it serves as a "surrogate parent," instructing him how to become a dominant agent in the world.

Identifying with a supremacy belief has a heinous adjunctive requirement—the hatred of those who don't possess the alleged attributes of the superior; after all, one is superior only if someone else is inferior.

It would overreach credibility to maintain that a wish to be superior is a major cause of violent behavior. Nevertheless, it can serve as a lethal cru- **223** cible for the primary factors. Our minds are drawn toward belief systems that instruct us how to respond to compelling urges in our psyche. For the rage-impacted child, a belief in superiority can have deadly consequences.

Conceptual Inability to Understand Death as a Permanent State

This concept refers primarily to lethal violence committed by young children. For the young child, an empirical study by psychiatrist Paul Schilder and psychologist David Wechsler (1934) of seventy-six children between the ages of five and eighteen who were psychiatrically evaluated in the children's ward at Bellevue Psychiatric Hospital in New York shows that death does not necessarily signify the end of life. This is verified by an analysis of children's stories and fairy tales. They reveal a common theme: the protagonists of the stories wish a person he or she is angry at to leave their life-space for the moment but to quickly return to life when the person is needed. In these stories, then, a person dead or turned to stone one moment comes back to life in the next. As a child psychologist I observe a similar process in young children's exploratory behavior. In playing with toy figures, for example, children will shoot them down, look at the fallen figures for a moment, then pick them up and start a new game with the "resurrected" toys.

The idea that people killed are not permanently gone allows the child to dehumanize people. It is a normal developmental process found in all children. Nevertheless, it can have serious destructive consequences in that the notion can lead to aggressive behavior toward those the child momentarily hates, especially nowadays. In the past, due to the limitations of the child's physical strength, his hatred and anger rarely was a dangerous threat. In recent times, the availability of firearms to children has given youngsters a lethal power they physiologically lack.

Family Conspiracy

Some of the most troubling cases of violence committed by juveniles are those in which a youngster carries out an especially brutal crime, and when questioned afterward seems not only unremorseful, but genuinely unable to explain his actions. Clinicians have offered various explanations for this disturbing behavior including: amnesia, denial, and psychopathic indifference. But none of these psychological conditions seems to satisfy all of the important details of the cases. There is an explanation, however, that does.

Youngsters who murder with neither remorse nor the ability to explain their actions may do so as an unsuspecting agent of an adult who has slyly encouraged the youngster to kill for the adult's benefit—for example, to remove an unwanted spouse, or a rival, or to insure an inheritance. While it is usually only a parent who has sufficient emotional authority to commission a murderous act with a small child, virtually any strong love figure can manipulate a vulnerable older youth to commit a violent act (Johnson 1959).

THE STEPS TOWARD VIOLENCE

I have still left unexplained how the confluence of these primary and secondary factors results in violent outrage. Studying the lives of my destructive patients, discussions with colleagues, and reading cases in the psychological literature and popular media indicate that seriously destructive people carry around—as a result of suffering from the destructive factors—a repository of injustice, shame, and self-contempt. This precipitous burden fuels both contempt against the world and a sense of unreality. In short, they undergo a trance: a state of vagueness and detachment. The offender feels as if he were a spectator of his own actions: his thoughts are strange and "frozen"; he is carried along mechanically as an automaton; other people seem artificial—they lack affective "color" and vividness. As a result, the offender feels different from his usual sense of who he is, but is unwilling to struggle against the forces that surge within him. The steps toward violence can be outlined as follows[1]:

1. *Shame.* Feelings of shame and humiliation boil within him.
2. *Inarticulateness.* The perpetrator has a linguistic difficulty expressing his shameful hurt—both to himself and to others; instead he experiences self-contempt.

3. *Agitation*. His self-contempt gets converted into intense con-temptuousness, and he is restless and excitable.
4. *Excitement*. He feels energized as he searches for opportunities to express his contempt.
5. *Frenzy*. He experiences a heightened excitement in finding a vul-nerable victim—usually a person who subliminally reminds him of his own hurt and shame.
6. *Attack*. He violates his victim(s) with minimal deliberation.
7. *Quiescence*. The perpetrator feels serene and superior to his victims.

It is of interest to compare recidivists of destructiveness—those who have become acclimated to acting violently—with people who are only situationally violent. The latter are people, normally controlled and well behaved, who become violent under the extreme circumstances of fear, confusion, stress, and traumatic hurt—especially if the experience involves a serious injustice done to them or to a loved one. Because they are not apprenticed in violent expression, many more steps are required for them to overthrow the customary control of their emotions. The spe-cific steps such a person will undergo to commit a violent act are:

1. *Quiescence*. The person is in harmony with other people prior to a painful intrusion in his life.
2. *Intrusion*. An outrage is done to the subject or someone impor-tant to him.
3. *Injustice*. The subject regards the outrage as unjust.
4. *Anomie*. The subject experiences a sudden loss of trust in the social order.
5. *Shame*. The subject feels considerable shame and humiliation for having been mistreated, or for being a helpless observer of a loved one's abuse.
6. *Inarticulateness*. The subject is unable to express articulately his feelings of hurt and injustice.
7. *Self-contempt*. The subject feels self-hatred for the ineffectual way he has dealt with the outrage.
8. *Panic*. His feelings of self-contempt are intolerable; he under-goes strong autonomic nervous system reactions of fear, confu-sion, and intense anger.

9. *Contemptuousness*. Feelings of rage are directed by the subject at those whom he holds responsible for the outrage as well as those who did nothing to stop it.
10. *Rationalization*. Insofar as acting contemptuously is not a customary behavior, the subject needs to justify his angry impulses.
11. *Dehumanization*. Justifying his contempt makes it possible for the subject to temporarily dehumanize those he holds responsible or unhelpful.
12. *Numbing*. Dehumanizing the victim(s) allows the subject to be indifferent about his actions toward them; the transformation of consciousness he incurs is similar to that a butcher might assume in cutting up the carcass of an animal.
13. *Attack*. Violence is directed at the victim(s).
14. *Agitation*. Following the attack, the subject feels shame, regret, and remorse.

NOTE

1. No other clinician has described the specific steps toward violence.

REFERENCES

Acocella, J. 1998. The politics of hysteria. *New Yorker* (April 6): 64–79.

Benedek, E. P., and D. G. Cornell. 1989. Clinical presentations of homicidal adolescents. In *Juvenile Homicide*, edited by E. P. Benedek and D. G. Cornell, 39–57. Washington, D.C.: American Psychiatric Association Press.

DiIulio, J. J. 1995. Crime in America: It's going to get worse. *Reader's Digest* (August): 55–60.

Cornell, D. G. 1989. Causes of juvenile homicide. In *Juvenile Homicide*, edited by E. P. Benedek and D. G. Cornell, 15–16.

Eron, L. D. 1963. Relationship of TV watching habits and aggressive behavior in children. *Journal of Abnormal and Social Psychology* 67: 193–96.

Eron, L. D., et al. 1983. Age trends in the development of aggression, sex typing, and related television habits. *Developmental Psychology* 19: 71–77.

Ewing, C. P. 1990. *Kids who kill*. New York: Avon.

Federal Bureau of Investigation. 1999. *Crime in the United States: Uniform crime reports*. Washington, D.C.: Government Printing Office.

Goldberg, C. 1991. *Understanding shame*. Northvale, N.J.: Jason Aronson.

———. 1997. *Speaking with the devil: Exploring senseless acts of evil*. New York: Penguin.

———. 2000. Limitations to artistic creativity. In *Spirituality, creativity and transcendence*, edited by J. Miller and S. Cook-Greuter, 41–54. Westport, Conn.: Ablex.

Heide, K. M. 1992. *Why kids kill parents*. Columbus: Ohio StateUniversity Press.

Johnson, A. M. 1949. Sanctions for superego lacunae. In *Search Lights on Delinquency*, edited by K. Eissler. New York: International Universities Press.

Justice, B., and R. Birkman. 1972. An effort to distinguish the violent from the nonviolent. *Southern Medical Journal* 65: 703–706.

Kopp, S. B. 1973. The refusal to mourn. In *The Analytic Situation*, edited by H. M. Ruitenbeek, 123–29. Chicago: Aldine.

Leopold, N. F. 1958. *Life plus 99 years*. Garden City, N.Y.: Doubleday.

Levin, M. 1956. *Compulsion*. New York: Simon & Schuster.

Lidz, T., W. Mulvey, and L. Gardner. 1993. The prediction of future violence of patients treated in the emergency department. *Journal of the American Medical Association* 273 (June): 607–12.

Masters, B. 1993. Evil is as evil does: Jeffrey Dahmer. *GQ* (British edition) (March): 79–92.

Meyer, J. 1967. *Joseph Conrad: A psychoanalytic biography*. Princeton, N.J.: Princeton University Press.

Reinhardt, J. M. 1970. *Nothing left but murder*. Lincoln, Nebr.: Johnsen Publishing.

Rubinstein, E. A., et al. 1972. *Television and social behavior: Reports and papers*, volumes I–V. Rockville, Md.: Department of Health, Education and Welfare.

Schilder, P., and D. Wechsler. 1934. The attitude of children toward death. *Journal of Genetic Psychology* 45: 406–51.

Silberman, C. E. 1978. *Criminal violence, criminal justice*. New York: Random House.

Stearns, W. 1957. Murder by adolescents with obscure motivation. *American Journal of Psychiatry* 114: 303–305.

Vissing, Y. M., et al. 1991. Verbal aggression by parents and psychosocial problems of children. *Child Abuse and Neglect* 15: 223–38.

Weinberg, A. 1957. *Attorney for the damned: Clarence Darrow in the courtroom*. Chicago: University of Chicago.

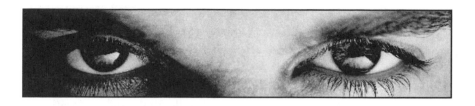

C.
BASIC EMOTIONAL
COMMUNICATION FOR
INTIMACY AND
INTERPERSONAL
CONNECTEDNESS

PEOPLE TODAY UNDERSTAND THEIR INTERPERSONAL NEEDS MORE explicitly and deeply than in the past. There is an expectation that each of us—rich or poor, young or old, well educated or not—is legitimately entitled to the best possible alliances with a right to walk away from unsatisfactory relationships.

Given one wish in life, most people want to be loved—to be able to reveal themselves entirely to another human being and to be embraced by that acceptance. But they also know that taking the emotional risks that allow intimacy to happen isn't easy—for example, one of two new marriages in the United States ends in divorce; countless others exist in name only.

In short, whereas intimate emotional encounter is the human experience most desired, it is at the same time arguably the most feared and avoided. When psychotherapy practitioners closely examine the underlying motives that impel their most difficult cases, they are likely to find that serious addictions like alcoholism, drug abuse, and eating disorders are due to self-medication to innoculate their clients from seeking and failing at intimate relating. Similarly, child and spousal abuse and every type of social probia, to say nothing of sexual problems such as the most common manifestations of male impotence and female frigidity, are indicative of their clients' difficulties with emotional closeness.

Practitioners who treat these psychological problems find that most of their clients feel incompetent to create an intimate alliance regardless of facility in other areas of their lives — intellectual, social, vocational. Few suffer well an inability to secure intimate fulfillment. Self-esteem and the feeling of living well is dependent upon being desired, understood, and appreciated by others. Moreover, a sense of security is bolstered by the awareness of caring others to whom one can turn in time of need. Repeated failure to foster caring from significant others leads directly to the feelings of inadequacy, intense loneliness, and destructive behavior toward self and/or others (Goldberg 1997a).

My thesis here is that the difficulties with intimate relating is responsible for much of the pervasive sense of alienation and existential exhaustion that characterizes postmodern society. Reflective of this malaise, the first international study of major depressive illness, discussed in chapter 1, reports that there has been a steady increase in clinical depression throughout the world in the twentieth century.

THE JOURNEY IN SEARCH OF SELF

There is a need today for socioemotional educational programs that can enable people to minister to their own and significant others' loneliness and despair (Goldberg 1999). To be successful in this endeavor, these programs must work confluently with the alienated individual's need for a personal journey. The journey in search of self is a venerable tradition found in all cultures, in which the seeker examines the course of his existence by means of a continuous series of developmental challenges.

For many the journey is solitary and lonely. We live as we dream, the British novelist Joseph Conrad claims — alone. But it need not be so. Personal growth is best achieved in an open, sharing, and trusting relationship in which both partners are present and involved in seeking an increased awareness of their own identities. In other words, each needs to explore, experience, and come to terms with the contradictory attitudes, assumptions, and ways of being that each has unwittingly assumed in allowing others to define her selfhood.

A cogent "paradox" is implicit in the relationship of those who travel together: how each agent in an intimate relationship may pursue his own journey and fulfillment while at the same time serving as a cooperative partner to the other. D. H. Lawrence, the British writer, describes the ideal intimate relationship as two people who are separate stars, but are more brilliant for their coming together.

BASIC EMOTIONAL COMMUNICATION

In this section I discuss a special type of dialogue which is designed to enhance the interpersonal connectedness of partners in an intimate relationship. I label the endeavor "Basic Emotional Communication" (BEC). It is a dialogue that spells out the specific principles I have alluded to in the clinical studies I have presented.

Dialogue is essential to our nature. We are captive of the verbal concepts our language provides us to shape the parameters in which we define and come to know ourselves and others. It is articulate language, after all, that enables us to be *sentient*: that is to say, capable of understanding others and creating a caring relationship with them. In my clinical and personal experience, couples who achieve desired intimacy in their relationships develop a *private language* with which they work out issues of closeness and constructive boundaries. BEC is designed to enhance relational communication in such a way that the private language of the partners becomes a highly articulate and emotionally stimulating exchange.

BEC consists of an ongoing dialogue between two people involved in a significant interpersonal relationship. This alliance can be between spouses and lovers, of course, but it as relevantly can be intimate encounters between any pair or group of people for whom an increased emotional sanguinity is desired by all.

BEC is positive, self-affirming, and respectful of each other's con-   **231** cerns. It is also psychologically oriented without dredging up the past, and spiritual without the infringement of religious dogma. Admittedly, it is not a quick, simple palliative for self-doubts, anxiety, and stress. It will lead the participant beyond easy answers for life's issues to the expectation of heartfelt responses.

An advanced educational degree is not required for the comprehension of BEC principles and concepts. Any relatively intelligent person involved in an intimate relationship (or, at least, one she seeks to develop into an intimate relationship) can use it profitably, providing that she is able to accept the notion that people are not entrenched personality types; they can modify how they relate to one another with personal effort.

The overall aim of BEC is to create a climate in which the needs and desires of each partner are both heard and responded to—emotionally as well as cognitively. To achieve this aim, an ongoing constructive momentum is required. An energetic analogy of this process would be to keep a Ping-Pong ball in continuous motion on a table through the continuous strokes of each of the two players. The exchange requires that neither player try to cast the ball out of reach of the other by hitting it too hard, too lethargically, or with a tricky movement, otherwise the ball will hit the floor and cease to be in motion; the exchange will end.

There is no set way that BEC should be taught. In working clinically, I conversationally discuss one or more of the principles that pertains to a conflictual issue which is impeding my work with a client. Twenty-five BEC principles are presented here in a progression that moves from "obvious" considerations to more subtle interpersonal and existential processes:

1. *Keep your statements brief*. To converse does not imply that two people are engaged in an authentic exchange. Daily conversations, as the French writer La Rochefoucald points out, frequently are two juxtapositioned monologues, "each is thinking more about what he intends to say than what others are saying—and we never listen when we are eager to speak."

Elaborate and tangential statements are apt to cause your partner to lose the essence of your communicative intent. Clear and terse statements by you make it more convenient for your partner to respond immediately.

2. *Give feedback for clarity*. A person is defined by his statements and actions. He is undefined to the degree that he remains passive and

undisclosed. The more self-defined a person is, the less others need to interpret him. Consequently, to the extent that you address descriptions of yourself by your partner that are inaccurate, constricting, or inauthentic definitions of how you intend to present yourself, you are able to define yourself in a constructive way.

It is useful, therefore, to periodically "play back" (summarize) what you have heard from your partner as objectively as you can. This provides a verbal mirror for your partner to reflect on what he is presenting to you and how it is received.

3. *Appreciate the nonverbal language you and your partner communicate.* Each person continually conveys signals — directly (verbally) and indirectly (nonverbally) — about what she wants and expects from others. Because much of what is elicited is nonverbal, people are largely ignorant of the messages and the attitudes and moods they foster in others. To become aware one must reorient oneself to one's bodily being. In the monitor of one's physical postures one detects discrepancies between what one verbally and nonverbally is communicating.

4. *Keep the momentum going in the dialogue.* A relationship feeds on the balance of energies contributed by the partners. You cannot, therefore, allow the exchange to abort by you becoming upset, angry, and tuning your partner out of your interest and responsiveness.

5. *Use active terms in the dialogue.* People experience themselves and others in terms of the conceptualizations employed in the language they use to communicate. The excessive use of passive terms reveals the passive use of self and the speaker's perception of himself as tentative-in-the-world, which leads to a loss of momentum in the dialogue. The use of active, dynamic terms and descriptions (i.e., the use of the first and second person, and active verbs), in contrast, helps to keep the momentum vibrant in an exchange.

6. *Speak directly and personally to your partner.* Assume that your partner has no previous information about you, so that the other must get to know you entirely on the basis of what you are willing to reveal in each specific encounter you have together. Partners, such as couples married for many years, may resist this directive. Once they begin to practice it, however, they usually find that they don't know each other nearly as well emotionally as they have assumed.

7. *Make "I" statements rather than "you" statements.* To move yourself   **233**

and your partner toward direct, positive statements of needs and desires, take active ownership of your statements about your presence in a dialogue. This endeavor will minimize your tendency to make statements that are critical and blaming, implying that you are the righteous person in a relationship, whereas your partner is the saboteur.

8. *Make personal statements out of your questions.* Most people try to get to know another person factually; they ask endless questions as if they were interviewers seeking to write the other's life story. To the extent the "interviewer" doesn't trust his own feelings and judgments about the other, he compares his factual information with what he knows about other people. On this basis he seeks to make sense of who his partner seems to be. However, endless questions, which require excessive intellectual reflection, tend to dissipate the momentum in a dialogue. Your personal statements indicate your willingness to be direct with your partner. Take the risk! Trust your own intuition and respond personally to your partner!

9. *Move from statements of needs to a statement of preference.* Necessity and preference are often confused conceptually as well as emotionally. Most people can meet their basic needs in order to survive, but they don't experience the "permission" to acquire more than survival provisions. Consequently, many people force themselves into positions of isolation, desperation, and despair in order to secure human contact and concern. You don't have to need a caring response from your partner to want it and have a legitimate right to ask for it.

10. *Make statements of your present needs rather than focusing on the frustrations of the past.* Conflict in intimate relations often centers around arguments about what a partner did or did not do in some previous encounter. Behavior that occurred in the past is no longer available for modification; it is from the start concluded (fixed) and closed (non-negotiable). Only the present and future are open and available. A statement of your present feelings moves the exchange onto an emotional and experiential plane in which the needs and desires of both partners are available to explore, share, and negotiate.

11. *Make statements of your desired expectations rather than of what you hope to avoid.* Psychologically, it is easier to initiate new behaviors than it is to terminate old patterns. Hence, it is necessary for you to explicitly inform your partner *what* new behaviors by your partner would be

gratifying to you rather than focus on behaviors of his you want terminated. To accomplish this you need to regard your partner as capable of responsible and rational agreement or disagreement with your requests. Using a "constructively selfish" approach, you ask directly for what you want and don't apologize for your wants, and certainly don't "protect" your partner from the "selfishness" of your requests.

12. *Specify exactly what you want and when it is most needed.* Psychologically, an individual can best adjust his behavior in a situation in which he knows specifically *when* these acts are most crucial to his partner, as opposed to an interpersonal regime in which he is expected to adopt new behaviors, pervasively terminating existing ones.

13. *Be aware that the depth and quality of your interpersonal involvement in an intimate relationship is dependent on your interpersonal risks.* An irrational fear militates against open communication of the needs of many of the couples I work with in psychotherapy. Their fear is that by direct communication of their needs, they give their partner the opportunity to hurt them in a way less possible when needs are expressed indirectly. It is as if these couples regard emotional risk as situations in which they have more to lose than gain. Their assumption is irrational because it fails to recognize that indirect communication will not prevent the other from locating one's vulnerabilities, it will only make it more difficult for the caring partner to respond to one's deeper needs.

14. *Use subjective clauses of speech which perpetrate active intent toward your partner rather than those which cause cessation of action and of sharing.* Beware in yourself of the tendency to use "negative qualifying" subjunctive clauses in your dialogue with your partner when you are feeling fearful. The use of the term "but" is a ubiquitous manifestation of this passive communicative tendency. For example, "I want to get close to you, *but* I am afraid ("... *but* I don't know how," or "... *but* I don't know if it is safe," and so forth). A rather different psychological attitude is expressed by changing "buts" to "ands." For example, "I want to get close to you *and* I am afraid." A more open and courageous sentiment is evinced by admitting the fear and including it in the struggle to become more intimate. In other words, "but" clauses are statements of isolation and closure. When contained in statements about intimacy they imply the problem with intimacy is entirely that of the speaker, which she must somehow overcome by herself. Since inti- **235**

macy is an expression of a shared endeavor, the difficulties of one of the partners is a legitimate concern for both. "And" clauses invite sharing.

As I have already indicated, attempts at emotional closeness are often desperate reactions to the fear of abandonment and loneliness. Negative subjunctive clauses also play a crucial role in the desperation of loneliness. For example, it is rare that a person alone feels lost, empty, or desperate at the first moments of being alone. Rather, these adverse emotions are contingent upon a *subjunctive clause* in which the person alone judges and evaluates his state of being and comes to the conclusion that his aloneness is likely to be permanent. In other words, loneliness and desperation comes from the statement to one's self, "I am not with anyone at this moment, which is all right, *but* I fear that this condition will continue. I will always be alone. I cannot bear that thought!"

15. *Periodically attempt new modes of behavior with your partner.* The cautious intellectualized person becomes isolated and detached in a dialogue because she feels a need to express only statements about which she feels relatively certain. This cautious stance erodes the dialogue until it loses its momentum. A basic emotional exchange is intended to be an opportunity for you to explore uncertain, uncomfortable, and threatening aspects of yourself with a trusted partner. It is particularly relevant "to do something different" when you feel dissatisfied with an intimate relationship rather than wait for your partner to initiate change. After all, you are the one who is feeling dissatisfied.

To the extent that a person feels the necessity to maintain typical modes of behavior, he is threatened by a loss of the essence of his "real" self. But to the extent that he is willing to attempt new behaviors periodically, he experiences energy and expansion of self in ways that are likely to be more authentic than his habitual self. In other words, no one ever changes and becomes someone else. We can only "change" and become more of who we actually are.

16. *Say no, but never say never!* View the dialogue as an experiential laboratory in which you are searching for awareness of who you and your partner are rather than a situation in which your personal limitations are to be judged and morally condemned. Let your partner know where you are at the moment, but leave the possibility of modification, especially in accommodating your partner's requests, open for the future. In fact, if you experience yourself unable or unwilling to meet

the needs of your partner, don't say never. Let her know exactly when you will respond to her requests, or, at least, when you would be willing to seriously reexamine these requests with her.

17. *View your strong negative feelings in a dialogue as indicators of your suppressed intentionality.* If in an exchange you feel bored, misunderstood, or uncared about, you are advised to act constructively rather than withdraw from the exchange and wait for your partner to change the dialogue. Interpret feelings of discomfort not as a warning that the exchange is ill-advised, but as an indication that you have allowed some important personal attribute to become suppressed.

18. *When you experience unfulfilled satisfaction from your partner, initiate the very behaviors toward your partner that you wish from her.* If you feel unloved, for example, it is likely that you are treating yourself as unlovable. Most people unwittingly treat others as the other conveys she deserves to be treated (which is very different, of course, from how she consciously wants to be treated). This is why many people complain that they get the same kinds of responses regardless of with whom they are involved. An astute person recognizes that one acts lovingly toward another only partially to evoke caring responses from the other; as important, caring for others elicits desirable responses in oneself.

19. *Act with your partner as if he is the person with whom ideally you would like to be involved and as if you are the person you ideally intend to be.* I view personality as a process—not a fixed entity. A person becomes that who he seeks to be through action and intent rather than from intellectual introspection of his past vicissitudes. Similarly, a person is shaped toward becoming the kind of person we seek her to be when she is treated as if she were already that person. In short, our intent toward our partner serves as a role model for the desired attributes we seek in our partner.

20. *When examining conflict in an intimate relationship, avoid interpretations and value judgments.* Employing psychological interpretations and moral value judgments of your partner's behavior causes an imbalance in the relationship. This informs your partner that his behavior needs to be morally restructured according to your idiosyncratic view of what is right and proper. Blaming interpersonal difficulties in the relationship on the psychopathology of your partner rather than recognizing the complexity of the task and helping your partner with these difficulties in a constructive way is destructive, of course, to attempts at inti- **237**

mate relating. Describe the nature of the conflict in as objective and functional terms as you can.

21. *Recognize that you and your partner are not responsible in an intimate relationship to any external agent or system of morality.* In a relationship in which there is conflict, each of the partners attempts to manipulate the other based upon the authority of external systems of morality. Functional dialogues result from recognizing the self-generative nature of emotional closeness: intimate relationships require explicitly negotiated norms established together by the partners.

22. *Be prepared to renegotiate the terms of your interpersonal relationship as an ongoing process in your dialogue.* Each person in his or her own way tries to escape the awesome responsibilities of creative and destructive capacities. Each, some more than others, acts as if she were a mere player entrusted to perform some inscrutable author's dictates, unequipped to rephrase, modify, reinterpret, or modernize a single line in her life script or to act impromptu in the exigencies of her daily life.

Because the dialogue between you and your partner represents a contractual agreement between just the two of you, it should when necessary be open to renegotiation in order to improve your functioning together. For example, a societally sanctioned way for canceling out acts of inequality, insensitivity, and mistreatment is to say "I'm sorry!" This too-often-perfunctory statement usually does not assuage adverse feelings. But people usually allow it to stand, nevertheless. In Basic Emotional Communication the recipient of the apology asks for proper redress of a grievance rather than a perfunctory apology.

23. *Avoid asking for or giving declarations of essence.* Many of the depressed clients I treat in psychotherapy are caught up in the tragic "romantic" trap of saying, "I don't really care how he (or she) treats me, as long as I know he (or she) really loves me," and "I don't care whether the relationship ends or not as long as I know he (or she) loved me." Love, like any other emotional quality, is not a singular essence that is captured by a declaration. It is a series of specific ways of relating to another person. In an intimate relationship the partner who refuses to ask directly for specific equitable and caring responses from her partner is left with an empty declaration.

24. *Your full presence in a dialogue comes from the encouragement of denied and underrepresented aspects of your personality.* Creative growth, as the ancient Greeks well understood, requires the reconciliation of oppo-

sites. Advancement in psychological maturity is thwarted by one's failure to harmoniously amalgamate psychologically antagonistic trends in one's personality. Too much emphasis given to one side or the other of these natural dichotomies fosters personal imbalance and tension, creating conflict between the partners.

A person's energetic presence in a dialogue comes from the harmony and balance of natural rhythm—passivity and activity, thought and emotion, intense involvement and objective observation, and so forth. Each partner can enable the other to be more fully present by enabling the other to experience those aspects of himself that are underrepresented in their dialogue.

25. *Ask for compensation to restore balance and equity in an intimate relationship.* We live in an age in which people are not wont to act toward us in ways we regard as just or fair. One's usual reaction to these acts of inequality is feelings of shame, anger, and resentment. Your unacknowledged untoward feelings toward your partner impede intimate and cooperative endeavors. It is your responsibility to yourself, as well as to your partner, to educate him about his responsibilities to you. When you ask your partner for interpersonal compensation for unfair treatment, and you do so with a legitimate sense of entitlement, balance and equity are restored to the relationship, which helps to dissipate anger and other adverse feelings from contaminating your interactions.

COMMUNICATION WITH DESTRUCTIVE PEOPLE

Obviously, dialogue with a destructive person imposes added difficulties—and even dangers—to one's daily dealings with people. It is important, therefore, to recognize that one is dealing with a destructive person. People who have committed destructive acts in the past are far more likely to do so again than someone without a history of such behavior. However, we live in a world in which most of us continually come into contact with strangers—people whose histories we don't know. It is to our advantage to be able to detect clues that we are interacting with a person who has strong destructive tendencies.

THE EVIL WE DO

In working with the destructive people I have described in this book, I became aware of ten "tip-offs" for detecting potentially dangerous people in personal relationships as well as in my professional duties. These indications are:

1. More than other people, a destructive person is likely to shift radically in his attitude and behavior toward you, almost in the blink of an eye. One moment, the two of you are having a warm, pleasant conversation, the next, he lashes out at you with a bitterness that seems completely unrelated to your interaction. My clinical experience suggests that this startling behavior is sparked when you unwittingly communicate a word, idea, or feeling that has a strong shaming effect upon him. Once this happens, there is no easy way to reason with and disarm his anger.

2. Typically, a destructive person tries to draw you into a scenario that is based on his exciting and/or disturbing fantasy about you rather than upon your actual preferences. One giveaway clue is his claim that your existence is boring and meaningless because you are either unpassionate or too cowardly to take risks to enhance your life. He, on the other hand, leads an exciting life and can make yours the same.

3. No matter what you do or say, it isn't right in his eyes. He accuses you of attitudes and motivations that are not consistent with your sense of yourself. If you protest or try to defend yourself, he is unmoved, acting as if he knows you better than you know yourself.

4. The sheer magnitude of his displeasure with the way he describes your behavior—a claim that you find inaccurate—suggests that he is reacting to you as a feared and hated person from his past.

5. His attitude and behavior reek of resentment and contempt. His desire for revenge is heavily rationalized—his victims, he reports, get what they deserve.

6. He regards other people as very different from himself. You should be especially concerned if it becomes apparent that he is unable to recognize that others deserve the same respect and protection he does.

7. He seems to take pride in admitting that his values and morals are regarded by conventional society as heinous. In fact, he justifies his morality as the product of his strength, his cleverness, and his superiority, while disdaining other peoples' behavior as a product of fear and inferiority.

8. The only topics he will discuss and the only issues he will respond to are those in which he is highly knowledgeable and competent. He adroitly eschews everything in which he is less than superior.

9. He admits only one discrepancy between his ideal personal identity and his present identity: other people misunderstand him and as a result don't recognize his superiority and social value.

10. Unable to tolerate his own hurt and vulnerability, he tries to hide his personal weaknesses from himself as well as from others.

THE PSYCHOLOGICAL TREATMENT OF DESTRUCTIVE PEOPLE

I have shown in the case studies in this book how as a psychoanalyst and psychotherapist I have dealt with clients who exhibited the tendencies I have enumerated above. The underlying assumption of my treatment approach is that the destructive client's behavior is a product of his unacknowledged shame and despair (Goldberg 1997b). Therefore, to dialogue with a destructive client in a constructive way, his shame and despair must be treated first. There are seven essential steps I typically address in working with destructive people. They are:

1. *The client learns to recognize the presence of shame in the ways he becomes distressed and unhappy.*

The purpose of the first step is to help the client gain specific, trustworthy ways of recognizing the messages from himself and from others that broadcast his feelings of self-blame and worthlessness. A person recognizes his shame once he can designate a specific set of thoughts and feelings with that label. I estimate that over 90 percent of the time when we are shamed we are unable to properly identify what is bothering us. Shame is usually misidentifiable as a physiological discomfort or mislabeled as guilt or other emotions.

In early sessions of clinical work I trace with the client those shaming messages to their original source. By exploring the client's current traumatic patterns of relating to people with how others have treated him in the past, the client becomes aware that his earlier profu- **241** sion of negative criticism and harsh judgments have evolved into a present *punitive inner negative voice* that rarely affords him the acknowledgement that he has ever done anything praiseworthy. Instead, his reproachful inner voice hurls the same accusations at his adult behavior as hurtful others did during his tender developmental years. By keeping a notebook or journal to record the judgments of the inner voice the client is usually startled by the frequent incident of his reproaching voice and how readily feelings of despair accompany its shaming presence.

   2. The client shares his sense of shame with a concerned and caring other.

   In addition to regular analytic or psychotherapy sessions with me, I encourage the client to discuss his suppressed shameful feelings with at least one caring person of his acquaintance. The purgation of heretofore hidden shameful feelings enables him in the presence of a concerned other to root out, closely examine, and then repudiate painful feelings about himself that are inaccurate, unreasonable, and unfair. In regard to shameful self-accusations that are more accurate, the client—with the guide of the other's life experiences—is given an opportunity to recognize his *pluralistic ignorance*. In other words, the shame-vulnerable person in the process of sharing his adverse feelings is startled to realize that he is not alone in his distress. Many, if not most, people struggle with feelings of self-contempt and despair. The client's isolation is a result of the misconception that he is alone in his shame and despair. While a psychotherapist may point this out, it is usually more easily believed by the client when said by a friend. Well-conducted support groups are useful here. In private practice and in institutional work I frequently used group psychotherapy to treat destructive patients.

   3. The client must discover his "hurt" voice and give it support.

   Because the client's punitive inner voice has inundated his sense of self with shame and despair, he has been unaware of the tentative but authentic voice of his child and adolescent longings. Shame and despair result from the bitter disappointment that the client experiences upon recognizing that he has lost or has never had a clear direction about how to live his life meaningfully and well. I encourage him to express the sadness and loneliness he has harbored from his failure to achieve the intimacy and closeness he has always craved.

4. The client learns the language of articulate emotion in order to give his "hurt" self a clear voice.

Once the client finds the precise negative messages that he is continually broadcasting to himself, it is time to start changing these hurtful and shaming messages. To give him a different voice, a new language must be learned. It is the language of *emotionality*—the principles of BEC are examples. Reading poetry, evocative literature, and drama may help the poorly educated client develop a language of emotionality.

A very essential dimension of the therapeutic encounter has to do with my teaching the client not only how to use emotionally expressive and meaningful words to communicate his inner needs, but also for me to provide a discretionary guide for when it is appropriate and when ill-advised to express openly and directly his innermost feelings to others.

5. The client defines himself to his "hurt" voice as the person he intends to be.

I discuss with the client the importance of giving his "voice of longing" clear and legitimate entitlement and vibrance by speaking to others as if he already were the person he seeks to be. As I indicated previously in this chapter, we begin to become the person we intend by acting as if we were that person.

6. The client halts the vicious cycle of being humiliated, feeling ashamed and hiding from oneself and others, then feeling additional shame and weakness for one's cowardice in dealing with one's conflictual issues.

To stop this destructive pattern, the client uses the newly acquired skills from the preceding five steps to repair existing relationships and to explore challenging and healthy new ones. The client is encouraged to define himself positively and insist that other people behave toward him in decent and nonhostile ways.

7. The client helps others heal their shame.

To overcome the magnification of self-importance, which I discussed previously as a serious adverse side-effect of psychoanalysis and psychotherapy, the client needs to recognize that the world doesn't begin and end with him. This final step encourages the formerly toxically shamed client to help others deal with their shame and despair. In effect, the client applies what he has learned to help himself to assist **243** others, and as result, enhances his sense of equity and balance in how he lives his life. These altruistic activities are best achieved by participation in areas of life that in the past he avoided.

REFERENCES

Cross-National Collaborative Group. 1992. The changing role of major depression: Cross-national compassions. *Journal of the American Medical Association* 268: 3098–3105.

Goldberg, C. 1997a. Chautauqua Institution lecture: The responsibilities of virtue. *International Journal of Psychotherapy* 2: 179–91.

— — —. 1997b. *Speaking with the devil: Exploring senseless acts of evil.* New York: Penguin.

— — —. 1999. Psychoanalysis and moral apathy. *International Journal of Psychotherapy* 4: 329–36.

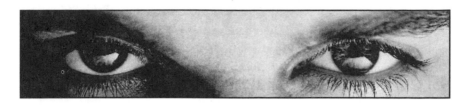

GLOSSARY

Agency. An individual's experience of freedom of choice based on the feeling that she is capable of behaving as the person she intends to be is called *agency*.

Apperceptive sense. A person who responds to a situation, not in a naive and uninitiated way, but guided by previous experience with aspects of the new situation, is said to be using his apperceptive sense.

Attachment theory. Child development researcher and psychoanalyst John Bowlby indicates that to speak of a child as "attached to, or has an attachment to, someone means that he is strongly disposed to seek proximity to and contact with a specific figure and to do so in certain situations, notably when he is frightened, tired or ill" (John Bowlby, *Attachment* [New York: Basic Books, 1982], 371).

Bicameral mind. According to Professor Julian Jaynes of Princeton University, prior to 10,000 B.C.E. in human history, auditory hallucinations served to orient and direct humankind not yet intellectually evolved enough to exercise deliberate personal self-control. In other words, when a person from that period thought he heard the voice of a god telling him what to do, the voice actually originated in the person's right brain and was heard in the left, as if through a radio transmitter. (Julian Jaynes, *The Origins of Consciousness in the Breakdown of the Bicameral Mind* [Boston: Houghton Mifflin, 1990])

Borrowing shame. The ways that people, particularly children, acquire their feelings of shame are usually quite subtle. Borrowing shame refers to an unaware person taking on and assuming the ashamed feelings of someone important to him or herself.

Countertransference of analyst. Both analyst and client behave at various moments in analytic sessions as if the other participant in the encounter is a person from his or her past. Countertransference refers to the analyst's responses toward the client, as a result of regressed or suppressed feelings, as if the client was someone else.

Depersonalization. Psychological conflict may cause a person to lose her sense of reality. During her depersonalization the event seems dreamlike, her body detached and withdrawn from the experience.

Depth psychology. Schools of psychology that derive from Sigmund Freud's theories are called *depth psychologies*: they seek to uncover dynamic psychic events that are not readily apparent to the psychologically untrained observer.

Epiphenomenal events. Events often seem linked to one another, but are not. *Epiphenomena* refers to events that appear to be but are not causally related.

Existential psychology. According to humanistic psychoanalyst Rollo May, existential psychology "does not purport to found a new school as over and against other schools or to give new techniques of therapy as over and against other techniques. It seeks rather, to analyze the structure of human existence—an enterprise which, if successful, should yield an understanding of the reality underlying all situations of human beings in crisis" (Rollo May, *Existence* [New York: Basic Books], 7).

Humanistic psychology. Humanistic psychotherapist James Bugenthal describes the task of humanistic psychology as "the preparation of a complete description of what it means to be alive as a human being. . . . Recognizing that such an ultimate description is an orientating goal, not an imminently expected attainment, the humanistic psychologist concerns himself with those aspects of the human experience which have importance in daily living" (James Bugenthal, *The Challenges of Humanistic Psychology* [New York: McGraw-Hill], 1967, 7).

Identification denial. To the extent that a person finds certain aspects of his personality unacceptable to his personal identity, let's say, unreasonable anger, detachment, or narrow-mindedness, he is apt to find his threatening attribute in (an)other person(s), rather than in himself. For example, the analyst who feels bored or finds his client resistant may on close examination find that his conflict with the client is due to his unwillingness to recognize certain important similarities between himself and his client.

Idiographic data. Psychological research is either nomothetic or idiographic. The former consists of an investigation of a selected number of attributes of a large number of subjects. The latter refers to evidence based on an in-depth investigation of a few subjects.

Inner negation as a psychological defense. This psychological defense is a form of denial, in which the subject immediately or quickly afterwards repudiates a thought or feeling that she has expressed.

Intrapsychic process. Western psychology as a conceptual and scientific enterprise regards the skin-encapsulated self as its primary unit of concern. Intrapsychic events refer to the psychological processes that occur "inside" that unit. Moreover, the term usually implies that these processes are not readily available to conscious scrutiny.

Introjection as a psychological process. *Introject* refers to the mental process in which the infant incorporates parental commands and prohibitions and those of other significant others into the self. The infant-as-adult behaves as if these values were of its own invention.

247

Legitimate entitlement. Legitimate entitlement denotes a healthy sense of self: implied is that the subject is entitled to find and to gain friendships with the most appealing, interesting, and worthwhile people available. This entitlement is based on the subject's feeling that she is able to provide the best interpersonal exchanges with those with whom she seeks friendship and intimacy. It can be contrasted with narcissistic entitlement which refers to the subject's pleading, demanding, manipulating, or some other desperate seeking of interpersonal and material resources on the basis of one's privation, illness, inferiority, or so forth.

Magical thinking. The primitive belief that wishing for or merely thinking about an event has the power to make the event actually happen is called *magical thinking*.

Metapsychology. *Metapsychology* is used here to refer to Freud's major theoretical notion: all psychological events have a corresponding physical and chemical base. This base, according to Freud, because it is the language of the natural sciences, is fundamental and must be the ultimate explanatory discourse for human behavior.

Moral masochism. Freud claimed that many of his patients didn't experience their feelings of guilt directly; instead, they suffered from illness, financial loss, failure in romance, or some other punishment for their unconscious feelings. Freud referred to this behavior as *moral masochism*.

Narrative truth. Freud assumed that the actual events of the patient's past could be captured and accurately described by the analysand if the proper analytic technique was applied to the patient's report. Neither Freud nor any other analyst has been able to design such a veracious analytic tool. Increasingly, analysts have come to doubt Freud's assumption about historical truth in psychoanalysis. Most now regard the patient's report as a product of his attempt to make meaning of his life in the context of his relationship with the analyst. This report is called *narrative truth*.

Normative data. Normative data refers to scientific attempts to ascertain the degree and patterning of attributes of interest to the investigator. In the Western psychological tradition, the investigation of one or a few traits of a large number of subjects is usually preferred to that of the holistic study of a few subjects. Normative data, therefore, typically consists of discrete factors rather than holistic evidence.

Ontological concerns. *Ontology* refers to a priori notions about the essential nature of existence. As these assumptions appear unable to be empirically verified, they are based upon belief rather than hard evidence.

Overdetermined event. Psychoanalysts claim that complex behavior cannot adequately be explained by any single causal factor, such as a perpetrator committing a violent act because he disliked what was said to him by the victim. Other important variables are also involved—for example, the victim reminded the assailant of a police officer who had brutally beaten him; moreover, his wife had deserted him, after telling him that he was inadequate as a man, and so forth.

Paradigmatic leaders. Important historical figures, such as Socrates, Moses, Jesus, Mohammed, and Buddha, who in both their public and private lives inspired their followers to affirmative social and moral behavior are referred to as *paradigmatic leaders, paradigmatic* referring to example or model.

Personal identity. An individual's personal identity consists not only of the sense of who he currently is, but also of beliefs and desires about who he should be and what he can become. From this context, every action and interaction on his part may be judged in terms of the information it provides for either substantiating or disconfirming the self the individual desires to be.

Personal statement. Personal statements are verbal and/or nonverbal communications in which the informant conveys her perceptions and judgments in a direct and undisguised way. They generally refer to statements about someone with whom the informant has a significant relationship.

Personal strategies. Individuals greatly differ in their willingness to withstand anxiety and uncertainty in quest of the resources they seek in life. *Personal strategies* refers to the notions people have about how to secure the objects of their wants and desires in tandem with the degree of anxiety and uncertainty they are willing to endure.

Phenomenological data. Evidence that is based on a subject's naive response to an event is called *phenomenological*. This data contains minimal interpretation and evaluation.

Phylogenetic explanation. Psychologists have borrowed the notion from biological theory that certain behaviors are inexorably set in human development. This patterning of behavior is thought to be a rehearsing of humankind's primitive ancestry.

Preoedipal period. According to psychoanalytic theory, the preoedipal period in a child's life is that in which he has the closest and most exclusive relationship with his primary caretaker. As the term suggests, it precedes the oedipal years.

Recovery ethics. The values and attitudes that are crucial in a criminal offender's overthrowing his antisocial, immoral life is referred to as *recovery ethics*.

Reductionistic explanation. A theory is a model of behavior that tries to approximate what is operative in the actual behavior. But no psychological theory at the present time can comprehensively explain all instances of a complex behavior. As such, psychological theories are compromises of one sort or another. However, some theories are more overly simplistic than are others. Reductionistic explanations are those that try to account for complex behavior by one or two factors.

Regression as a psychological defense. *Psychological regression* refers to the less mature psychological activity of a person who is undergoing severe psychological conflict. In a regressive state, the person is less aware of his feelings and motives than he is normally. He is more able to blame others rather than taking responsibility for how he influences his situation.

Resistance analysis. Resistances in psychotherapy are those interactions between therapist and client in which they are not working cooperatively together. Resistance analysis refers to an examination of the factors that have interfered with constructive therapeutic work.

Solipsistic assumptions. Certain assumptions people make about the world are limited to that person's personal experiences. And the subject is unwilling to reexamine these assumptions in the light of other peoples' experiences and expertise. These assumptions are solipsistic.

Superego. The superego is that part of the mind that incorporates the values and attitudes of the subject's parents with that of society-at-large. Accordingly, the superego may be in conflict if there is a significant discrepancy between the standards of society and those of the subject's parents.

Suppression as a psychological defense. *Psychological suppression* refers to a defensive strategy in which a person in psychological conflict pushes the motives for his dysfunctional behavior out of consciousness. According to psychoanalytic theory, these motives are retrievable.

Teleological explanations. *Teleology* is employed here to refer to a person's sense of meaningfulness and purpose as a product of what she is directing her existence toward. In other words, rather than implying that one's present behavior is compelled by what has happened to one in the past, the concept implies that one's present behavior is predominately impelled by what one anticipates in the future.

Transference in psychotherapy. Human development relies on stimulus generalization: the adaptive capacity to apply what one has learned in one situation to other situations that contain similarities. Transference in psychotherapy is a form of stimulus generalization in which the strong affects a client has experienced with significant people in the past (or outside of psychotherapy) are felt toward the psychotherapist—with little or no conscious recognition of the stimulus generalization on the part of the client.

Unacknowledged shame. Shame that is suppressed by the subject because it is based on the painful sense that the subject is incapable of establishing a system of shared meanings with other people and as a result has lost and may never regain an interpersonal bridge with significant others is called *unacknowledged shame*.

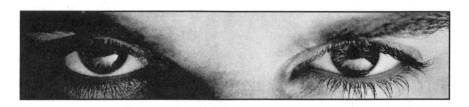

NAME INDEX

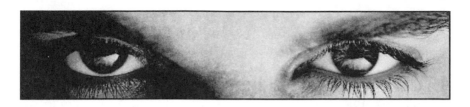

SUBJECT INDEX